SPEAKING
SCARED
SOUNDING
GOOD

PUBLIC SPEAKING FOR THE PRIVATE PERSON

PETER DESBERG, PhD

SQUAREONE
PUBLISHERS

Cover Designer: Jeannie Tudor
Editor: Carol A. Rosenberg
Typesetter: Gary A. Rosenberg

Square One Publishers
115 Herricks Road
Garden City Park, NY 11040
(516) 535-2010 • (877) 900-BOOK
www.squareonepublishers.com

Library of Congress Cataloging-in-Publication Data

Desberg, Peter.
    Speaking scared, sounding good : public speaking for the private person /
Peter Desberg.
        p. cm.
    Includes bibliographical references and index.
    ISBN-13: 978-0-7570-0262-5 (pbk.)
    ISBN-10: 0-7570-0262-5 (pbk.)
    1. Public speaking. 2. Public speaking—Psychological aspects. I. Title.

PN4129.15.D46   2007
808.5'1—dc22

                                                                    2006026985

Printed in the United States of America

10   9   8   7   6   5   4   3   2   1

CONTENTS

PART THREE

Broadening Your Presentation Skills

Appendices

INTRODUCTION

You are reading this book for one reason: The thought of public speaking makes you nervous, *really* nervous. You've heard other people speak effortlessly and fearlessly in different situations and in front of audiences of all sizes, so what's wrong with you? Why do you, and you alone, suffer from stage fright? As you read *Speaking Scared, Sounding Good,* you'll discover that there isn't anything wrong with you. You are not alone. Even the best speakers among us sometimes get stage fright.

In their bestseller, *The Book of Lists,* David Wallechinsky and Amy Wallace point out that the fear of public speaking is the number-one fear in America. The fear of dying comes in at number five. What this suggests is that most Americans would rather die than talk in public! If you've ever been called on to speak in front of an audience, you may understand why—that racing heart, narrowing throat, and profuse sweating sure make you feel like the end is near, but it's painfully slow in coming.

You'll be glad to know that you don't have to suffer like this. A little reading and practice can help you overcome these dreadful feelings that hold you back from reaching your true potential as a speaker. The program presented in this book is based on proven methods that have been tested on hundreds of people, just like you, who have gone through my stage-fright workshops or consulted with me individually. The techniques and exercises throughout this book are easy to do and will have you successfully managing the fear that wells up inside of you whenever you are faced with the prospect of speaking in public. The more you know about why you have stage fright, the easier speaking in front of others will be.

> "... people's number one fear is public speaking. Death is number two. Does that sound right? This means to the average person, if you go to a funeral, you're better off in the casket than doing the eulogy."
>
> —*Jerry Seinfeld*

Woody Allen once said, "Any theory that you can put in a nutshell belongs there." Well, here is why people get stage fright *in a nutshell:* Everyone wants to perform well in front of an audience. If you *think* the audience won't like you, you'll be afraid to get up in front of them. You'll feel even worse if a negative evaluation of your performance could result in personal or professional problems.

This book explains the general causes of stage fright and helps you identify the specific causes of *your* own fears. You will be coached to handle your fears at three levels—through your emotions, your thoughts, and your actions. You will be guided through helpful exercises at each level. This will give you a wide selection of skills for dealing with stage fright under any condition—personal encounters, interviews, sports or music performances, and most important, public speaking.

In going through this book, you will need to follow a simple procedure. First you read it, then you try it. There is a difference between reading and learning. Reading is a passive process, while learning is an active one. This book will not be a passive experience for you; it's not a book to cuddle with under your blankets. You will be asked to work with the book in designing and carrying out your own improvement program.

I will be your coach throughout these pages, but you will learn to control your fears on your own. You will do a lot of thinking about and imagining what it is like for you to speak in public. What you'll likely discover is that the thinking and imagining process actually causes most of your stage fright. As you practice the various exercises throughout the book, you'll learn to tap

into and record your thoughts and fears. This will help you pinpoint your specific needs and will help you design your own treatment. Each chapter begins with a "Big Idea." As you read through the chapter, reflect on how it relates to the "Big Idea."

No matter the level of anxiety you currently experience when faced with public speaking, you'll learn how to control your fear and get through a presentation. If you diligently practice the lessons in this book, your fears will be reduced and you might even find yourself beginning to enjoy public speaking. Opportunities will arise as you begin to present yourself with more confidence.

I truly enjoy speaking in public now, but it wasn't always like that. When I was a student, I was sure there was no worse torment. When faced with giving a speech, I felt like a five-year-old boy whose angry mother had just shouted, "Just wait till your father comes home!" For me, this dread lasted throughout graduate school. However, after years as a university professor who practices public speaking daily, I've learned how to do it, and I do it well. Now, I challenge myself by playing the guitar and singing in front of live audiences. Yes, it makes me anxious, but I have learned to turn my anxiety into excitement and my fear into anticipation—just as I will teach you to do in this book.

When you are preparing to begin a diet, you must first step on the scale to determine your starting point. In this case, your scale is your Anxiety IQ. Grab a pencil, turn the page, and let's see how much stage fright is weighing you down. . . .

THE HOW-SCARED-ARE-YOU? QUIZ

Before you read another word of this book, take this quiz to determine how afraid you are to speak in public. Your total score represents your current anxiety quotient (AQ).

When you have finished this book and have participated in all the various exercises, you'll quiz yourself again to see how much you have improved.

DIRECTIONS: For each statement, select the answer that best describes you and record the corresponding point value in the space provided. (Although these statements are focused on speaking in public, you can substitute any type of performance to determine your level of anxiety in that area.)

1 I avoid situations in which I must speak in front of people.

0 Never   1 Sometimes   2 Often   3 Always   _____

2 I am afraid I will draw a blank during my presentation.

0 Never   1 Sometimes   2 Often   3 Always   _____

3 I think the audience will be bored by my presentation.

0 Never   1 Sometimes   2 Often   3 Always   _____

4 When I speak in public, I experience breathing problems, such as shortness of breath.

0 Never   1 Sometimes   2 Often   3 Always   _____

5 I get nervous speaking in front of people who are as competent or less competent than I am.

0 Never   1 Sometimes   2 Often   3 Always   _____

6 I think people in the audience will ridicule my presentation.

0 Never   1 Sometimes   2 Often   3 Always   _____

7 The potential consequences of my presentation make me nervous.

0 Never   1 Sometimes   2 Often   3 Always   _____

8 I think I will deliver my presentation poorly.

0 Never   1 Sometimes   2 Often   3 Always   _____

9 I think others will dislike me when I speak.

0 Never   1 Sometimes   2 Often   3 Always   _____

10 I am affected by the size of the audience.

0 Never   1 Sometimes   2 Often   3 Always   _____

11 I have difficulty concentrating while delivering my presentation.

0 Never   1 Sometimes   2 Often   3 Always   _____

12 People feel sorry for me when I make a presentation.

0 Never   1 Sometimes   2 Often   3 Always   _____

13 Speaking in front of strangers makes me nervous.

0 Never   1 Sometimes   2 Often   3 Always   _____

14 The audience will sense that I don't know my material.

0 Never   1 Sometimes   2 Often   3 Always   _____

15 I think there is something about me the audience will dislike.

0 Never   1 Sometimes   2 Often   3 Always   _____

16 I get embarrassed when I speak in public.

0 Never   1 Sometimes   2 Often   3 Always   _____

17 I sound disorganized when I make a speech.

0 Never   1 Sometimes   2 Often   3 Always   _____

18 I expect to be put on the spot and challenged by the audience.

0 Never   1 Sometimes   2 Often   3 Always   _____

19 I tremble or shake when I speak in public.

   0 Never   1 Sometimes   2 Often   3 Always   _____

20 I do not rehearse enough for my presentations.

   0 Never   1 Sometimes   2 Often   3 Always   _____

21 Even if I perform well, the audience will find fault with me or my presentation.

   0 Never   1 Sometimes   2 Often   3 Always   _____

22 Once I've started my presentation, I feel anxious.

   0 Never   1 Sometimes   2 Often   3 Always   _____

23 I expect to make a lot of mistakes during my presentation.

   0 Never   1 Sometimes   2 Often   3 Always   _____

24 I expect the audience to reject my point of view.

   0 Never   1 Sometimes   2 Often   3 Always   _____

25 When delivering my presentation, I feel like an observer.

   0 Never   1 Sometimes   2 Often   3 Always   _____

26 I get nervous when I must be spontaneous in front of an audience.

   0 Never   1 Sometimes   2 Often   3 Always   _____

27 I get distracted very easily during a presentation.

   0 Never   1 Sometimes   2 Often   3 Always   _____

28 I become preoccupied with my physical symptoms of anxiety during a presentation.

   0 Never   1 Sometimes   2 Often   3 Always   _____

29 Just thinking about speaking in public makes me panic.

   0 Never   1 Sometimes   2 Often   3 Always   _____

30 I get nervous when speaking in a new setting or different location.

   0 Never   1 Sometimes   2 Often   3 Always   _____

TOTAL: _____

INTERPRETING YOUR AQ

If you have an AQ of **41–90**, you have a **high level of stage fright**.

People with scores this high often go to great lengths to avoid speaking in public, sometimes to the detriment of their careers. Chances are, you worry about giving a speech weeks or even months ahead of time. Just thinking about the task probably makes you very anxious.

If you have an AQ of **21–40**, you have a **moderate level of stage fright**.

You are probably seeking relief from the discomfort you've associated with public speaking. This book can help you figure out why and how you get stage fright, and more important, how you can control it.

If you have an AQ of **1–20**, you have a **low level of stage fright**.

Good for you! You are probably a high achiever and picked up this book because you want to get that extra edge when you speak in public. This book can offer you ways to become even more comfortable on the speaker's platform and will show you how to expand your repertoire of public speaking skills in social and work environments.

PART ONE

UNDERSTANDING YOUR FEAR OF PUBLIC SPEAKING

The BIG Idea

Your emotions are a direct result of what's on your mind. If you *think* you will give a bad speech, you will be afraid to give that speech. Just thinking about it negatively weeks before the scheduled date can make you tremble. This is because your negative thoughts cause your fear.

1

WHAT REALLY CAUSES STAGE FRIGHT?

When I ask my university students how many of them are afraid to speak in public, about 40 percent of them typically raise their hands. Then, I check to see if the ones who haven't raised their hands are being honest: I look around the room, making eye contact with nearly every student, and say, "Let's see . . . I'm going to pick someone at random to get up and give a quick two-minute talk—but first, how many of you are afraid you'll be picked?" The number of hands now shoots up to well over 80 percent!

Why is that percentage so high? I'm sure you know the answer. For many people, the thought of speaking in public makes them uneasy and apprehensive, sometimes to the point where they cannot function. This translates into a fear of public speaking, technically termed "glossophobia." Even if you've practiced a speech over and over again, and felt like you knew it pretty well, the moment you have to get up in front of an audience to talk, you get *stage fright*—acute nervousness or anxiety that can vary in severity depending on the circumstances.

Understanding where these fears come from and how they work will start you on the path toward dealing with them and controlling stage fright. Moreover, this understanding will guide you to a place where you can learn to harness your fears to energize your presentations.

A CLASSIC CASE OF STAGE FRIGHT

I'd like to introduce you to Barbara G. to help you better understand how stage fright works. Barbara is waiting to give a speech at her leadership meeting. . . .

The Case of Barbara G.

I hope I don't come off sounding like a complete jerk! My temples are throbbing. . . . I'm not sure my opening joke is going to go over. . . . I can barely breathe. . . . Why don't they just call me up there now? . . . Forget these endless announcements and introductions. . . . Maybe it won't be so bad this time . . . and I won't forget all the . . . oh, no . . . there's the regional manager.

Recently promoted from chemist to manager, Barbara was usually very confident. Speech giving was the task she disliked most about her new managerial position. She believed that with each new leadership meeting she ran, there was a greater chance she'd expose her poor communication skills.

I've got to focus on my first three points. . . . They're the key to my talk. . . . Oh God, there's Richard . . . he's been salivating over my job. . . . He looks so smug. . . . Please don't let me forget my opening . . .

When Barbara's name was announced, a new wave of panic swept over her. She thought of her opening joke and decided it wouldn't get any laughs. As she rose from her chair, her attention wavered between her shaking knees, the people in the audience, and how important this talk would be for her career. Suddenly concerned she had forgotten her opening points, she tried to run through them in her head. Then, as she reached the podium, she had a flashback of the disastrous talk she'd given at last year's promo meeting.

Why is Richard smirking? . . . Look at my hands; they're shaking. . . . What's Richard whispering to the regional manager? . . . My throat feels like it's closing up. . . . I've got to calm down! . . . I can't remember anything. . . . Are the two of them laughing? My throat is so tight. . . .

Although Barbara looked calm on the outside, her insides were in knots and her thoughts were scattered. As she attempted to present the three basic ideas of her speech, she realized she was already discussing the third point but had failed to mention point two. Her thoughts raced ahead to how this failure would affect the balance of her speech. When she tried to go back to the second point, she tripped over her words. Poor Barbara!

Barbara G. was experiencing stage fright in a big way! As her case so clearly illustrates, just thinking that your performance will go poorly and that you'll be evaluated negatively as a result can cause stage fright.

The audience can be as small as one person—if that person's opinion and assessment of your performance are important enough. For example, if you ask for a raise, your boss becomes an important audience of one. When you invite someone to join you for a cup of coffee, you are also speaking to an audience of one. Your audience can be large or small; it just depends on how *you* view it. For many people, stage fright can well up before and during a job interview, a public speech, a sports performance, an important business call, or a boss's review of a report. This doesn't happen only to shy or insecure people; anyone can experience these fears—and when they do, they usually go through the same type of thought processes. Let's take a look.

THE FIVE STAGES OF THE STAGE-FRIGHT CYCLE

There are five stages in the stage-fright cycle. Reviewing them will give you a good picture of how stage fright starts and builds momentum. Understanding the mechanics of stage fright will make it easier to understand what causes it and then how to control it. As you read about the five stages, remember that they form a repetitive cycle. Although there is a clear beginning, once it starts, it just keeps going around in a big circle until the talk is over or the speaker faints.

1. You Predict Something Bad Will Happen to You

You make thousands of predictions every day. They happen so quickly that you barely know you are making them. You've been making predictions all your life; they are just part of the way you think. *Why did the chicken cross the road? Because she predicted she would get to the other side.* Is this just a silly joke or does it describe what you do constantly throughout your day?

You probably don't realize it, but you make several predictions even when deciding something as simple as whether or not to see a movie. Here are just a few of them: *The movie will be enjoyable, it won't be a hassle getting into the theater, and the parking lot will be safe.* If you predicted the opposite—*the movie will be awful, the theater will be overcrowded, and a mugger is waiting for you in the dark parking lot*—you'd never leave your house to see another movie. Because making predictions is such a basic part of how you think, they happen automatically and you don't even notice you're making them unless a particular prediction is strange or disturbing.

To develop a fear of public speaking—or any performance for that matter—you have to predict things might go wrong. You may predict that you'll forget what you're going to say, that you'll appear and sound disorganized, or that you'll bore the audience. You may also predict that after giving a crummy talk, people will laugh at you behind your back, or you won't get the raise you were hoping for, or you will lose your job. Where do these fear-provoking thoughts come from? Sometimes, they come from your own past failures and even from observing other people's failures. In other cases, they might simply be the result of a creative and overactive imagination. There's more on this later.

Although Barbara G. was not a particularly nervous or insecure person, she firmly believed she wasn't good public speaker. She predicted

Stage 1. You predict something bad will happen to you.

she would forget important parts of her talk. That would be enough to frighten anyone who was about to give a speech. But were Barbara's predictions reasonable? She believed they were; after all, they were based on her own history. She'd had a bad experience in a similar situation the year before. To add fuel to her fears, she predicted her poor talk could ruin her career.

Why do thoughts about stage fright have so much power over us? Can't we just relax and think about marshmallow bunnies? The answer is no, because our brains are wired for survival. We'll always notice negative thoughts before positive ones because those are the thoughts that are designed to keep us safe—negative thoughts alert us to impending danger. Because of the survival value of noticing the negative, you take your fear-provoking thoughts very seriously. (Chapter 6 takes a deeper look at our efforts to protect ourselves and how and why this sometimes backfires.)

As you will notice, you don't just make one prediction and then stop. You keep making predictions every time you receive new information. Each new event and each new piece of information you take in will affect your predictions and create new, updated ones. Stage 2 will present you with a new question based on these updated predictions: You know that sticks and stones can break your bones, but can thoughts harm you?

STAGE 2

2. Your Fear-Provoking Thoughts Make You Anxious and Afraid

Anxiety is the way your body responds to danger. The rush of adrenaline you get in dangerous situations—referred to as the "fight-or-flight response"—gives your body that extra burst of energy it needs to flee danger or stay and fight. So, what's the problem? Here it is: The fight-or-flight response is triggered even when you just *think* you are in danger. Fear is caused by *interpreting* that you are in jeopardy. If you are *not* in danger, but truly believe you are in harm's way, you *will* feel anxious.

I'm shaking like a leaf, and my heart is pounding.... I must really be in trouble or my body wouldn't be doing this!

Stage 2. Your fear-provoking thoughts make you anxious and afraid.

According to the world-renowned psychiatrist Dr. Aaron T. Beck, there is a simple recipe for how a person becomes frightened. If you are in what you perceive as a dangerous situation and believe that you don't have the resources to cope with it, you will be scared. Your reasoning doesn't have to be accurate; you just have to *believe* it's accurate. For example, if you have a fear of snakes and were to see a bent twig in the right light, you'd panic until you realized it was just a twig. As long as you believed it was a snake, it didn't matter that it was just a stick. Likewise, if you believe you will get up in front of an audience and look foolish, you will make yourself anxious and afraid.

Because Barbara G. predicted she would do badly in her talk, she became anxious and frightened. Her heart was beating quickly, she was short of breath, her legs were weak, her hands shook, and her throat was tight. She believed her predictions, so her body responded to her beliefs. Clearly, Barbara's thoughts produced her uncomfortable feelings. For more on how this works, see "I Think, Therefore I Feel" on page 14.

3. Your Anxiety Symptoms Confirm Your Predictions and Increase Your Anxiety Level

STAGE 3

Once you predict that your speech will turn out poorly, you'll look for evidence to support your prediction. The first jolt of adrenaline—that feeling of overwhelming anxiety—is strong evidence that your fears are justified. Your anxiety is *proof* that things are really as bad as, or even worse than, you feared. After all, if the situation weren't dangerous, your body wouldn't be in such an uproar—or so you've convinced yourself.

When Barbara G. noticed her intense physical symptoms, they proved to her just how bad things really were. *She became afraid of being afraid.* Knowing that physical symptoms are *real*, she was certain the danger she *predicted* she was in must also be real. Once Barbara noticed the physical feedback from her body, her next wave of predictions became much more intense, which then led to even more intense physical symptoms.

Stage 3. Your anxiety symptoms confirm your predictions and increase your anxiety level.

4. Focusing on Your Fears Becomes a Distraction

STAGE 4

Anxiety steals part of your attention away from your presentation and places it on the symptoms of your fear—your pounding heart, your clammy skin, your shaking hands, and so on. This leads to one of the major culprits in your case of stage fright, *your brain.*

Our brains are wired to perform only one complicated mental task at a time. For example, if we were in the middle of a conversation and got into your car, you'd be able to continue the conversation as you started the car and drove away, no problem. However, if it were an unfamiliar rental car, you would need to familiarize yourself with the placement of the ignition, gearshift lever, parking brake, and so on. Our conversation would probably come to a grinding halt while you figured out how to start the car.

I Think, Therefore I Feel

When it comes to speaking in public, just *thinking* about something going wrong can produce strong, uncomfortable emotions. For instance, you only have to *think* you will forget part of your speech to feel intense panic—even weeks before you make the actual presentation. To help you understand this concept, I want to share with you my favorite example of how thoughts can change how we feel. Imagine yourself in this situation:

You're late for an important meeting, and you're stuck in traffic. It's a very hot day and the air conditioning in your car is broken. The sweatier you get, the more upset you are over how late it is. You start dwelling on how the other people at the meeting will view your tardiness and the sweaty mess you've become and how embarrassed you'll be. You creep along, but somehow you finally reach your destination. As you circle the enormous parking lot, you see that every space in the lot is taken. You think to yourself that you'll never find a spot and start to panic.

You drive around to the front of the building in time to see an elderly man exiting through the front doors. You pop your head out the window to ask if he will be leaving a parking space. He says yes, and for a minute, you feel relieved. But the man walks very slowly, and you're out of patience and silently blame him for making you even later for the meeting. After what seems like forever, the man gets to his car in the very last row. He moves very slowly, but—finally—you see his taillights go on and he inches his way out of the spot. Just as you are preparing to pull in, a car zooms in off the street and swipes the space you've been waiting for. Now you're fuming. "That inconsiderate selfish jerk!" you shout to yourself. "How dare he?!"

Did the driver's actions make you angry? You might think so, but I disagree. It's not the driver who made you angry. It is what you thought to yourself

that made you angry. It is your evaluation of the situation that created the anger, not the driver's actions. You may not agree with me, so let's go on with the scene so you can see that what I'm saying really does makes sense.

Okay, so you're fuming and you're getting ready for a fight. The man who took your space opens his door, gets out, and runs around to the passenger side of the car. He opens the other door and carries out a small, injured child. As he runs past your car, he slows down long enough to say, "I'm sorry . . . my son is seriously hurt and I've got to get him to the doctor."

What happens now? Your anger evaporates in less than a heartbeat. You've reinterpreted, or rethought, the situation and decided that his need was way greater than yours. You feel bad for the boy and perhaps ashamed for being angry at the driver. Your reinterpretation caused your anger to vaporize. Now do agree that your thoughts lead to your emotions?

To further clarify this concept, let's take this example in a different direction. Rewind to where your spot just got taken: You jump out of your car and stand there in the parking lot with your hands defiantly on your hips. All four doors of the offending car open and four large, gruff-looking men get out. What happens to your anger now? It immediately turns to fear. Once again, you have rethought the situation. This time, you interpreted the situation as dangerous to you. It doesn't matter that these guys had no intention of harming you. They were actually undercover officers responding to a bomb threat in the building. If you had arrived on time for your meeting, you'd be in perilous situation right now. Once you learn this, you feel relieved.

So, you see, the rule is it's not what actually happens, but how you think about, or interpret, the event that determines your emotions.

Try this test. Start counting the number of words on this page, and while you do so keep repeating the word "ridiculous" to yourself. You'll notice that it's virtually impossible to do both of these simple tasks at the same time. And, if you can't do these two simple tasks at the same time, imagine what the effect would be if you allow your fears to distract you while trying to perform a complicated task like giving a speech.

When you give a talk, it's very important to focus your attention on your topic, not on your anxiety or its physical symptoms. Stressing over who is in the audience, how much you're sweating, or whether or not you'll remember parts of your speech is very distracting. Distractions interfere with your memory and create havoc on any type of performance.

Barbara G. was clearly distracting herself. Her attention was split four ways: 1) she was thinking about her talk; 2) she was monitoring the reaction of certain people in the audience; 3) she was assessing her own state of anxiety; and, 4) she was dissecting her own deteriorating performance. The more she allowed her attention to be divided, the more focus she lost. It's no surprise she began skipping parts of her speech and tripping over her words.

Stage 4. Focusing on your fears becomes a distraction.

The more attention you give to your current state of anxiety, the less you'll be able to concentrate on your performance. This will cause problems for you such as forgetting what you want to say. This usually leads to—let me say this in the most technical term—*messing up*. Distractions are the nightmares of every performer. The mistakes you make because of these distractions will affect your next round of predictions in the cycle.

5. You Make Mistakes That Justify Your Anxiety and Lead to Even More Negative Predictions

STAGE 5

Every mistake you make causes you to make a new set of predictions that are now based on new evidence—your mistakes. These predictions now say, "I'll never be able to regain my composure; I'm going to keep messing up." For some people, this level of anxiety sends them into a tailspin from which they cannot recover. Others eventually adapt during their speech and find a way to stumble through their presentations.

Keep in mind that this is a cycle, so it just keeps going around with each update. New information keeps coming in, causing you to further modify your predictions.

When Barbara G. confused the order of her main points, she panicked, evidence that her fears were coming true. Each mistake added to

Stage 5. You make mistakes that justify your anxiety and lead to even more negative predictions.

her distraction, leading to even more mistakes. Each mistake also led to a new round of predictions, which led to even worse physical symptoms. The recognition of her mistakes, the disorganization brought on by the distractions, and the increasing discomfort of her physical symptoms all led to even worse predictions that kept the cycle going and growing.

Summary of the Stage-Fright Cycle

As you've learned, the five stages of the stage-fright cycle continue flowing and repeating. At each stage, anxiety increases as it builds on the stage that came before it. It's a cycle that doesn't really end, but just keeps using the information it gets to keep things going. Here is a review of what happens in each of the five stages:

Stage 1	• You constantly make predictions about everyday happenings.
	• You aren't always aware that you are making predictions.
	• You are mostly aware of the negative predictions because of the fear they cause.
Stage 2	• Your negative predictions result in a change in your emotions, and you *feel* afraid.
Stage 3	• Feeling afraid is proof to you that your predictions are accurate.
	• Your next round of predictions is even more negative.
Stage 4	• The more your anxiety distracts you, the more likely you are to make mistakes during your speech.
Stage 5	• Mistakes lead to even worse predictions, and the cycle repeats itself.

It's time for you to complete the first exercise in this book. Exercise 1.1 will help you recognize these five stages in your case of stage fright.

EXERCISE 1.1. Identifying the Five Stages of Your Stage Fright

In this exercise, you will prepare to give a speech. This exercise works best if there is an upcoming event at which you will have to perform. If you don't have to speak anytime soon, think about the next presentation you will have to give, or make one up, and prepare for it. Research the topic, prepare your speech, and practice delivering it as if you were going to be speaking soon.

Once you've rehearsed your presentation, record yourself giving it. A video camera works best, but a tape recorder will do. The more you can make your practice situation like the actual performance conditions the better. Aim to put as much pressure on yourself as possible to simulate the feeling of a real situation. For example, it's a good idea to ask a few friends to play the part of the audience during the taping. If you don't have an audience, simply visualize one. While it's true your imagined audience or your friends aren't the actual audience you'll eventually be facing, you may be surprised by how tense you become during the practice speech.

Once you begin your speech, don't start and stop the recorder, and don't rewind and start over from the beginning. Just keep going no matter what happens.

When you're finished, examine your recorded performance and identify each of the five stages. Try to recall and relive each stage as it occurred. In the space provided below, write down all the thoughts you remember having during each stage.

Stage 1. What predictions did you make?

_____

_____

_____

_____

_____

_____

_____

Stage 2. What physical symptoms of anxiety did you experience as a result of those predictions?

_____

_____

_____

_____

_____

_____

Stage 3. What were your thoughts when you noticed you were anxious?

_____

_____

_____

_____

_____

_____

_____

_____

Stage 4. What distracted you while you were giving your speech?

_____

_____

_____

_____

_____

_____

_____

_____

Stage 5. List any actual mistakes you made during your performance.

_____

_____

_____

_____

_____

_____

Feedback for Exercise 1.1

Although no two people have identical reactions to public speaking, you may find it helpful to compare your answers to that of other people who have also gone through this exercise. The following are some of the most common responses to the above questions:

Stage 1. The most common predictions people make are:

- I'll forget my material.
- The audience will think I'm incompetent.
- My physical signs of anxiety will show.
- I'll harm my career or position as a result of my speech.

Stage 2. Most people report experiencing these physical symptoms:

- Rapid heartbeat
- Shallow breath
- Wet, clammy hands
- Dry mouth
- Tight throat
- Shaking

Stage 3. When they notice their symptoms of anxiety, most people report thinking about the following:

- My heart was pounding so much, I could hear it in my head.
- I was thinking about how nervous I must look to the audience.
- I was sure the audience could see sweat pouring off my brow.

Stage 4. Common distractions reported include:

- My hands were shaking so much that I couldn't take my attention off of them.
- A plane went overhead and I panicked because I'd lost my place.
- A person in the front row looked bored (or rolled his eyes, or laughed, or talked at an inappropriate time).

Stage 5. Actual mistakes made during a performance often include:

- I paused for too long because I couldn't remember what came next.
- I used a number of fillers like *hmm, ah, you know,* and *let's see.*
- I presented my points in the wrong order.

Now, review your recording again and use these examples to help you examine each of the five stages of stage fright you experienced. Did you find the place where you first began to get tense? Were you able to remember what predictions you made to bring that tension on? Were you able to identify any of the distractions, either mental or physical, that affected your presentation? Did you make any mistakes? If so, try to remember what you were thinking about just before you made each mistake. You will be using this information in the next few chapters to help you learn to manage your anxiety and, as a result, speak better under pressure.

While doing Exercise 1.1, you probably relived some of your more unpleasant moments in front of an audience. This is good, because now you've had a chance to examine your fears of public speaking. There are three main ways you might have developed these fears: 1) by having one or more bad experiences yourself (a learned fear); 2) by observing someone else having a bad experience (also a learned fear); or, 3) by being instinctively afraid (obviously, an instinctive fear). Do you think all fears are basically the same? Where do they come from? Let's take a look in the following sections.

LEARNED FEARS AND INSTINCTIVE FEARS

There are two kinds of fears: learned fears and instinctive fears. Instinctive fears are wired into your brain at the factory. Some common examples of instinctive fears are fear of unexplained loud noises, fear of loss of balance or support, and fear of pain. Other examples include fear of the unknown and fear of new situations.

Like Pavlov's dogs, when we learn to associate a neutral thing with an instinctive reaction, our response to both will be the same.

Learned fears are another story. You develop learned fears by creating associations between neutral objects or situations and instinctive fears. As the famous Russian physiologist, psychologist, and physician Ivan Pavlov demonstrated, when we associate a neutral thing with an instinctive reaction, our response to both will be the same. In his well-known example, Pavlov created an association in dogs between food and the ringing of a bell. Once the association was made, the simple sound of a ringing bell caused the dogs to salivate. In much the same way, commercials teach our kids to salivate at the sight of those yellow arches by associating them with succulent burgers and fries. Are you afraid of cotton? T-shirts are made of cotton, and you can wear one all day long and remain relatively calm. But what happens when your doctor dabs a piece of cotton in alcohol and rubs it on your arm? You immediately tense up. You've associated the cotton with the shot you're about to get. (Get the point?) Associations like this are very powerful.

Under the "right" conditions, people can even learn to like painful things. For example, back in my university days, my friend who played center on the football team told me he liked to hit and be hit. "I like the contact," he said. This surprised me, because being hit by someone who weighs more than 250 pounds hurts—but my friend looked forward to it. Why? Because he had learned that such contact was part of the game he loved. His coaches praised him, his fans cheered, and the girls swooned. In the end, this painful contact became something he liked. In fact, many of the celebrities I've worked with tell me how they've learned to turn their anxiety into excitement. They look forward to that first jolt of adrenaline, which others find "painful." Rather than frightening them, it energizes them. They've learned that tension feels good—the same way a bungee jumper eagerly anticipates the "adrenaline rush" that comes from being in a potentially perilous situation.

For most people, the cause of stage fright is a series of learned fears and predictions that warn them about the terrible things that can happen to them during, or as a result of, their presentation. But, remember, you can simply be afraid of stepping on a stage *without* ever having had a bad experience in that particular type of situation and without making a fear-provoking prediction. In this case, the situation is new to you and seems instinctively dangerous.

Whether your fears are instinctive or learned, you'll learn how to deal with both types to get you over your fear of public speaking in much the same manner, since they have basically the same effects. Keep in mind, however, that the longer you do nothing about your fears, the more situations you'll find yourself avoiding. This is because fears generalize and spread the way many diseases do. Has your fear of public speaking crept into other areas of your life? See "Is Your Fear Spreading?" below.

WAS YOUR FEAR LEARNED THROUGH OBSERVATION?

Here is an agonizing example—one of many—of how I *learned* to make awful predictions and developed stage fright simply by observing someone else's failure. For me, this example crystallizes all of the most agonizing aspects of public speaking and places the speaker under the largest of magnifying glasses.

Is Your Fear Spreading?

If you are afraid to speak in public, you've probably discovered that your fear is not limited to just that one situation. Once you develop a fear, it doesn't remain connected only to that situation, person, or activity. Fears have a tendency to generalize, or spread, to other similar situations, people, and activities. For instance, if you are afraid to speak in front of a large group, you may develop a fear of speaking in front of a small group, although this fear might not be quite as intense. Then, the fear may generalize to other situations where you must perform in front of a group—for example, conducting a meeting, giving a toast at a wedding, or performing on the tennis court with spectators. The general rule is, the more similar a situation is to the one you are afraid of, the more you will be afraid of the new situation. That's why tackling your fear is so important.

When I was in the eighth grade, we were forced to go through a painful ritual like so many who had gone before us—the dreaded school dance. The boys hung out on one side of the gymnasium, and the girls on the other. While the other boys and I watched the girls dance with one another (no boy had yet ventured across the floor), one of the boys finally summoned up the courage to ask a girl to dance. Picture these three versions of the outcome; it doesn't matter which really happened:

Case 1—Mild Rejection

A boy walks across "no-boy's-land" to ask a girl to dance. He feels every boys' eyes on his back as he faces the sea of girls. Knowing that the whole gym is watching, he asks one of them to dance. Smiling politely, the girl says, "I'm sorry, I'm a little tired now, maybe later." He turns away and now has to make the long walk back to the boys' side and tell his curious friends what happened. Sure, the situation is slightly embarrassing for him, but not so bad that he won't try again, either later that night or at some other dance.

Watching this, I imagined myself in his place and decided that, for now, he'd been brave enough for the both of us. Maybe I'd try later, or maybe not.

Case 2—Moderate Rejection

A boy walks across the dance floor to ask a girl to dance. This time, in a loud voice, the girl responds, "No way!" then turns back to her friends and continues talking. The walk back to the boys' side after this defeat is excruciating. He won't try this again for quite a while; if he does, he'll likely be filled with anxiety.

Watching this, my jaw drops. I lean back in my chair, comforted by the knowledge that there's no chance something like this will happen to me because I'm not going to leave the safety of my chair.

Case 3—Serious Rejection

Again, same situation: This time, the girl laughs in the boy's face and says over the music, "Yeah, like I'd actually dance with a geek like you." As he makes the painful walk back to the boys' side, he can hear the girl and her friends laughing. Very few of the boys will talk to him now because no one wants to become a geek by association. The odds that this boy will ask a girl to dance again before he is a university sophomore are very low.

I huddle in a corner with the rest of the boys, and we talk about basketball.

These examples clearly show that the worse the experience, the more difficult the recovery. Now, here's where is gets interesting: in each case, only one boy was doing the asking. Did the other boys learn anything by watching him? Yes, many of us shared his painful experience just by imagining ourselves in his place.

You may be afraid to speak in public and find yourself perplexed by it because you've never had a bad experience doing it. As the school dance example shows, you may have learned this fear by observation rather than by direct experience. We'll revisit this topic in Chapter 3. Meanwhile, Figure 1.1 summarizes how a fear of public speaking develops.

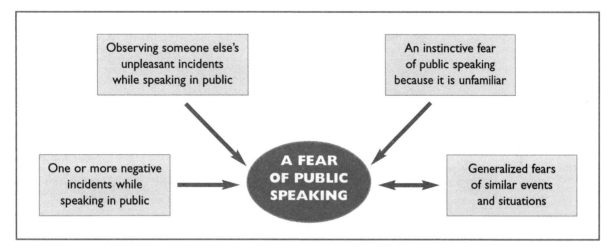

Figure 1.1.
How a Fear of Public
Speaking Develops

Now that you have looked at each stage in the stage-fright cycle and examined how fears can be learned or instinctive, you are ready to examine the most common cause of stage fright—you guessed it, a fear of a negative evaluation or rejection.

A FEAR OF A NEGATIVE EVALUATION OR REJECTION & THE MISSING PIECE OF THE PUZZLE

The most common cause of stage fright is a fear of a negative evaluation or rejection. Does it come as a shock that you don't want people to think you are boring, stupid, disorganized, or incompetent? And why would an audience think of you that way? Because of what they see you do and hear you say. But while you're giving your speech, you have no way of knowing what they're thinking. That's the missing piece of the puzzle. You can't truly know. For example, let's say you're sweating a lot. The audience *might* think you're sweating because you are incompetent and can't hide how anxious it makes you feel. Or they *might* just as easily think you're sweating because you are so emotionally committed to what you are saying. The point is, whether you're sweating or not, you can't read the audience's mind. Unfortunately, that won't stop you from *imagining* what they are thinking. Your interpretations will be colored by your predictions and fear-provoking thoughts. It's really all in your head. Don't worry. You'll soon learn how to conquer this common fear by putting things in the proper perspective.

Feedback after a speech, on the other hand, is another thing entirely. If you are negatively evaluated or, worse, rejected, that can put a real damper on things. But don't worry about this either. Later, I'll also show you how to put this type of feedback to good use.

WHAT YOU HAVE LEARNED AND WHERE YOU ARE GOING

In this chapter, you've learned the causes and mechanics of stage fright. It's very important to be aware you are making predictions that lead to your fear-provoking thoughts. Keep a small notepad or voice recorder handy so you can record these predictions when they happen while they are still fresh in your mind.

In the next chapter, you'll learn exactly how to identify *your* particular fear-provoking thoughts to help you get a handle on them. You may already be aware of some of them, but you'll probably be surprised to discover some fears you weren't even aware you had.

IDENTIFYING YOUR FEAR-PROVOKING THOUGHTS

There's a wonderful expression in boxing, "You never see the punch that knocks you out." In much the same way, you will not be able to rid yourself of fears caused by thoughts you don't see coming your way. Because fear-provoking thoughts can be difficult to identify, this chapter will guide you through a series of exercises to help you find the crippling thoughts that are keeping you from comfortably presenting yourself to others. Throughout the remainder of this book, you will use this information to help control and eliminate your fear. The results from these exercises will be your blueprint. Each exercise helps you to look at your stage fright in a different way. There is no one-size-fits-all approach. One or more of these exercises will help you break through and identify your fear-provoking thoughts.

To warm you up and get you into the right frame of mind, this chapter begins with another example of how thoughts lead to emotions. Because you can be more objective about other people's thoughts and fears, we'll look at the case of Mary S. Mary's example will serve as a model of the thought process you'll be using in this chapter's exercises to begin identifying your own fear-provoking thoughts.

Don't allow yourself to be caught off guard by your fear-provoking thoughts.

ANOTHER CLASSIC CASE OF STAGE FRIGHT

The Case of Mary S. is an example of stage fright in a woman with a very small audience—her husband. We'll take a look at the problem, the investigation, and the solution. At first, you'll see that Mary was unaware of the negative predictions she was making, as is often the case. Her fears distracted her so much that she couldn't function in the situation. Finally, by learning to identify her predications and fear-provoking thoughts, she was able to work through the unreasonable ones.

The Case of Mary S.—The Problem

Mary S. was a biology major at a local university. She was in her early forties and had recently returned to school. She came to me for help with what she called her "math phobia." However, when she described to me the scariest math-related scene she could imagine, it occurred to me that her problem might be stage fright. Here's what Mary imagined: *I'm taking a math test and my professor is looking over my shoulder as I work on the problems. I'm extremely uncomfortable—it's pure torture.* In this scene, the professor is Mary's terrifying audience of one.

Next, I asked Mary how she went about studying for math tests. She told me that her husband often helped her study. Then, I asked her to describe a typical math session with her husband: *He's an engineer and loves math. He's very good at breaking down complicated problems into simple steps and explaining them clearly. He has the patience of a saint and is always encouraging. He's a perfect tutor.*

When I asked Mary to tell me what was going on in her head while her husband was helping her study, it took her a while to put words to her thoughts. Then all of a sudden, they just exploded out of her. Here are just a few of them:

He's so patient and helpful. He could teach anyone, anything . . . unless that person were really stupid. I'm just not following what he's saying . . . he's going to think I'm an idiot. How can an intelligent man like him love an idiot? Oh, God, I'm going to lose my husband. And, if I don't pass this math course, I won't be able to pass my physics and chemistry courses—oh no, I'm going to flunk out of school. I'll never get any further in my career! I'm going to lose everything—my husband, my degree, and my chance to have a successful career.

The Case of Mary S.—The Investigation

While Mary was trying to concentrate on understanding her math lessons, she was constantly distracting herself with her fear-provoking thoughts. She explained that whenever her husband tried to help her, she felt like a loud, screeching sound was going off in her head, preventing her from focusing. If you were Mary, you'd find it difficult to concentrate on your math lessons too if your whole life was crumbling around you the way Mary was imagining her life was crumbling around her. Mary's fear-provoking thoughts—that her husband would discover she's stupid, that she'd be abandoned, and that she'd get nowhere in her career—made it almost impossible for her to understand the work.

As you may recall from Chapter 1, thoughts become more powerful when you find evidence, such as physical symptoms, to support them. When Mary realized that she wasn't learning her math lessons and was becoming more and more confused, she became even more anxious—her anxiety was *real proof* she was failing. Compounding her fears were the problems her failure at math would cause: divorce, flunking out of school, and career limitations. Mary found herself in a vicious stage-fright cycle: the more anxious she got, the less she could concentrate on her task. The less she could concentrate, the more anxious she got. Negative thoughts lead to negative feelings. Then, those feelings lead to new negative thoughts. It was an endless cycle for Mary. With some work, she came to see the *real* problem: It was her thoughts, *not* an inability to understand math, that were causing her learning difficulties.

The Case of Mary S.—The Solution

When we first started working together, Mary was completely unaware of the many predictions she was making—as many people are—even though her predictions led to such intense fears. Her mind was stuck on self-descriptions like "stupid" and "unteachable." It never occurred to Mary that she was preventing herself from learning by focusing on her fears while she should have been focusing on learning her lessons. She was totally unaware of her dire predictions because her attention was focused on the physical symptoms of anxiety, on the "screeching" in her ears, and on her negative opinions about her math intelligence.

As Mary and I began talking about her situation, she discovered that whenever she told herself she was in danger, she became frightened. This is what caused her stage fright. It didn't matter whether she *really* was in danger of losing her husband and her chance at education. What mattered was that she *believed* she was in danger of losing them. Mary learned that controlling her stage fright involved learning how to accurately distinguish between situations that really are dangerous and safe situations in which she only *believed* she was in danger. As she came to believe that her husband was there to help her rather than evaluate her and that he would never give up on her, she was able to calm down and focus on the math lessons at hand. She learned to ask questions when things were unclear. The more she was able to understand her math lessons, the more evidence she had to disprove her original fear-provoking thoughts about being *unable* to learn math.

Mary eventually earned her biology degree and went on to graduate school. And she had a proud husband at her graduation. None of this would have happened if she hadn't learned how to tap into her negative thoughts, disprove them, and then control them. She had to learn to listen to the "voices" in her head just as you are about to do.

LISTENING TO YOUR INTERNAL DIALOGUES

You talk to yourself all the time. Everybody does. Because the talk goes on inside your head, it's silent. Sometimes you are aware of it, but more often, you are not. A common example of internal dialogue is what happens when you want to do something you know you'd enjoy but it's bad for you. It's sort of like the cartoons where a devil and angel pop up on the shoulders of a character in a moral quandary and argue the merits of their opposing sides. You want to eat that piece of chocolate cake, but you are supposed to be dieting. If you tap into your thoughts carefully, you might hear something like, "Tomorrow, I'll run three extra miles on the treadmill to work it off." Or "I don't see my mother very often and it makes her so happy when I eat what she serves me—so for her sake, I'll eat it." Or you might simply say, "Mmmm. That looks sooo good . . . one piece won't spoil my diet too badly."

Internal dialogues occur alongside whatever else you are thinking about, and they often go unnoticed. They usually become more obvious during stressful situations when it's necessary to concentrate harder. You'll find that you evaluate yourself more harshly during these dialogues. And, while you're tearing yourself down, it becomes easier to accept your evaluation as true, which is yet another problem. Then, to make matters worse, you don't test these ideas out to determine if they really are true. To make matters better, start by listening to your internal dialogue to identify your fear-provoking thoughts. The balance of this chapter should help you on your way.

LEARNING TO IDENTIFY YOUR FEAR-PROVOKING THOUGHTS

When it comes to public speaking, most people share similar fear-provoking thoughts. This is a lucky break for you. It will make Exercise 2.1 easier for you to complete. You won't have to answer the question "What makes you afraid?" right away. Instead, you'll be able to choose from a list of other people's fear-provoking thoughts to identify those that apply to you. This exercise is just a warm-up for figuring out your own thoughts from scratch, which you will do in Exercise 2.2.

EXERCISE 2.1. Selecting Relevant Fear-Provoking Thoughts

The following is a list of common situations in which people get nervous while speaking. Place an "X" next to any of the fear-provoking thoughts you've had in similar situations.

Public Speaking

The following statements were made by people who were about to speak in front of an audience.
Which do you identify with?

____ I will probably forget what I'm supposed to say.

____ I'm going to appear disorganized.

____ They're going to see my hands tremble.

____ Everyone is going to think I'm boring.

____ A lot of people in the audience know more about this topic than I do.

____ People are going to feel sorry for me.

____ I'm going to sound stupid.

____ I'm unprepared.

____ People aren't going to take my presentation (or me) seriously.

____ I'm going to make people feel uncomfortable.

____ They will hear my voice quaver.

____ I'm going to come off as cold, distant, and unlikable.

____ I'm not going to be able to answer the questions they will ask me.

____ I'm not going to get the promotion (get elected, pass the class, and so on).

Talking to a Boss

The following statements were made by employees who were just about to talk to their bosses about various issues, ranging from presenting new ideas to asking for a raise. Which do you identify with?

____ I'm going to choke under pressure.

____ I'm going to sound incompetent.

____ I'm going to seem like a loser.

____ I'm going to put my job in danger.

____ My boss will think I don't have the necessary abilities to perform my job.

____ I'm going to forget my purpose and start to ramble.

____ I'm going to sound like I'm kissing up to my boss.

____ My boss will think he or she has overestimated me.

____ I'm going to lose my temper.

____ I'm going to laugh nervously.

____ My ideas will sound lightweight.

____ I'm not going to achieve my goals for this meeting.

Interviewing for a Job

The following statements were made by people who were about to go on an interview. Which do you identify with?

____ I won't understand some of the key questions.

____ I'm either going to say too much or too little.

____ I'm going to wilt under pressure.

____ I'm going to sweat too much.

____ I'm going to seem desperate.

____ I'm going to wear the wrong outfit.

____ If I'm asked about my weaknesses, I won't be able to come up with any believable ones.

____ I'm going to sound stupid.

____ I'm going to quarrel with the interviewer.

____ I'm going to sound insincere.

____ I won't have the right qualifications for the job.

____ I'm going to give the wrong answers.

____ I have the wrong image for this job.

____ I haven't done enough research and preparation for this interview.

Feedback for Exercise 2.1

There are forty statements in this exercise. If you marked more than thirteen, it's clear you get pretty anxious when faced with an audience. As you review your selections, can you find any patterns in what makes you afraid? In other words, did you select mostly statements that deal with your abilities, your physical symptoms, or how you will be evaluated? Try to determine which type of fear each of the items you selected represents and note whether or not you've selected one type more often than the others. The more statements you identified with, the easier it will be to see a pattern.

Once you've completed Exercise 2.1, you will be ready to search your mind for your own personal fear-provoking thoughts. Exercise 2.1 should have helped familiarize you with the types of critical self-statements that lead to stage fright. Armed with this information, you should have a better idea of what's going on in your mind during your internal dialogues.

It's time to take off the training wheels and identify your own fear-provoking thoughts by asking yourself five key questions that will help you unlock them. One of the reasons skilled interviewers like David Letterman and Barbara Walters are so successful is because they know which key questions will open up new areas of discussion, often resulting in a response that surprises even the person being interviewed. The questions in Exercise 2.2 are designed to do just that.

EXERCISE 2.2. Identifying Your Fear-Provoking Thoughts

As you answer the following questions, keep in mind that the fear of negative evaluation or rejection is a common thread that runs through all thoughts related to stage fright. One key to identifying your fear-provoking thoughts is to recognize a fear of negative evaluation or rejection during your own internal dialogues. Also be on the lookout for any harmful predictions you think you can do little or nothing about it.

Ask yourself the following questions and record all of your responses in the space provided. (These are tough questions, so if you have some trouble getting started, first read the feedback for this exercise for some assistance.)

1. What will happen when I speak in public?

_____

_____

_____

_____

_____

2. What past experiences have I had in this type of situation and what were the consequences?

_____

_____

_____

_____

_____

3. What have I seen happen to other people in similar situations?

_____

_____

_____

_____

_____

4. What's the worst thing that could happen to me in this situation?

_____

_____

_____

_____

_____

5. If the worst thing were to happen, what would happen then? And then what? And so on.

_____

_____

_____

_____

_____

_____

_____

_____

_____

Summarize Your List of Fear-Provoking Thoughts

Use all of the information you've recorded above to make one consolidated list of your fear-provoking thoughts. Combine duplicates in any manner you think will be most helpful. (Keep this list handy since you'll be referring to it in upcoming chapters.)

_____   _____

_____   _____

_____   _____

_____   _____

_____   _____

Feedback for Exercise 2.2

I. What will happen when I speak in public?

If you are having difficulty getting warmed up, rephrase this question. For example, ask yourself "What might go wrong during my presentation?" Some of your predictions might be "I will forget part of the speech," "I will sound disorganized," or "The audience will think I'm boring." If you have difficulty coming up with a lot of predictions here, imagine that you are about to be called up to a platform to speak or recall a specific talk you gave. The more pressure a particular talk offered, the better choice it is for this exercise.

To give you an idea of where your vulnerabilities lie, see how many of your predictions fell into each of these three categories:

1. Things you will do incorrectly, such as forgetting information or losing your place.

2. Physical symptoms, such as sweating or voice quavering, that will embarrass you in front of an audience.

3. Negative reactions from the audience, such as thinking you are dull or repetitive.

This first question usually uncovers a lot of information. It is a good starting point, but it will rarely take you far enough. The next four questions help you probe a little deeper.

2. What past experiences have I had in this type of situation and what were the consequences?

Your past experiences will certainly have a large effect on your predictions. Try to dredge up any examples of negative things that may have happened to you during past presentations. Try to recall the predictions you made, what actually happened, and what the consequences were. Sometimes, it's not what happened to you in the past, but the consequences of what may happen that are really worrying you.

Past experiences—particularly failures—play an important role in stage fright. You may already have some believable evidence that whatever you are afraid of can happen to you because it already has! Experience is a great convincer.

Don't limit yourself to what happened; also include the consequences of what happened.

When answering this question, go back as far as you can. For example, if I were answering this question, I might think back to my personal humiliation in seventh-grade math class when I was called up to the chalkboard to work out a math problem. With each mistake I made, the giggles and whispers behind my back grew more and more intense. Incidents like this lay the foundation for a life of presentation fears. So, go back to the beginning if you have to.

As you look over your list of past incidents, reflect on those that seemed to recur. Can you identify repetitive patterns? Are any early incidents related to your current fears? Which incidents stick out in your mind? Have any of these past experiences made it into your dreams?

3. What have I seen happen to other people in similar situations?

This question is an extension of question 2. Observing what happens to someone else can be as powerful as your own direct experience. If you've been witness to someone else's bad experience with public speaking—even if you never had such an experience yourself—it might be enough to make you think that something like that could happen to you.

Bring to mind the worst things you've seen happen to other speakers—such as mean-spirited questions from the audience, freezing up, and shaking noticeably. Think about how those incidents affected your feelings and thoughts about speaking in public yourself.

When answering this question, don't be too fussy about the similarities between the situation and your own. Any situation in which you have observed someone mess up, fail, become embarrassed, or be humiliated will work for this part of the exercise. Also, you don't need to limit yourself to situations you've witnessed personally. Even a story about someone's failure could be influencing your thoughts. Once you've taken this question as far as you can, you'll be surprised by how easily you can make a connection between these situations and your own.

4. What's the worst thing that could happen to me in this situation?

This is a more intense version of the previous questions. When answering this question, be sure to also include the worst possible consequences of the worst things that could possibly happen. This category is often the most valuable one—particularly for pessimists and perfectionists. Anything that could possibly happen is fair game, so go ahead and take this question to the limit.

Imagining the worst-case scenario often helps you tap into that gray area between rational and irrational thoughts. It lets you examine cases in which you think your fears may be exaggerated, but they still make you anxious. You may be reluctant to voice some of these fears because they sound too extreme, but you still worry about them. Use this exercise as a safe harbor to express those things you think probably won't happen but could.

5. If the worst thing were to happen, what would happen then? And then what? And so on.

Take each negative prediction you've made so far and ask yourself this basic question: "And then what would happen?" Record the answer to that question, then ask yourself again, "And then what?" Continue this process until you can't come up with any more consequences. Here is an example of how to do this:

Situation: *After having been promoted, you are about to run your first departmental meeting.*

Negative prediction: *The department personnel are going to think I don't have the experience to lead because I can't express myself clearly.*

The worst possible outcome: *My performance at the meeting will be poor and ineffective.*

And then: *The people in my department won't respect me.*

And then: *I'll be ineffective as a leader and won't have the confidence to give them work assignments.*

And then: *The work won't get done and will reflect badly upon me.*

And then: *I'll be called into my boss's office to discuss the poor outcome of the department.*

And then: *This will give me a chance to rectify the situation.*

Doing this will show you that, in many cases, the consequences soon become trivial or you will have a chance to work things out somewhere down the line. The goal here is to keep asking these secondary questions "And then what?" until the situation becomes harmless.

It is foolish to avoid thinking about your fears, even though this can bring immediate relief. Even when you successfully avoid thinking about them, you'll always have that nagging feeling that something isn't quite right. So, press forward by asking yourself what would happen if a particular fear were to come true. You'll often find that the fear loses some of its power over you.

The most important thing to ask yourself is, "If that happens, would I survive?" You will be surprised to discover that you can tolerate the results of most bad experiences involving public speaking. This will greatly weaken the fears and make them much more manageable.

While doing Exercises 2.1 and 2.2, you may have discovered that just thinking about having to talk in public and imagining what could go wrong have made you tense. If it did, you are beginning to realize that you hold the key to your own relief. *If you have learned to make yourself anxious, you can learn to make yourself calm.* Learning to recognize your fear-provoking thoughts will show you how you can control and eliminate them. Let's go even more in depth and try to discover what you are most afraid of when it comes to public speaking.

Which makes you more afraid?

WHICH ARE YOU MORE AFRAID OF?

There are two very different types of stage fright. The first one has to do with how well you think you will perform in front of your audience. The other deals with whether you think your audience will like what you do. You can have either type of fear, or both. Most people experience some of both types. By paying close attention to your fear-provoking thoughts, you will discover which you fear more. Let's take a look at these two types of fears, beginning with the one you are probably more familiar with.

Fear of Failing in Front of an Audience

One common fear that public speakers often have is that they don't know their information well enough to effectively present it to their audience. This is a tricky fear because it depends on two things: 1) how well the speaker can recall the knowledge, and 2) how much the speaker knows about the topic compared with the audience's knowledge. For example, a student may study very hard and know the information in his or her presentation very well, but becomes intimidated when attempting to explain and discuss that information in front of his or her professor, who is perhaps an expert on the subject.

How well you know your information will certainly affect how well you remember it and deliver it, especially under pressure. The better you know your topic, the less chance you will forget it. Remembering your information is very important, but it does not guarantee your audience will enjoy your presentation, which brings us to the other type of fear.

Fear of Not Being Accepted by an Audience

My favorite example of a fear of not being accepted by an audience is what comedians call "flopsweat." Flopsweat is one of those terms that defines itself. Comedians worry that they will flop instead of making their audience laugh. Although successful comedians are usually very competent, some of them admit to being terrified night after night. They worry that evening's audience won't think their routine is funny, in which case they will be humiliated on stage. Virtually all comedians have been on stage at one time or another—perhaps early in their careers—only to be rejected by a silent audience. Since nobody really knows whether an audience will laugh at a particular joke, comedians experience the possibility of flopsweat on a regular basis.

When it comes to public speaking, you may not worry whether or not your audience finds you funny. In most cases, you hope they won't!

Some of the more common fear-provoking thoughts surrounding not being accepted include the fear your audience won't find you warm, interesting, persuasive, knowledgeable, and so on. We all want audience approval, and ultimately, we want them to like us and what we have to say. In Exercise 2.3, you will identify some of your fear-provoking thoughts specifically relating to the audience's acceptance of you.

EXERCISE 2.3. Identifying How Others See and Accept You

In this exercise, you'll be thinking about how acceptable you are to your audience. The way you view yourself and the way you think you are being viewed greatly determine how you will present yourself. For each of the pairs of descriptive words below, circle the number that shows how you think an audience would rate you personally.

Awkward	1	2	3	4	5	6	7	8	9	10	Poised
Boring	1	2	3	4	5	6	7	8	9	10	Interesting
Distant	1	2	3	4	5	6	7	8	9	10	Caring
Dumb	1	2	3	4	5	6	7	8	9	10	Intelligent
Forgettable	1	2	3	4	5	6	7	8	9	10	Memorable
Incompetent	1	2	3	4	5	6	7	8	9	10	Competent
Lifeless	1	2	3	4	5	6	7	8	9	10	Charismatic
Remote	1	2	3	4	5	6	7	8	9	10	Involved
Repulsive	1	2	3	4	5	6	7	8	9	10	Attractive
Tiring	1	2	3	4	5	6	7	8	9	10	Amusing
Unskilled	1	2	3	4	5	6	7	8	9	10	Talented

If you're feeling brave, ask friends and/or colleagues to use this form to evaluate you. This is not for the feint of heart, but it can be very revealing, especially when you compare it to your own evaluation.

Feedback for Exercise 2.3

Identify items that you have scored higher than 8 and lower than 3. These items represent extreme scores and show you which adjectives you think *accurately* describe you, one way or the other. Next, identify items you have scored 6 or above. These represent positive views you have of yourself. Also, identify the items you've scored 5 or less. These represent negative views you have of yourself. Your views strongly affect your predictions about how you think the audience will accept you. They will guide your actions and affect how you prepare for your presentation. As you read through the book, you'll learn how to determine if your estimates are accurate or exaggerated, and which ones you may be able to work on to help make your audience more accepting of you.

ARE THE CONSEQUENCES OF YOUR SPEECH FRIGHTENING YOU?

Let's examine your predictions about the importance of your talk. Will a bad speech threaten your job, your chance of getting a promotion, or your chance of getting a date with someone who means a lot to you? If you think a bad speech will lead to disaster, you will be very afraid to give it. The more you predict that negative consequences will result from a bad presentation, the more stage fright you will have. This is the point at which many people's fears become unreasonable. People often exaggerate how badly their lives will turn out if their talk goes poorly. If you were speaking in front of a large audience, you might normally feel some mild to moderate stage fright. But if you believe your job depends on a successful presentation, chances are you'd feel some extreme stage fright. If you thought it meant never being able to work in your field again, you'd most likely find yourself in a state of panic.

Think realistically about how the results of your next presentation might affect you. Could it affect your career, your relationship(s), or the way you think about yourself? Oftentimes, everything depends on how *you* see things—in other words, it is totally subjective. You will learn how to gain perspective on these subjective views of stage fright in Chapter 3. Meanwhile, let's take a look at the Case of Jud H. to see how the potential consequences of a speech can play a role in one's degree of stage fright.

The Case of Jud H.—Low Level of Stage Fright

Jud H. moved to a new neighborhood. When his son's teacher heard that he was an aerospace engineer, she asked if he would speak to her eighth-grade science class about the possibilities of space travel. This was a subject Jud knew very well, and he loved to talk about it. The audience—a class of thirteen-year-olds—was not a threat to him. He was confident that he knew more about astrophysics than any kid in the class. He also understood that if his talk went badly, the consequences would not affect his career. In any event, the likelihood of a successful talk was quite high. Not surprisingly, he gave the talk with confidence and received spontaneous applause from the class. When he finished the talk, the students asked him many questions, which he was well prepared to answer. He thoroughly enjoyed the experience.

The Case of Jud H.—High Level of Stage Fright

Jud H. was also scheduled to give a presentation at the aerospace company where he'd recently been hired. He was concerned about making a good impression on the other engineers and considered this his "coming-out party." He believed he was an effective talker in one-on-one situations, but he'd never felt comfortable talking in large professional settings. He usually avoided public speaking in professional situations whenever possible. A few days before his talk, Jud learned that several of the vice presidents, as well as the CEO of the company, were planning to attend his presentation.

Based on how important the outcome of his presentation was to him, Jud actively dreaded giving this talk for two weeks, and his wife complained about how irritable he'd become. He convinced himself that his audience of new colleagues would think he was a "lightweight" and unworthy of holding an esteemed position in the company. When Jud finally made his presentation, he experienced feelings of panic. Later, he could barely remember anything he had said.

When Jud and I examined the differences between the situations, he concluded that he wasn't a "bad" public speaker. He realized that his performance and his feelings leading to it simply depended on the situation and how he viewed the consequences.

In Exercise 2.4 on the following page, you will identify what you believe the consequences of your presentation will be. Remember, the more you exaggerate how important the outcome of a speech is, the more nervous you will become. If you can put each presentation into the proper perspective, you will approach the situation more calmly and greatly increase your chances of sounding good.

HOW DO YOU DEFINE THE SITUATION SURROUNDING YOUR SPEECH?

By now, you should be getting the message that having stage fright is not a personality trait. Some people believe that when it comes to stage fright, there are *haves* and *have-nots*. The *haves* get nervous in front of any audience, and the *have-nots* never get nervous. This is not true. Stage fright is not a mental disorder or a personality trait that you either have or don't have. Virtually everyone experiences stage fright at some time or another. *It depends on the situation.*

It's not that people automatically get nervous talking to other people —they get nervous depending on how they define a situation. This is yet another way for you to examine how you view stage fright. Instead of looking within yourself or out at the audience, now look at different aspects of the situation surrounding your talk. This provides another perspective for examining your own stage fright and how it comes about.

What part of public speaking makes you nervous? Since every situa-

It Ain't a Trait
Stage fright is not a mental disorder or a personality trait that you either have or don't have. It depends on the situation.

EXERCISE 2.4. Identifying the Consequences of Your Presentation

In the space provided below, list the consequences of an upcoming presentation or speech. Be sure to answer the following questions:

1. What are the possible immediate or short-term consequences of your presentation? Will you feel embarrassed? Will this ruin an opportunity for you? Will it cause awkwardness between you and your friends or colleagues?

2. What are the possible long-term consequences of your presentation? Will it affect your career? Will it affect any social or work opportunities? Will it leave indelible memories that people will refer to for years?

3. How reasonable are your predictions of the results? Keep in mind that it's not uncommon to exaggerate the importance of a talk. We'll be spending some time on evaluating the reasonableness of your fears in Chapter 3, but for now, try to be as objective as possible when answering this question.

Immediate/Short-Term Consequences

_____

_____

_____

_____

_____

_____

Long-Term Consequences

_____

_____

_____

_____

_____

Feedback for Exercise 2.4

Examining the results of this exercise helps you to further identify your fear-provoking thoughts. You may discover that you are causing yourself more anxiety by telling yourself that the results of a bad presentation will devastate your life. Many people are brought up with the belief that any form of failure is catastrophic. This is the kind of belief that seems so obvious on the surface that it's rarely questioned. This exercise helps you realistically examine both the short- and long-term effects to determine if you are just panicking or if there is a substantial reason to fear the consequences.

tion is different, it might be the size of the audience, how well you know the people in the audience, how well you know your material, or even how well you slept the night before. Each time you give a talk, the situation is different. Here's a short list of factors that affect the situation: the authority of the people in the audience, how prepared you are, experts in the audience who know more than you about the subject, whether or not you have to use a microphone, what you ate before the presentation, how tight the waistband on your pants is, and a few thousand other things.

Don't be fooled into believing the stage-fright myth that size matters. There is a common belief that the degree of stage fright depends on the size of the audience—in other words, the larger the audience, the greater the fear. Like many myths, this one is often untrue. While the size of the audience may increase a speaker's tension, a large audience can also energize a speaker and make him or her try harder. Here's an example:

A friend of mind is a successful studio guitar player. After a trip to Detroit, he told me that he had played at the Pontiac Dome without experiencing any fear whatsoever. Can you imagine playing in front of 50,000 people and not being afraid? Then came the strange part. The following week, he performed at a local club in Los Angeles with an audience of 300. He told me he was so nervous that he could hardly hold on to his guitar pick. After we discussed the situation, we came to a few conclusions.

Small audiences can provide a sense of intimacy and comfort, or they can make a presenter feel like he or she is under a microscope.

In Detroit, with bright lights in his eyes and the audience of strangers somewhere in the distance, he had nothing to lose. He was concerned only with entertaining them with his music. However, in the small Los Angeles club, he knew more than half of the people watching him. Many of them were also guitar players and were listening to his music very carefully. He considered the club gig a much riskier situation, one that could affect his reputation and future job opportunities.

In Exercise 2.5, you will determine the situational factors that play a role in your case of stage fright. Like my guitar-playing friend, you may discover you feel more comfortable in front of an audience of strangers, or you may discover you'd prefer an audience of people you know.

EXERCISE 2.5. Identifying Situational Factors

In the spaces provided below, identify an event where you spoke or performed well *without* experiencing strong anxiety or fear. For example, maybe you once told a group of your friends about a movie or sporting event you went to and were able to answer their questions.

Next, try to identify the aspects of that particular situation that made you feel comfortable and confident. Perhaps you've known all the people who were listening to you for a very long time and they did not pose a threat to you. Or maybe you knew more about the event than they did so there was no chance of contradictions or challenges.

Now, identify an event where you did experience a lot of stage fright. For example, maybe you asked your boss for a raise or gave a speech in your community, and it went poorly. Identify the situational factors you think may have been responsible for your anxiety, such as financial consequences or the chance of being criticized for making mistakes.

Successful Performance

Event: _____

_____

Situational factors: _____

_____

_____

_____

_____

_____

Unsuccessful Performance

Event: _____

_____

Situational factors: _____

_____

_____

_____

_____

_____

Review your responses, and use them to answer the following questions:

1. What types of people make you most afraid?

_____

_____

_____

_____

_____

2. What sort of things are you uncomfortable discussing or doing?

_____

_____

_____

_____

_____

3. What size groups seem to affect you most?

_____

_____

_____

_____

_____

Feedback for Exercise 2.5

Identifying situations in which you were comfortable helps you see firsthand that you don't *always* experience stage fright. This allows you to identify the various situational factors that are present when you do experience it. It's good to be aware that you don't *have* stage fright but that you *experience* stage fright in certain situations.

Also try to figure out why and how the two situations were different from each other. What factors were missing in the successful performance that allowed you to remain calm? Were there one or more things that made you nervous in the unsuccessful performance? The more specific you can be, the more helpful the information will be in designing your plan to overcome your fear of public speaking.

WHAT YOU HAVE LEARNED
AND WHERE YOU ARE GOING

In this chapter, you learned that fear-provoking thoughts are sometimes difficult to identify. However, you also learned a number of ways to tap into your internal dialogues to put words to what is making you afraid. The information you've generated in this chapter will be very useful to you. Identifying your particular fears will help you customize the remainder of the book. The next step is to evaluate your fear-provoking thoughts to determine if they're reasonable or not.

The BIG Idea

Your fear-provoking thoughts might be based on real-life experiences and may actually be reasonable. On the other hand, they might be the result of exaggeration and/or shaky logic. Identify the thinking process that fuels your fear-provoking thoughts.

3

EVALUATING YOUR FEAR-PROVOKING THOUGHTS

A friend of mine was planning to ask his boss for a raise, but the idea of doing it was stressing him out. When I asked why, he said, "Well, my boss might bring up the few times I came in late, or he might think I'm not dedicated enough, or he might get angry that I'm asking for a raise and demote me, or . . ." At that point, I interrupted him to say that solving his problem would be a "snap." I suggested he wear a thick, loose rubber band around his wrist, and each time he *imagined* what his boss *might* say, he should snap the rubber band. The next time I saw him, his wrist was almost as red as his face, but he understood my point. *Just because he believed something might happen did not mean it would happen.* When he finally asked for the raise, he was turned down. But not for the reasons he'd imagined. The company's earnings were so low at the time that there was no room for a raise for anyone in the company, including the boss. None of the things my friend imagined—the things he feared might happen—actually happened.

For a while, I toyed with the idea of including a rubber band with this book. I pictured the advertisement, FREE WITH THIS BOOK: STATE-OF-THE-ART BIOFEEDBACK DEVICE THAT HELPS YOU CONQUER STAGE FRIGHT! But the information in this chapter is more powerful than a rubber band. It provides you with a set of tools to help you analyze your fear-provoking thoughts and divide them into two categories: 1) reasonable fears based on actual evidence, and 2) imagined fears that come from your mind. I certainly won't make light of the fears based on your imagination since that's where fear generally lives. They are no less frightening than reasonable fears. In fact, they might be even more powerful. However, it's important

FREE!
state-of-the-art
biofeedback
device

to understand that your imagination may be causing you to exaggerate, overgeneralize, and bend logic.

Each tool in this chapter gives you a different way to examine your fears in a new light. My clinical supervisor gave me some words to live by, "Our job is really to get people to see the same thing in a new way." By the end of this chapter, you will be as indebted to him as I am. You'll learn how to evaluate the evidence you use to support your fears and determine if it is valid. You'll learn to create alternative ways to think about your fears, and use worst-case scenarios to examine them. You'll also learn to identify several flaws in your logic. Next, you'll examine and evaluate your reactions to the various characteristics of a situation, and finally, you'll rate how reasonable your fears are. Let's begin by examining the evidence on which you base your fears.

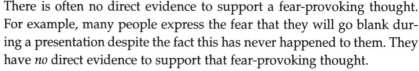

SUPPORTING EVIDENCE

"Just the facts, ma'am"

There is often no direct evidence to support a fear-provoking thought. For example, many people express the fear that they will go blank during a presentation despite the fact this has never happened to them. They have *no* direct evidence to support that fear-provoking thought.

We're going to examine the strength of the evidence supporting your fear-provoking thoughts, but first, let's take a moment to consider the case of Janice M. Janice was worried she would become disorganized during a seminar presentation. But, as it turned out, she had *never* actually become disorganized while speaking in public. When I pushed her to provide evidence to support her fear-provoking thought, she recalled being witness to a classmate's poorly delivered presentation. "It was awful," she said. "Everyone in the class was embarrassed for her. They felt so sorry for her. I'd die of shame if that ever happened to me."

Janice's classmate's experience was the only evidence supporting her fear-provoking thoughts. When she realized that there was very little direct proof to support her fear, she was able to release it.

Once you make yourself afraid to speak in public by thinking fear-provoking thoughts, you end up putting most of your attention on the fear itself and never challenge the fear to determine if it's reasonable. If you can determine that your fear is not based on anything that has happened to you, you should be able to let it go.

There are three different sources of evidence on which you base your fears—direct experience, direct observation, and indirect experience. Let's take a look at each one to help you determine what you've based your particular fears on.

Direct Experience

The most reasonable fears are those that are based on firsthand evidence, or direct experience. In this case, you have experienced an event with bad results. For example, if you were once bitten by a dog, you have a pretty good reason to be afraid of dogs. You probably know the fear isn't totally reasonable since people have positive interactions with dogs all the time. However, the fact that they don't get bitten means little to you because *you have been bitten*. Similarly, if you once stepped up to the podium and were so nervous that you really did forget everything you were going to say, it's understandable to fear that it will happen again. Rest assured, you can overcome reasonable fears based on direct experiences, but it will take a little work. Just keep reading and partaking in the exercises throughout this book.

In most cases involving direct experience, however, the evidence supporting your prediction will probably be exaggerated. You may have made things out to be much worse than they actually were. In this case, it's a little easier to disprove your fear-provoking thoughts.

To determine if your fear-provoking thoughts are based on direct experience, identify specific events and try to recall exactly what happened and how bad the experience was. Record as many details as you can, and keep this record handy. You'll need it later when you're formulating your plan to conquer any fears based on direct evidence.

Consider each of your fear-provoking thoughts, and like an investigator, keep searching your memory banks for direct evidence. When you find it, try to determine if it's really enough evidence to support your fear-provoking thought. For example, if you recall that your hands shook for a few minutes during an interview, this is not enough evidence to support the fear that your legs will give out while you're up at the podium. Keep investigating and cross-examining yourself to get the evidence you are looking for or until you recognize the lack of evidence.

It's helpful to approach weak evidence with a good sense of critical humor. For instance, say to yourself in the most sarcastic voice you can muster, "That's it? My hands shook for a couple of seconds? And because of this, I'm panicking for a month? That's not enough evidence!" You may then rest your case. It is important for you to see the absurdity of being so afraid based on so little direct evidence to support that fear.

Once you've developed a fear-provoking thought, it's easy to be swept up in the heart-pounding panic that it causes. You must stop this downward spiral and demand to see the evidence. At best, you'll probably discover that you've exaggerated an actual event, or you may realize

Once you've developed a fear-provoking thought, it's easy to be swept up in the heart-pounding panic that it causes. You must stop this downward spiral and demand to see the evidence.

that the fear is not based on anything that actually happened to you. So let's take a look at fears based on direct observation.

Direct Observation

Evidence that is based on something that happened to someone else, or direct observation, rather than direct experience, may seem reasonable on the surface. If it happened to someone else, why can't it happen to you? And if it was only mildly humiliating for them, who is to say it wouldn't be twice as humiliating for you? That's your imagination talking. In Janice's case, she observed her classmate's humiliating event. Although Janice wasn't the speaker, the whole experience was very intense for her, maybe even more intense than it was for her friend.

When you realize that you are basing your fears on something that happened to someone else, try to investigate further. How did that person react after the humiliating event? Was she able to face people from the audience, like friends or colleagues, after the humiliating event? Most important, did she continue to inhale and exhale—in other words, did she survive? Although you are sure that she would have died of shame, that didn't happen, did it? The situation often looks worse from the outside.

Regardless of the humiliation you witnessed, you must remind yourself that this has not happened to you. There is no direct evidence that you will forget your speech, or shake or stammer, or whatever else your imagination has convinced you might happen. Fears based on direct observation are simply not reasonable.

Indirect Experience

"I never exaggerate, I just remember big."
—Juan "Chi-Chi" Rodriguez

In the case of indirect evidence, you've only *heard* about something that happened to someone. You probably realize that as stories about events are told again and again, they become exaggerated and embellished. For example, each time I tell someone how good I was at basketball in high school, my ability to play under pressure becomes more and more legendary. (It was pretty amazing.) People have a tendency to retell events in a manner that makes them sound more awesome than they really were. So, be wary of taking other people's accounts of humiliating performances and traumatic consequences at face value. In any event, like fears based on direct observation, fears based on indirect experience are unreasonable.

If you've ever consulted an attorney on a matter in which you've been unfairly treated, you probably began by listing the many ways you'd been wronged and how you want to get even with the person who wronged you. Then, the attorney asks, "What evidence do you have to prove that you were wronged?" It's not enough to list your complaints. You need to back them up with solid evidence. This is what you will be doing in Exercise 3.1. In this case, you are going to be the judge, the jury, and the opposing attorney. You need to examine the logic behind your fears to determine if you really have supporting evidence. For example, like I said before, if you've been bitten by a dog, you have a relatively reasonable reason to fear dogs. However, if you've simply noticed that dogs have sharp teeth, that's very weak evidence to support your fear.

EXERCISE 3.1. Examining the Supporting Evidence

In Chapter 2, you identified your fear-provoking thoughts. Now, imagine that you are being told that your fears are baseless. It's your job to provide evidence that your fear-provoking thoughts should be taken seriously. Do this by making as strong a case as possible to support your fears. Provide specific supporting evidence, including dates, places, times, and names. Be sure to identify the source of the evidence as well. Once you've done this, you'll examine the data to determine if it is substantial enough to support your fear of speaking in public.

Fear-Provoking Thoughts Under Investigation

_____

_____

_____

_____

Supporting Evidence

From Direct Experience: _____

_____

_____

From Direct Observation: _____

_____

_____

From Indirect Experience: _____

_____

_____

Feedback for Exercise 3.1

To examine the evidence on which you've based your fears, answer the following questions:

- Is there actual data to support your fears—for example, specific events, specific outcomes, or specific instances of forgetting or losing your place?

- Are any of the examples of evidence actually your interpretations of what happened rather than real outcomes. If you find yourself writing things like "I felt like everyone was bored," then be wary. Your interpretation is not as valid as having had someone walk up to you afterward and say, "Wow, that was really boring."

- If someone came to you with the same evidence, would you take it seriously?

The key here is to get yourself to distinguish between fact and opinion. Keep challenging the facts until you rule out the false ones.

Now that you have examined the evidence you've based your predictions on, let's look at how you can see your fear-provoking thoughts in a different light.

CONSIDERING ALTERNATIVE EXPLANATIONS

We often treat our predictions as if they are facts. For example, let's say your friend doesn't show up for a lunch date and doesn't call. Those things are facts—she doesn't show up and doesn't call. If you conclude that she did those things because she is selfish or because she doesn't want to be your friend anymore, that's your interpretation of the situation. Truth was, her cell phone battery died and she was stuck in traffic. What a shame you upset yourself with your predictions.

A good way to combat making upsetting predictions like that is to come up with alternative *possible* explanations to explain the facts. A possible alternative explanation in the case of the no-show friend might be that she had some sort of emergency. "Possible" is the key word here. If you can doubt your fear-provoking thoughts even a little bit, you are well on your way to reducing their influence over you. Let's examine the case of Cheryl M. I asked Cheryl to generate a list of alternative explanations for a poor talk, and this took a great deal of pressure off of her the next time she was faced with public speaking.

The Case of Cheryl M.

Cheryl M. had a negative experience during a staff meeting at which she was discussing the company's projected goals for the next two years. She had been quite anxious during the talk, and the staff members had seemed disinterested and fidgety. Cheryl attributed her poor performance to her inadequacies as a public speaker. However, when I pushed her to provide alternative explanations for her poor performance and the audience's reaction, here's what she came up with:

- I did not have time to familiarize myself with the data and prepare adequately.
- The vice president did not make the projected goals clear enough, so I had difficulty discussing them with my staff.
- The meeting took place after lunch on a Friday, when everyone was thinking about their weekend plans.
- The staff hates projection meetings because things change so fast in the industry that they are never meaningful. They rarely pay attention or bother being polite.

Just considering alternative explanations for the poor outcome of her talk helped Cheryl feel better. It didn't change the facts, but she recognized that there were other possible explanations for the audience's response to her talk besides her imagined inadequacies as a public speaker.

Try to determine if you've locked yourself into seeing a situation from only one side. In Exercise 3.2 on the following page, you're going to try to come up with alternative explanations for something that went wrong. Once you see that there are indeed some alternate ways to interpret an event, you'll find that the fears stemming from it will begin to have less of an effect on you.

SELF-TESTING AND LOGICAL FLAWS

When people are afraid, they begin to think less clearly. To express this relationship, we commonly hear expressions like "He lost his head" or "He cracked under pressure." Anxiety and logic rarely go hand in hand. In this section, you will examine how logical flaws can creep into your thinking when you are focused on your fears. Logical flaws often lead to poor conclusions. Therefore, in evaluating your fear-provoking thoughts, it is essential to examine your thinking processes.

First, it is important to be aware of your tendency to self-test. We all

EXERCISE 3.2. Exploring Alternative Explanations

Think back to a time when you gave a poor presentation or think about an upcoming presentation where you've predicted things will go wrong. Consider a few of the fear-provoking thoughts associated with the real or imagined event, and record them in the space below. Once you've done this, come up with believable alternative explanations for what went (or might go) wrong.

What went wrong: _____

_____

_____

Alternative explanation: _____

_____

_____

What went wrong: _____

_____

Alternative explanation: _____

_____

_____

What went wrong: _____

_____

_____

Alternative explanation: _____

_____

_____

Feedback for Exercise 3.2

As you examine your alternative explanations, the key feature to look for is plausibility. As long as each alternative makes sense to you, it will help you avoid getting locked into seeing things from only one viewpoint. Review Cheryl's alternative explanations on page 49. Notice that each one of her alternative explanations makes sense and is reasonable. Each would explain why things didn't go so well for her during the presentation.

test ourselves, and we do it all the time. Sometimes it's a trivial test with no real significance. For example, "If I can throw this wad of paper into the trash can from here, I'm good." But sometimes the tests are big. For example, "If I can get this client, I'll be on the fast track at work, and someday I'll achieve great success!" Some of our tests are reasonable, and some aren't. The important factor in self-testing is making sure that the test is reasonable, or logical. Take a look at the following examples and try to determine which self-test is unreasonable. Here's the situation: Gerald D. is going to be making a presentation to the CEO and the board of trustees of his company. There's a lot of pressure on him, and he's very nervous.

> Self-test 1—If the board members linger after my presentation to ask questions and if I get a luncheon invitation, that's proof my presentation was a success.

> Self-test 2—If I present all eight of my main points in order, I will have accomplished the goals of my presentation.

It should be pretty clear that self-test 1 is the unreasonable one. There are many reasons the board members might not remain after the presentation that have nothing to do with the quality of the presentation. However, if Gerald is insecure, he can bend and twist the logic to feed his fears. In other words, "no questions or lunch dates equals failure."

In general, the more insecure you feel about a situation, the more often you will self-test. If you are very unsure of yourself, you are much more likely to push for feedback after a talk, and then skew the feedback to fuel your insecurity. Moreover, the more insecure you feel, the more unreasonable your tests will become. You will likely use any negative event as proof that your talk did not go well. If a couple of people leave early or if no one asks questions or they ask too many questions, you can use this as evidence that your presentation didn't go well. I hope it's clear that this is bad evidence.

Take note when you self-test to determine if your insecurities are interfering with your logic. To help you figure this out, let's examine four common logical flaws that are common to people who experience a lot of stage fright. If you can learn to identify these logical flaws in your fear-provoking thoughts, you can go a long way toward controlling your fear of public speaking. With this information, you can examine the data you are using to determine how logical your thought process is. This material is based largely on the work of Aaron Beck, the father of cognitive therapy, and Dr. David Burns, a leader in cognitive behavioral therapy methods. For more information along these lines, consider reading *Feeling Good: New Mood Therapy* by Dr. David Burns.

Unreasonable Self-Test

Reasonable Self-Test

LOGICAL FLAW 1

1. Overgeneralization

Overgeneralizing requires very few, or even one, bad experience. For example, if you've had one bad experience during a presentation and now you think *all* your future presentations will turn out the same way, you are overgeneralizing. Typically, overgeneralizing requires very little data in order to reach a conclusion. A key to identifying overgeneralization is to look for words like "always" and "never." Sally C.'s case provides a good example of logical flaw #1.

The Case of Sally C.

Sally C. was a music student who was performing at her senior recital. In the middle of her performance, she blanked out on the piece she was playing and couldn't pick it up. Humiliated, she ran off the stage in tears. Based on that incident, Sally was sure she would *never* be able to remember her music under pressure again. The basic flaws in her thinking are obvious. She had very little data to support her negative prediction. She'd had only *one* bad experience and was making all of her new predictions based on it. She didn't consider any of the positive data—the hundreds of times she had remembered and played the pieces perfectly. In her mind, those successful performances didn't count anymore. She was sure she'd *always* be plagued by forgetfulness during her performances and would *never* have a successful performance ever again.

LOGICAL FLAW 2

2. All-or-Nothing Thoughts

When you have all-or-nothing thoughts, you are thinking in extremes without acknowledging that there may be a middle ground. Everything is described in an absolute fashion. However, the world usually comes in all shades of gray. Rarely is anything purely black or white. A key to identifying all-or-nothing thoughts is to look for extreme language. Words like "greatest" and "worst" are good examples. Let's look at John T.'s case for an example of all-or-nothing thoughts.

The Case of John T.

John T., a college tennis player, believed there were only two types of tennis players: great ones and awful ones. The great players were the ones who could beat him. The awful players were the ones he could beat. Whenever he was up against a "great" player, he'd get very nervous and play poorly because that player was so much better than him. Whenever he was up against an "awful" player, he felt like he was wasting his time. Poor John rarely enjoyed playing because of these all-or-nothing thoughts.

Are all your friends saints or are they all scoundrels? Is your car a top-of-the-line luxury vehicle or a broken-down wreck? Is your office perfectly organized or is it in complete chaos? Chances are that none of these extremes are accurate. Evaluating things as being either black or white isn't reasonable. So, it's likely that you won't forget every part of your speech or remember every detail perfectly every time you make a presentation.

To avoid falling prey to your all-or-nothing thoughts, evaluate different aspects of your performance by rating them from 0 to 100. Rather than making the absolute statement that your performance was a total failure, you'll begin to see the shades of gray. This ranking strategy may work even better if you give descriptions to a range of numbers. For example, you can call 90–100 a great speech, 75–90 a good one, 60–75 an average one, and so on. This can also help you gauge your improvement.

3. Disqualification of the Positive

LOGICAL FLAW 3

When you base a conclusion on poor or no information despite good evidence to the contrary, you are disqualifying the positive. Quite often, when a person holds an idea about himself, he'll often look for evidence to support it. And, when there's really no supporting evidence, he will actually distort the evidence until it fits his point of view. The Case of Ernie A. is an example of someone who disqualifies the positive. Despite the fact that people would tell him how well he had performed, Ernie was sure that whenever he gave a presentation his nervousness and anxiety were written all over his face for his audience to see and this would spoil his performance. There is a basic rule about human perception that feeds into this flaw. We notice what's wrong before we notice what's right. This, as you know, is a basic survival skill.

The Case of Ernie A.

Ernie A., a marketing coordinator, did not want anyone to notice how nervous he was at the monthly staff meetings. After the meetings, his colleagues would always compliment him on how calm and self-assured he seemed to be during his presentations. He disregarded this feedback from others, convinced that his nervousness was clearly visible. He distorted the compliments he received by telling himself that if he didn't look so nervous, people wouldn't feel obligated to compliment him.

Ernie ignored all outside evidence to the contrary, using his own emotions and distorted beliefs as his only supporting evidence.

To avoid this logical flaw, consider all of the feedback you receive—the positive as well as the negative. Try to believe the position rather than disqualifying it because you personally feel it's unjustified. Accept it graciously and allow yourself to feel good that someone has expressed a positive opinion of your performance. I realize that this is easier said than done. In fact, there is mounting scientific evidence that it is difficult to get people to change their minds, especially when it involves changing their own model of how the world really works. For a very interesting look into this subject, consider reading *Changing Minds: The Art and Science of Changing Our Own and Other People's Minds* by Howard Gardner.

LOGICAL FLAW 4

4. Magnification and Minimization

In this logical flaw, failures and fears are magnified out of proportion, while successes and strong points are minimized. In general, people have a tendency to dwell on the negative no matter how small or insignificant it is and tend to ignore or deemphasize positive factors. Jim Y.'s case is an example of a person who ignored his past successes whenever he experienced even the slightest of setbacks.

The Case of Jim Y.

Jim Y., a young comedian, had just completed a week of performances at a local comedy club when he came to me for help. He told me he was terrified to go back on stage after his miserable failures during the one-week engagement. Upon further probing, I discovered that he'd been enormously successful six out of the seven nights. On the night that wasn't enormously successful, the audience had given him a lukewarm reception. When people asked him how his week had gone, all he could talk about was how badly he'd done based on that single night's performance. When his friends who'd attended all his performances pointed out how successful the other six nights were, he dismissed their comments and turned his attention back to the "off night."

If you tend to magnify the negatives and minimize the positives, it's essential to learn how to balance the way you view your personal history. I'm not saying you should ignore bad performances. Simply be sure to consider both the good and the bad to get an accurate picture of how you did. The goal is to use your existing data to point you in the right direction for change.

It is not important for you to be able to name and define each of these logical thinking flaws. Rather, you should notice that they all share certain basic similarities. They emphasize the bad, ignore the good, and are prone to serious exaggeration. In Exercise 3.3, you will identify the logical flaws in the fear-provoking thoughts you have already identified. You will be given examples of logical flaws, and you will try to fit them to your predictions.

EXERCISE 3.3. Uncovering Logical Flaws

This exercise includes a list of the various types of logical flaws that most often result in unreasonable predictions. Examine your fear-provoking thoughts and the evidence you are basing them on. Try to determine if you can identify these logical flaws in your thought process. Place an "X" beside each logical flaw you have detected and record examples in the spaces provided.

____ Exaggeration

_____

_____

_____

_____

____ Use of words like *always* or *never*

_____

_____

_____

_____

____ Discounting positive evidence

_____

_____

_____

_____

_____

_____ Overemphasizing negative evidence

_____

_____

_____

_____

_____ Having only extreme points of view

_____

_____

_____

_____

Feedback for Exercise 3.3

Review your answers and try to identify extremes in your thinking. Also, look for a lack of balance in the way you interpret what happens to you or what you predict. If it seems like you only consider the negative, this is a tip-off that your logic is flawed. Let's revisit the case of Cheryl M. (see page 49). Cheryl did this exercise, and the following was the outcome:

X Exaggeration

I wasn't just going to forget some information; I was going to "freeze up."

X Use of words like *always* or *never*

Every time I speak, the same things are always going to happen.

X Discounting positive evidence

Even if a few of the presentations I made worked out okay, there were still a lot of times when I had problems. I can never be comfortable because they can always come back at any time.

X Overemphasizing negative evidence

My rapid heartbeat was proof that I was extremely nervous even if I didn't necessarily sound that way.

X Looking at only extreme points of view

Everyone in the audience pitied me. I hate it when the audience feels sorry for me.

After doing this analysis, Cheryl learned that she wasn't a terrible speaker, but she only paid attention to the problems she encountered. She discounted all of her good presentations. The good ones outweighed the bad ones and most of her talks actually went pretty well.

DISSECTING THE CHARACTERISTICS OF THE SITUATION & EVALUATING YOUR REACTION

As you now know, a fear of public speaking depends a lot on the situation, and each situation is unique. Even if you make the exact same presentation ten times in a row, it will be different every time—there will be new faces in the audience, the room may be larger or smaller or hotter or colder, you may have gotten more or less sleep the night before, and so on. The list of variables is virtually endless.

The importance you assign to each part of the situation determines how much anxiety you feel. The following sections examine each part of the situation to help you determine which characteristics really are fear provoking and which parts you may be exaggerating the danger of. As you read, try to bring to mind an anxiety-provoking performance and determine how each characteristic of the situation relates to it.

I. The Audience

SITUATIONAL FACTOR I

The people who make up your audience can play a major role in determining your level of stage fright. The members of the audience may determine how you will be evaluated. Will you be evaluated positively or negatively? Do they have the experience and training to know the difference between a good job and a bad one? The two most important things to consider about your audience are how competent they are and how important they are.

If there are people in the audience who are very competent and really know the topic you're discussing, you will probably get nervous—especially if you think they know more than you do. If members of the audience are informed, well trained, and discriminating, they will be in a position to know whether you do a good job or a bad job. For an example of how the type of audience can affect someone's anxiety level, see "Music, Maestro, Please" on page 58.

If the audience includes influential people, you can expect to be nervous. If their power or status relates directly to the topic of your presentation, the effect becomes even stronger. And, if your future can be affected by the outcome of your talk, the situation will be even more stressful. For example, if you are giving a presentation on your company's new marketing policy and your boss is part of the audience, your anxiety level will probably be high. However, if your promotion is on the line, chances are your anxiety level will be tenfold. And, if your job is actually at stake, you can expect serious anxiety.

Music, Maestro, Please

I was once fortunate enough to have the opportunity to interview Paul Salamunovich, the former conductor of the Los Angeles Master Chorale. He had taken his choir to Rome and performed in St. Peter's Square before the Pope, the entire College of Cardinals, and thousands of people. He told me that during the performance, he'd felt very calm and totally enjoyed the concert without feeling any fear.

A month later, however, he took the same choir to Atlanta to perform the same recital for the annu-al convention of the American Choral Conductors. He'd admitted to shaking like a leaf during the performance—same choir, same music, but a totally different level of fear. Why?

Maestro Salamunovich knew that the Pope and others would simply enjoy the concert and never notice a missed beat. But in Atlanta, every choral conductor would immediately take note of even the slightest mistake, and, what's more, they'd discuss it later!

Think back to a nerve-wracking presentation. Were there people in the audience you'd consider experts on your topic? Did their presence add to your discomfort? Also, were there any important people present who could affect your future? Were you consciously aware of them during your talk? The answers to all of these questions show the extent to which you permit the composition of the audience to affect your level of fear.

It's important to know that a speaker's perception of how the audience can affect his or her future is often exaggerated. Fears based on exaggerated consequences are easily challenged once their foundation is clear. The following sections discuss the major "audience factors" that can influence your level of stage fright. Try to evaluate how accurate your particular audience-related fears are.

A Strange Audience versus a Familiar One

Some people are more relaxed in front of an audience that includes people they know, and others feel more relaxed in front of total strangers. In the case of people you know, you may feel more nervous because a bad performance will likely be discussed or even held up to ridicule in your social and/or work circles. In other cases, you may fear performing in front of strangers because they don't know where you're coming from, unlike your friends and coworkers. Strangers know nothing about you until you begin. During your last speech, how familiar were you with the people in the audience? Did the familiarity, or lack of it, affect you?

The Size of the Audience

In general, the level of stage fright increases with the size of the audience, but as you already know, this is not a hard and fast rule. Some people actually prefer a larger audience because it seems impersonal and anonymous. There's no need for constant eye contact or personal interaction. In that case, their level of stage fright decreases with the size of the audience. Either way, size matters!

Think about how the size of an audience affects you. Do you get nervous in front of large groups, small groups, or all groups? How does the size of the group affect you?

The Audience's Reaction

It's not uncommon to become anxious if people in the audience begin to fidget, whisper to one another, or show other signs of a lack of interest. The more you interpret these actions as signs of disinterest in your presentation, the more stage fright you will feel. Some speakers look over the audience's heads, rather than at them, to avoid eye contact and feedback.

How much do you monitor the audience members' reactions? Does it distract you very much? Do you use their reactions to determine how well you are doing? If they fidget, do you think it's because they don't like your presentation?

2. Being Evaluated and/or Judged

SITUATIONAL FACTOR 2

It's not uncommon to feel nervous if you know you are being evaluated. If your performance is being videotaped or if there are judges or critics in the audience with clipboards and pencils, you'll probably get more nervous than if the audience members are just there to learn or be entertained. If the judges share their notes at certain times and smile or frown at the same time, you might find yourself unnerved. Imagine the pressure Olympic gymnasts experience. They perform for a brief time, knowing that a series of judges will soon be holding up score cards that will determine their future. If they don't perform well, they have to wait and train for four more years to get another chance, if they can get through the Olympic trials.

There are times when you are one of several people making a pitch or presentation to get an account or new client. You may be running for an office and have to make a speech as a candidate. You may be asking for a raise or a promotion, or interviewing for a new position. In all of these cases, you know that you are being evaluated. This will add pressure to the situation. How have you handled this kind of pressure? Were you able to focus on the topic at hand? How were you able to deal with the pressure of being evaluated?

3. Being the Center of Attention

In general, the closer you are to being the center of attention, the more butterflies you will likely feel fluttering about in your stomach. For example, if you were performing as part of a choir, you'd probably feel much calmer than if you were singing a solo. When you are the speaker or a featured speaker, you'll be the center of attention. All eyes will be watching you. If you stop talking, there's silence. Compare that to just being a member of a panel discussion with five other panel members and a moderator. Whenever you share the spotlight, your fear will be related to the number of people you share it with. The more people performing with you, the less stage fright you will experience. Have you ever been the "whole show"? How did this affect you?

4. The Uncertainty Factor, or the Novelty of the Situation

It's not uncommon to be nervous in a new or unfamiliar situation. It stands to reason that a person will perform better when he or she knows what to expect. For example, if you have never worn a microphone, you might find it unnerving. You may wonder what will happen if you clear your throat or make a bodily sound, such as a spontaneous burp, while you're wearing it. You may wonder how you'll know if you're speaking loud enough or too loud. Likewise, what if you have notes prepared, but there's no table or podium on which to place them? Anything out of the ordinary can be quite scary, even terrifying.

Consider someone who plays tennis for fun and feels very comfortable during a tennis match with a friend, even if a few people stop to watch. However, if this person were to enter a tournament with spectators, a referee, and a commentator, his or her comfort level would likely drop dramatically. Likewise, giving a talk under conditions that you are not used to can be very difficult. Think back to a time when you gave a speech—was there anything new or unfamiliar that you had to get accustomed to? How long did it take? Did you ever feel comfortable in this novel situation?

Perhaps you found yourself in a new and unfamiliar role that affected your comfort level. For example, being a PTA member who shares thoughts and ideas at a meeting is different from being the PTA president who is running the meeting. Maybe you've recently been promoted or elected to a new position and had to take a leadership role with people who had formerly been your equals. If this was the case, you should become more comfortable as the novelty wears off.

Now that you are more familiar with some of the situational factors, Exercise 3.4 will help you determine which of these factors has a role in your case of stage fright. There's a good rule in psychology—*You can't solve a problem before you have identified it*. This exercise will help you figure out how you are viewing different situations. This will give you insight into how you construct your fear-provoking thoughts and will provide you with the information you need to evaluate them.

Exercise 3.4. Identifying Situational Causes of Your Stage Fright

Think back to a time when you gave a poor presentation or think about an upcoming presentation where you've predicted things will go wrong. Fill out the form below to identify how you are affected by each part of the situation. Place an "x" next to each situational factor you think has a strong influence on you. Then, for each checked item, write a short description of how that situation affected, or will affect, you.

Situation

___ You are the center of attention for all or part of the presentation.

_____

_____

_____

___ The audience contains powerful or important people.

_____

_____

_____

___ The audience includes very competent people.

_____

_____

_____

____ There are strangers in the audience.

_____

_____

____ There are family, friends, or colleagues in the audience.

_____

_____

____ You are in front of a large audience.

_____

_____

____ You are in front of a small audience.

_____

_____

____ People in the audience are fidgeting and look bored.

_____

_____

____ You are clearly being evaluated.

_____

_____

____ The setting is new to you—for example, you are seated on a panel or you are on a stage
with a microphone.

_____

_____

____ The role you have is new to you—for example, you are the emcee at a fundraiser.

_____

_____

Feedback for Exercise 3.4

You should now have some idea which situational factors specifically contribute to your stage fright. Let's continue to use the Case of Cheryl M. (see page 49) as an example. Take a look at her answers to this exercise.

Situation:

✗ You are the center of attention for all or part of the presentation.

I was the center of attention because I was the only speaker. I was holding the meeting and everyone's eyes were on me. This made me nervous.

✗ The audience contains powerful or important people.

My supervisor, colleagues, and the vice president attended the meeting. I felt extremely pressured to sound good in front of them.

✗ The audience includes very competent people.

Everyone in the meeting was qualified and competent. This put additional pressure on me to come across as qualified and competent too.

___ There are strangers in the audience.

✗ There are family, friends, or colleagues in the audience.

Several of my colleagues are good friends of mine. If I screwed up my presentation, they'd feel really bad for me, and I'd be reminded of my screw-up whenever we socialize.

___ You are in front of a large audience.

✗ You are in front of a small audience.

It was a very small audience. It was scary for me because I knew them so well, and they were so physically close to me that I could almost "feel" what they were feeling.

✗ People in the audience are fidgeting and look bored.

The audience appeared very restless, and this made me worry about what I was doing wrong.

✗ You are clearly being evaluated.

My supervisor's presence at the meeting made it clear I was being evaluated. I wanted to look good in front of her, but felt extremely nervous about the outcome.

___ The setting is new to you.

X The role you have is new to you.

Since I've only been a manager for three months, running this meeting was a fairly new experience for me. The novelty of the role contributed to my anxiety.

Once Cheryl saw all of her responses taken together, she started noticing some patterns. A good deal of the fear she experienced came from her thoughts that the consequences of this talk would be long lasting. Because it was such an intimate setting, if she floundered or failed, it would not be forgotten quickly. She imagined that people would discuss it and reshape their views of her. Because there were a few very competent members in the group, she believed that she was very vulnerable. If she made any mistakes, they would be noticed immediately. Once she recognized these patterns, she was able to attack them head on.

IMAGINING THE WORST-CASE SCENARIO AND FACING IT HEAD-ON

A very powerful technique in evaluating your fears is to examine a worst-case scenario. Take a fear you are dealing with and imagine the worst possible thing that can happen. Once you have this scene, evaluate the consequence. Would it ruin you? Would it shame you? Would it lead to a loss of your career or valued job? Or would it simply be unpleasant—something you could ultimately handle? Using the worst-case scenario gives you perspective. It provides a context in which you can evaluate your fears in a "real world" sense. The idea is, if you can survive a worst-case scenario, you can survive a bad scenario even better. Armed with this knowledge, your fears will not become exaggerated. You can keep them in proportion.

Fred D. was the embodiment of the worst-case scenario. He believed in Murphy's Law—*Anything that can go wrong will!*—the way most people believe in religion. When the worst case came about, he recognized it and it actually helped him. Let's take a look.

The Case of Fred D.

Fred D. was usually very pessimistic and never failed to predict disaster in anything he attempted to do, so I was pleasantly surprised one day when he walked into my office in a fairly cheerful mood. When I asked him why he seemed so happy, he replied with a great answer: "Doc, I woke up this morning feeling as low as I have ever, ever felt. I have never been so depressed, and then something interesting happened. I realized that I couldn't sink any lower, and you know what? If this is the worst that it can get, I can take it. I'm going to be okay." That was just the beginning of Fred's progress. Today, Fred has a successful career and a lovely wife.

Now, whenever I work with a person who has an anxiety problem, I think of Fred. The first thing we do is put a "ceiling" on the fear. We look for a way to limit the extent of the problem so that the worst view of it would still be tolerable, maybe not great, maybe not even so-so, but tolerable. This puts a limit on the fear. We go about this by jumping right into the worst-case scenario of any situation. We play it through to see if it is *survivable*.

Let's do this now. Imagine that you get up in front of a group of people at work and you totally blank out. Not a single word passes your lips. You stand in front of them, shaking and quivering, for what seems like forever. You finally manage to stammer out a few nonsense words, then run out of the room in utter embarrassment. At first thought, you'd think that you would die of shame, but in fact, you've seen people in worse situations come back to work on Monday morning. They survived! There may have been some kidding, awkwardness, and maybe even pity, but they survived. Once you realize that you, too, could survive even that worst-case scenario, you can go on to consider what will *probably* happen.

Desberg's Maxim
Even if worse really does come to worst when you give your speech, you'll survive the ordeal.

First of all, it's almost impossible to go *totally* blank, but if you did, you could survive it. Thinking that you will forget *everything* is a pretty clear case of all-or-nothing thinking. So, what's likely to happen? A few stammered words, an occasional squeak to your voice, a little hand shaking, and maybe even a short pause or two to find your place. These possibilities become almost trivial when compared with the worst-case scenario. Once you realize that you will somehow survive the experience, your panic will be reduced to a normal level of anxiety.

Imagining the worst-case scenario can reveal a great deal of useful information. It can show you how remote the chances are of something catastrophic happening during your presentation. And that even if the worst-case scenario actually did happen, the consequences would be bearable.

In Exercise 3.5 on the following page, you will take a close look your worst-case scenario. Then, you'll figure out what the consequence would be if it really happened.

DETERMINING HOW REASONABLE YOUR FEARS REALLY ARE

With all the work you've done in this chapter, you are now in a position to look at all the data you've collected and determine how reasonable

EXERCISE 3.5. Exploring Your Worst-Case Scenario

In Chapter 2, you identified the worst thing that could happen during your performance and the worst possible consequence. In this exercise, continue the process of analysis by answering the following five questions.

1. What is the worst possible thing that could happen during your performance?

_____

_____

_____

_____

2. What is the worst possible consequence if it actually happened?

_____

_____

_____

_____

3. How tolerable would the worst possible outcome be?

_____

_____

_____

_____

4. What could you do to cope if "worse comes to worst"?

_____

_____

_____

_____

5. How likely is it that worse will come to worst?

_____

_____

_____

Feedback for Exercise 3.5

While doing this exercise, you can put your imagination and your sense of exaggeration to good use. Check to see if you figured out the absolute worst thing that could happen in the situation you selected. Here are Cheryl M.'s answers for comparison.

1. What is the worst possible thing that could happen during your performance?

I'll be so nervous that I'll totally freeze up and sound like a babbling idiot.

2. What is the worst possible consequence if it actually happened?

I would get demoted or even lose my job because they would see that I wasn't an effective manager.

3. How tolerable would the worst possible outcome be?

I suppose I could find another job somewhere else. If they demoted me, I could work hard to improve my skills and try to get reinstated, while I also looked for another job.

4. What could you do to cope if "worse comes to worst"?

If I freeze up, I could simply read from my prepared notes.

5. How likely is it that worse will come to worst?

It's doubtful that I'll really freeze up completely, but it's possible for me to come across as sounding disorganized. I could use cue cards to prevent that from happening.

By doing this exercise, Cheryl learned two valuable things about herself. She learned that if worse came to worst, she could come up with strategies to move forward, increase her skills, and progress. She also learned that the chances the worst-case scenario would actually come to pass were pretty slim. Keep in mind that except for poorly written sitcoms, worse rarely comes to worst.

they seem to you. Remember that just because something frightens you, it doesn't mean it's a reasonable fear. So be sure to be as objective as possible when doing Exercise 3.6 on the following page. You may find it helpful to role-play here. Ask yourself how your boss or colleagues might evaluate some of your fears. Or ask yourself how you might evaluate these fears if someone came to you for advice. Putting yourself in these different roles helps to increase your objectivity.

EXERCISE 3.6. Reasonableness Rating

Now that you have gone through the first five exercises in this chapter, you are ready to make an overall reasonableness rating of your fears. Reexamine your fear-provoking thoughts and determine how reasonable you think they are on a scale of 0 to 100 with 0 being unreasonable and 100 being reasonable. Is the evidence real or exaggerated? This is your time to become critical and tough. Carefully examine your fear-provoking thoughts to detect any instances of bias, distortion, or illogic.

Fear-provoking thought:_____ Rating: _____

Fear-provoking thought:_____ Rating: _____

Fear-provoking thought:_____ Rating: _____

Fear-provoking thought:_____ Rating: _____

Feedback for Exercise 3.6

Any fear-provoking thought you rated between 80 and 100 is a reasonable fear, according to your determination. Knowing exactly which of your fears are reasonable can help you tackle and overcome them realistically. In later chapters, you'll learn some relaxation techniques, how to set realistic goals, and how to prepare and, in some cases, over-prepare to minimize the effects of these fear-provoking, but reasonable, thoughts.

If your reasonableness ratings are in the 30 to 70 range, you're still not sure how to realistically evaluate your fears. In this case, the following chapter, which takes the evaluation of your fear-provoking thoughts a bit further, should help you overcome the uncertainty. You may want to redo the exercises in this chapter for some further, or deeper, insight.

Hopefully any fear-provoking thought you rated between 0 and 30 no longer frightens you. But if it does, you'll need to do additional work to lessen its effect on you. You will benefit from the reality-testing techniques provided in Chapter 4. Moreover, you'll learn how to use affirming self-statements to cope with any fear-provoking thoughts, both reasonable and unreasonable, that persist.

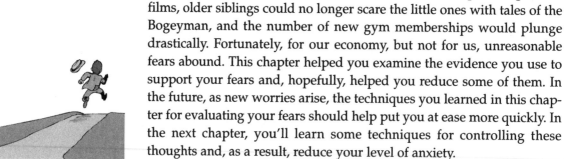

WHAT YOU HAVE LEARNED
AND WHERE YOU ARE GOING

If all of our fears were reasonable, Hollywood would stop making horror films, older siblings could no longer scare the little ones with tales of the Bogeyman, and the number of new gym memberships would plunge drastically. Fortunately, for our economy, but not for us, unreasonable fears abound. This chapter helped you examine the evidence you use to support your fears and, hopefully, helped you reduce some of them. In the future, as new worries arise, the techniques you learned in this chapter for evaluating your fears should help put you at ease more quickly. In the next chapter, you'll learn some techniques for controlling these thoughts and, as a result, reduce your level of anxiety.

4

The BIG Idea

Reality-testing strategies and positive self-statements can give you a firm handle on your fear-provoking thoughts and can help you get them under control.

CONTROLLING YOUR FEAR-PROVOKING THOUGHTS

I n the 1960s, a landmark experiment on creativity took place at the University of California–Berkeley. It was the single, largest study of its kind. The researchers studied artists and creative professionals from many fields and came up with two major traits that all creative people seem to share: the ability to tolerate ambiguity and suspend judgment, and the ability to operate without having to know and understand everything all the time. Ambiguity is difficult to deal with because the same event can be interpreted in many different ways. For example, a friend of mine who is a comedian told me about an interesting experience he'd had. He worked a job where he got lots of smiles and almost no laughs. At the end of the evening, he didn't know what to expect. He was pleasantly surprised when the club owner rehired him. He said, "They loved you. They were a *smiling* audience, not a *laughing* one, but a bunch of people wanted to be sure that you were going to perform here again . . . great job." Good thing my friend didn't let the lack of laughter affect his confidence level or his performance. He suspended judgment and tolerated the audience's ambiguous reception. In a sense, this chapter is all about tolerating ambiguity and suspending judgment.

To control your fear-provoking thoughts, you'll need to carry out experiments to discover what works for you and what doesn't. This task requires you to postpone your judgments for a time. As you wait for the results of your experiments, you'll need to deal with ambiguity. Moreover, you'll have to take a few risks when performing these experiments.

In essence, you'll be turning your life into a walking, talking laboratory. Each new occasion at which you must speak will serve as a new experiment. (Don't worry—you won't have to wear a white lab coat during your

To control your fear-provoking thoughts, you'll need to carry out experiments to discover what works for you and what doesn't.

presentations!) You'll take the ideas that have been worrying you out into the real world to test them out. With luck and practice, you should learn how to manage your anxiety so that speaking gets easier and easier with each outing. Let's begin with the concept of reality testing, which takes what you learned in Chapter 3 an important step further.

REALITY TESTING

As you've seen in previous chapters, sometimes it's difficult to judge how reasonable your fear-provoking thoughts are. You learned that these thoughts are interpretations of facts rather than facts themselves. It's sometimes difficult to determine how seriously you should be taking these fears. This situation calls for a little reality testing. In other words, you'll try to determine if your interpretations hold up under rigorous, scientific scrutiny. You'll get to use your favorite laboratory—you! Let's take a look at two types of reality-testing strategies, suspending judgment and shame attacking.

Suspending Judgment

As you now know, creative people have two important traits: 1) the ability to tolerate ambiguity and suspend judgment, and 2) the ability to operate without having to know and understand everything all the time. They can suppose and test out their ideas by acting *as if* they were true.

To suspend judgment, you must learn to avoid evaluating your performance and to *act* as if you are not afraid. Begin by identifying an area in which you are not held back by fear-provoking thoughts or stage fright. For example, it might be coaching your kid's soccer team, teaching Sunday school, or heading the social committee in your community or at work. Once you have identified such a situation, behave as if you are in that situation when faced with fear-provoking circumstances. This is what I instructed Lily B. to do. Let's look at what happened.

The Case of Lily B.

Although Lily B. was comfortable speaking during book club discussions, she was very uncomfortable giving presentations at work. When I asked Lily why she wasn't afraid to speak in front of the group members, she had a couple of reasons. First, she was sure she knew a lot about the book of the month, but even if she were to make a mistake or forget an important part, there wouldn't be any serious consequences. And second, she was confident that the club members liked and respected her.

With that in mind, I gave Lily the task of suspending judgment concerning her fears about speaking in work-related situations and instructed her to act as if she were in front of her club members. Lily reported back to me and said that approaching the stressful situation as if it were an enjoyable one in which she feels comfortable had reduced her anxiety considerably, and she had presented herself and her views well.

A shortcut version of this strategy is to act as if you are someone who you respect a great deal and who appears to perform fearlessly. Take on that person's confidence, poise, and charm. Practice "being that person" by using the same type of jokes, gestures, and phrasing. Make the types of decisions you think that person would make. In other words, approach the situation as if you are an actor who is impersonating someone with a lot of confidence and ability. You'll be surprised by how calm this makes you feel.

Shame-Attacking

Shame-attacking is an exercise in which you confront the shame or embarrassment you believe you will feel in front of others by doing something you wouldn't normally do, usually something silly. These exercises were developed by cognitive-behavioral therapist Albert Ellis, the developer of rational emotive behavior therapy (REBT), back in the 1960s. Shame-attacking exercises are very useful for testing fear-provoking thoughts that appear to be reasonable on the surface.

This experiment is a fairly straightforward process. Start by identifying something you think would embarrass you or make you feel ashamed if you were to do it. Then, actually go ahead and do it! It will be interesting to see if the act lives up to your predictions. If it doesn't, you can let the fear go and stop worrying about that type of situation. If the act is still uncomfortable, but not as bad as you feared it would be, you can at least diminish your fear of that type of situation.

The following are the steps involved in performing a shame-attacking exercise, which you will do in Exercise 4.1 on page 73.

1. Identify an action you can take that you believe will embarrass, shame, or humiliate you. Be sure you really believe the act will be humiliating. Also make sure that it's not something that will harm you or others. Moreover, be certain it's legal, moral, and ethical. Other than that, have fun with it.

2. Predict the results of actually performing the action. To get the most from this exercise, be as detailed in your prediction as possible. Later,

Walking a banana along the street as if it were a dog is a good example of a shame-attacking exercise.

you'll compare this prediction to the actual results. This can help you identify the extent to which you exaggerate and distort your predictions.

3. After identifying the prediction, actually do it. Take the action!

4. Compare the actual results with the predicted results. See how accurate or inaccurate your prediction was.

There's simply no better way to rid yourself of unreasonable fear-provoking thoughts than to test them out and show yourself just how wrong your prediction was. Let's take a look at the Case of Peter D. (that's me) for an example of a successful shame-attacking exercise.

The Case of Peter D.

Years ago, I was attending a practicum led by Albert Ellis. Ellis asked each participant to try a shame-attacking exercise that week. Ellis gave us examples of silly things like walking a banana along the street on a leash and riding on a crowded elevator and calling out each floor.

On the third day of the practicum, I was having lunch with three other practicum members. Two of them, Pam and Marcie, decided they were going to perform their shame-attacking exercise during lunch. Pam announced that she was going to perform her shame-attacking exercise by standing up after she had eaten her lunch and singing "Happy Birthday" to Marcie. Furthermore, she requested that the rest of our party remain silent, which would increase her embarrassment.

Marcie liked the idea and said that if Pam had the nerve to sing to her in the restaurant, the least she could do was make a short acceptance speech, which would be her shame-attacking exercise. They both agreed they would find these acts extremely embarrassing, which would fulfill the requirements of the exercise.

I was surprised to hear my own voice telling Pam and Marcie that their choices were not appropriate for this exercise. I told them that the song and speech were too contrived and theatrical, and not really personally embarrassing for them. I was surprised by how intense I became trying to explain to them why they shouldn't do it. After the two women got through calling me names, they assured me that their exercises were quite appropriate. At that point, my immediate thought was, "Okay, if they want to act foolish, let 'em. I'll just wait in the restroom until they're done."

Then I realized I was trying to persuade them not to do their shame-attacking exercises because *they would embarrass me!* I decided that for my own shame-attacking exercise, I would sit through the entire ordeal no matter how embarrassing it would be for me. Next, I needed to make a prediction about what would happen. My prediction was that everyone at the restaurant would ignore Pam and Marcie and stare at me. They would all think, "How could a cool guy like him be with people like that?"

After finishing her pizza, Pam got up and sang. If she was not nervous, then she did a very good imitation of a nervous person. Her hands were trembling and her voice was breaking. Interestingly, a few other people at nearby tables began singing along with her. When they noticed that no one else at our table was singing, they stopped and turned away, looking awkward and embarrassed. During all this, I looked around and noticed that I appeared to be invisible. No one seemed to notice that I was even there.

I got really mad at myself. I thought about the thousands of times I had stopped myself from doing things I wanted to do because of what people might think about me, even strangers . . . especially strangers. I realized that my predictions were way off, and I felt liberated enough to act like a fool in front of strangers from that moment on.

You've read about it—now it's time for you to try it. And, like one of my martial arts instructors used to say, "Make it real!" To us, this meant we'd have to block *real* kicks or punches to avoid getting injured. This made us focus completely on the exercise, which is what I want you to do. So, when you select your shame-attaching action in Exercise 4.1, be sure to make it real. You must truly believe the action will be shameful in order to get the benefit of this exercise. Trust me, it's worth the risk.

Exercise 4.1. Performing a Shame-Attacking Exercise

For this exercise, identify an action you can take that's neither harmful nor illegal but that will definitely embarrass you. If there's something daring or foolish you've always avoided doing (but secretly wanted to), make this an excuse to go ahead and do it. Not only is it a good excuse, it's therapeutic. If there's nothing in particular you've avoided because you feared it would embarrass you (which is highly unlikely), do your best to come up with something that will provoke shame. Then, complete each of the items below in detail.

1. Describe the task you will perform.

_____

_____

_____

2. Make a few predictions about the outcome of the task. What will happen? What will others think? How will you feel about it? What are the possible consequences?

_____

_____

_____

3. Perform the task. Don't hold back. Do it in its full form. Record the details.

_____

_____

_____

4. Assess the results of carrying out the task.

_____

_____

_____

5. Compare your prediction with the actual results, and determine if your prediction was reasonable or not.

_____

_____

_____

6. Identify how these results will impact your future.

_____

_____

_____

Feedback for Exercise 4.1

The key to this exercise is to make sure the activity is truly fear-provoking and you sincerely believe it will cause you embarrassment or shame. If doing the activity has no emotional impact, you won't learn anything. Also, be sure to carry out a full analysis of your predictions. By now, you should be pretty good at identifying the types of predictions you make when you think about doing something. Avoid trivializing the results of your shame-attacking exercise by saying the task wasn't all that fear-provoking in the first place. To avoid this problem, it's essential that you list all of your predictions before you carry out the act.

Using your life as a personal laboratory is a very powerful technique. When something works, you know it, understand it, and believe it. If you have a fear of public speaking, there's no more direct way than to test it out.

In the next section, you'll learn a different way to go about dealing with your fear-provoking thoughts—this time by "talking to yourself."

USING POSITIVE SELF-STATEMENTS TO CONTROL YOUR FEAR-PROVOKING THOUGHTS

Reality testing is one way to attack your fear-provoking thoughts; talking to yourself is another. I'm not suggesting you talk to yourself out loud as you walk down the street (unless, of course, that's your shame-attacking exercise). What I'm talking about here is the talk that you do internally—the things you tell yourself.

As you know, fear-provoking thoughts are internal dialogues that make you feel anxious. By using a similar approach, you can use positive statements to help you overcome many of your fears. I'm not asking you to chant pat slogans like, "Every day I'm getting better in every way." Instead, your self-statements will be unique to you because they will come from the data you've been collecting and the self-analysis you've been conducting so far throughout this book.

By now, you've discovered how habitual and automatic your thoughts are. Quite often you have the skills that would enable you to cope with a difficult situation, but for some reason, you don't use them. In some cases, these skills are temporarily forgotten under the stress of the moment. Positive self-statements, which you will learn to create, can serve as a reminder to use the skills you have during trying circumstances.

You have learned how easy it is for you to predict doom for an impending presentation. By selecting and rehearsing appropriately positive self-statements, you will remind yourself of the unreasonableness of some of your fear-provoking thoughts. For example, Joe H., an aerospace engineer, always worried that something would go wrong when he was asked to make a presentation to governmental review agencies. He had an unreasonable fear of leaving out small details. He decided to motivate himself by using the phrase "focus on the big picture." This reminded him of his unreasonable preoccupation with details. It helped him focus on what he had to do rather than on what could go wrong. The key to using positive self-statements is to make sure they have a basis in fact so they can counter the unreasonable thoughts you are having.

> "An affirmation is a strong positive statement that something is already so."
>
> —*Shakti Gawain*

When I was a graduate student taking my last series of doctoral exams, I became very nervous. The faculty had us believing that we should know everything about every area of psychology. From time to time, friends would try to make me feel better by saying things like, "Don't worry, you'll pass," or, "You're smart, relax." I listened to them and thought that they had no clue about the situation I was facing. The thing that calmed me down was talking to other graduate students and friends who had recently received their doctorates and learning some strategies for how to prepare for the exam. Then, I was finally able to say to myself, "You are well prepared and know how to con the faculty into believing that you actually know what you are talking about." My self-statements were based on something tangible and accurate.

Positive self-statements are the result of countering or disproving your unreasonable thoughts. Once you have discovered why a particular fear-provoking thought is unreasonable, the positive self-statements you come up with then become your reminder for what you will do and how things will probably work out. Furthering the work you did in Chapter 3, take each of the steps below to learn how to create positive self-statements from your various fear-provoking thoughts.

1. Realistically Appraise the Situation

Turn back to your list of the fear-provoking thoughts you identified in Chapter 2. Try to identify any information you can use to contradict those fear-provoking thoughts. For example, if you are predicting failure, try to recall similar situations in which you performed well. Then, come up with some positive self-statements. Here are some examples of fear-provoking thoughts and positive self-statements:

Your audience wants you to succeed! If you remind yourself of this often, you should start to feel more comfortable when you're in front of them. Remember, they're on your side.

Fear-provoking thought: The audience will think I don't know my material.

Positive self-statement: I know more about this than the audience does.

Fear-provoking thought: Situations like this always make me nervous.

Positive self-statement: I've done this before, so I'm not going to be as nervous as I've been in the past.

Fear-provoking thought: The audience is going to pity me.

Positive self-statement: The audience wants me to succeed.

Fear-provoking thought: I'm going to lose the audience's interest.

Positive self-statement: If people in the audience look bored, I'm going to disregard it because I have no way of knowing what they're thinking.

2. Identify Weaknesses of Supporting Data

As you may recall from Chapter 3, when you are trying to discredit the supporting data for your fear-provoking thoughts, you need to consider the source of the data as well as how solid the data is. For example, Janet D. believed gender discrimination was rampant in her workplace, and it was holding her back and interfering with her presentations in front of male colleagues. However, when Janet investigated the situation, she learned she had very little data to support her assumption. Only one female coworker had mentioned a situation in which she had felt discriminated against and the issue had never made its way to the human resources department. However, from that one bit of data, Janet had formed a firm belief. She had never experienced discrimination herself.

Don't make the mistake Janet made: consider only direct experience when investigating the data that supports your fears. Then, examine your direct experience as it relates to your current, "reasonable" fear-provoking thoughts. Take the fears you can support and convert them into positive self-statements. Here are some examples:

Consider only direct experience when investigating the data that support your fears.

Direct experience: I failed to make a good presentation at the last meeting.

Fear-provoking thought: If I failed once, I'll fail again.

Positive self-statement: There's no proof I'll fail this time around. I can succeed.

Direct experience: One of my colleagues said I could have been more focused.

Fear-provoking thought: I'm not going to sound focused.

Positive self-statement: The past has no bearing. I will remain focused.

3. Identify Alternative Explanations

As you may recall, coming up with alternative explanations for things that went wrong during a presentation can do a lot to calm your anxiety when you are faced with a similar situation. When you consider alternative explanations for your fear-provoking thoughts, it will become much easier to face your audience. Here are some examples:

Fear-provoking thought: If an audience member yawns, it means he or she is bored by my presentation.

Alternative explanation: If an audience member yawns, it could be because he or she slept very poorly the night before.

Positive self-statement: If an audience member yawns, it will have no affect on me.

Fear-provoking thought: If people leave early, it's a sign I've failed in some way.

Alternative explanation: If people leave early, it could be because they have other appointments or need to get back to work.

Positive self-statement: If people leave early, it will have no affect on me.

Fear-provoking thought: The audience is going to think I'm a poor speaker.

Alternative explanation: I can't read minds and have no idea what the audience is thinking.

Positive self-statement: I will present myself as well as I can so that the audience enjoys my speech.

4. Survive the Worst-Case Scenario

Rarely will you ever have to face your worst-case scenario. But even if it were to happen, chances are you'd simply be distressed by the outcome rather than destroyed by it. It's quite unlikely that a terrible presentation will end in disaster. While it's true that you will not have gotten what you wanted out of the situation, chances are you will be given other opportunities to achieve your goals. When faced with your worst-case scenario fears, remind yourself of the following:

Positive self-statement: No matter what happens, I will survive.

Positive self-statement: *Distress* is not *disaster*.

Positive self-statement: I don't really believe the worst-case scenario will actually happen.

Rarely will you ever have to face your worst-case scenario. It's quite unlikely that a terrible presentation will end in disaster.

5. Identify Logical Flaws

After having read the discussions of logical flaws in Chapter 3, you should be pretty good at identifying which of them you have indulged in. Each time you identify a logical flaw in your thinking process, you become better at discounting it and, eventually, at avoiding it. Like Janet D. mentioned earlier, many people tend draw too general a conclusion, or overgeneralize, from small amounts of data. By now, however, you should know how to identify when there is not enough data to justify a fear-provoking thought. Here are some reasonable ways to deal with logical flaws and develop positive self-statements as a result:

Logical flaw: I'm either going to fail miserably or make a very positive impact on my audience.

Reasonable statement: I must stay in the gray area—not everything can be defined in black-or-white terms.

Positive self-statement: I will do my best to present myself well.

Logical flaw: After my last presentation, one of my colleagues told me he heard my voice shaking.

Reasonable statement: I must consider the positive as well as the negative. Several other colleagues told me I sounded great.

Positive self-statement: I will do my best to sound good while giving my speech.

Logical flaw: If I fail, I'll be ruined and will never work in my field again.

Reasonable statement: I must keep things in perspective. If I fail, I'm going to be embarrassed, not ruined.

Positive self-statement: The outcome of my presentation will not ruin me.

6. Remind Yourself of Your Skills and Preparation

Compose self-statements that reinforce the skills and techniques you have practiced. For example:

Positive self-statement: I will remember to breathe.

Positive self-statement: Closing my eyes for a moment will help me relax.

Positive self-statement: I am well prepared for this presentation.

Positive self-statement: I have prepared an outline.

Positive self-statement: I have practiced this speech a dozen times.

"Trust your hopes, not your fears."

—David Mahoney

The above are just some examples of how you can use your fear-provoking thoughts to create positive self-statements. You will want to make your self-statements unique and meaningful to you. This is what you'll be doing in Exercise 4.2 on the following page.

EXERCISE 4.2. Designing Positive Self-Statements

In this exercise, you will consider the evidence you've gathered to disprove your fear-provoking thoughts and form positive self-statements based on that evidence. Keep in mind the following rules when designing your statements:

- No more than four or five self-statements are necessary.

- Choose only the most relevant statements you think will have the most impact.

- Keep the statements short and simple so you can recall them easily.

- Make your statements positive so they inspire you rather than remind you of your fear-provoking thought—for example, "I can do this!" is better than "I will not fail!"

- Make your statements in the present tense. Positive self-statements are designed to help you in the present moment, not at some distant point in the future. The unconscious mind operates in a type of "constant present." It makes no distinction between past, present, and future.

- Make your statements in the first person to remind you that you are directly in control over your own behavior—for example, "I can," "I will," and "I am," rather than "You can," "You will," and "You are."

Keeping all of those things in mind, go ahead and create your positive self-statement in the spaces provided below.

Fear-provoking thought: _____

_____

_____

Positive self-statement: _____

_____

_____

_____

Fear-provoking thought: _____

_____

_____

Positive self-statement: _____

_____

_____

Fear-provoking thought: _____

_____

_____

Positive self-statement: _____

_____

_____

_____

Fear-provoking thought: _____

_____

_____

Positive self-statement: _____

_____

_____

_____

Fear-provoking thought: _____

_____

_____

Positive self-statement: _____

_____

_____

_____

Feedback for Exercise 4.2

An essential part of this exercise is to make sure your positive self-statements are believable—in other words, you should have some evidence to back them up. For example, there is no evidence to back up a positive self-statement such as "I will get the promotion." Also, positive affirmations like "Every day I'm getting better in every way" are not based on data, so they are hard to believe. Consider your evidence. A statement such as, "I will interview well because I am prepared" is believable because of all the time and effort you put into your preparation.

How and When to Use Positive Self-Statements

Once you've designed your set of positive self-statements, it is important to know how and when to use them. Although people may *know* how to handle a difficult situation, they don't always "activate" those skills when necessary. "Activation" means to put those skills to use when they are called for. Think of all the times when you have left a situation and said to yourself, "Oh, I should have said *this* or I should have done *that*."

Here are some suggestions to make sure you are able to call up your positive self-statements when necessary: Say your positive self-statements to yourself whenever you practice your speech or presentation. This way, you not only practice the statements themselves, but you also practice calling them up and using them during your actual presentation. Also, use your positive self-statements while you practice your relaxation exercises, described in Chapter 6. By doing this, you will associate a state of relaxation with your positive self-statements. This will increase their calming effect over you. Whenever you begin thinking fear-provoking thoughts, call up your positive self-statements. Use other reminders such as sticky notes on the bathroom mirror to remind you to practice your statements regularly. Remember, it's not enough just to have a list of positive self-statements if you are not going to use them.

WHAT YOU HAVE LEARNED
AND WHERE YOU ARE GOING

This chapter helped you translate your fear-provoking thoughts into actions. It's often a good idea to put an end to speculation by taking a little risk and evaluating it. You also learned how to control your fear-provoking thoughts by replacing them with positive self-statements.

In Part Two, you'll learn some important tools for helping you reduce your fear-provoking thoughts. We'll start with a discussion of setting goals.

PART TWO

TOOLS FOR REDUCING YOUR FEAR-PROVOKING THOUGHTS

5

SETTING GOALS

f you don't know where you're going, you may wind up somewhere else. I keep this maxim in mind whenever I set a goal. And you should too. Goal setting is a very important step in learning to control your fear of public speaking. By approaching your ultimate goal to effectively deliver your speech in small steps, it is much more likely you will be successful and pleased with the outcome. This chapter will help you develop logical, effective, and achievable goals. With the information you gathered in Part One, you can custom-make goals that will provide you with a blueprint for a successful presentation. You'll also learn how to evaluate when you've met your goals. Let's begin.

If you don't know where you're going, you may wind up somewhere else.

THE THREE ESSENTIAL PRINCIPLES OF GOAL SETTING

There are three essential principles to keep in mind when setting your goals: 1) Set goals that are directly under your control, 2) Base your goals on your fear-provoking thoughts, and 3) Make your goals specific so you can recognize when they have been accomplished. Let's take a close look at each of these principles below.

1. Set Goals That Are Directly Under Your Control

PRINCIPLE 1

Set your goals in terms of your own voluntary actions, not on the actions and reactions of others. Keep in mind, also, that your moods are *not* under your voluntary control; if they were, you'd never be sad or afraid again. So, don't set an unrealistic goal to completely eliminate your fears. Rather, set your goals on actions you can take that will help you feel better about making your presentation or delivering your speech. For example, setting a goal to be less afraid in the face of public speaking is unrealistic and is not under your control; however, setting a goal to practice your presentation for at least a half hour a day *is* under your control. Regular practice will help reduce your fear of speaking in public.

PRINCIPLE 2

2. Base Your Goals on Your List of Fear-Provoking Thoughts

Base your goals on your specific fear-provoking thoughts. For example, if you are worried that you will forget important details or key points during your presentation, make it your goal to improve your recall of the information through practice. If you are afraid you won't dress appropriately, set a goal to peruse clothing shops and ask salespeople for assistance. Or, if you are afraid the audience won't laugh at your opening joke or jokes, try them out on friends, family, and coworkers and ask for feedback. You can even set a goal to attend a few coaching lessons from a professional. Accomplishing such goals should lead to a reduction or elimination of your fear-provoking thoughts.

PRINCIPLE 3

3. Make Your Goals Specific So You Can Recognize When They Have Been Accomplished

Set your goals in terms of *specific* actions you can take and/or set dates by which you plan to complete certain tasks. Break down complicated goals into small, manageable steps. Plan what you will do today, tomorrow, and next week. When you have set a goal, determine what evidence you'll need to recognize when that goal has been met. For example, if your goal is to research the topic of your next presentation on the Internet, you can break this down into smaller goals. For example, your first goal may be to find and download five relevant articles. Your second goal would be to read those articles. Your third goal would be to take notes on those articles. And your fourth goal would be to work that information into your presentation. Breaking down a goal this way makes it easy to gauge your progress. You might also want to set a timeframe for accomplishing these smaller goals. For example, "Today I'll download the articles. Tomorrow I'll read them and take notes." And so on.

You will be using the three principles of goal setting throughout the rest of the book. To get you in a goal-setting mood, let's take a look at the Case of Judy S. and the Case of Bill H. They will give you some guidance in preparing your own goals in this chapter's exercises.

The Case of Judy S.

Judy S. was one of three final candidates in line to be interviewed for the position of CFO at a large corporation. She had worked hard for many years for an opportunity like this. However, when the day of her interview finally arrived, Judy was a nervous wreck. During the interview, her responses to the interviewers' questions were vague and unfocused. She felt awkward and uptight, and failed to present an effective, organized presentation of her past experience. She felt that the interviewers didn't get an accurate view of her personality. Needless to say, she didn't get the job.

Judy sought my help a few weeks before she was scheduled for another major interview. When I asked Judy what her goals were for the interview, she replied, "Goals? I only have one goal—to land the job of CFO!" I pointed out that "getting the job" was an unreasonable goal because it was not directly under her control. There was nothing Judy could do to *guarantee* she'd get the position. That decision was up to the people interviewing her. I explained that the first step in setting her goals was to identify her fear-provoking thoughts. Using her failed interview experience, Judy easily identified four issues that were worrying her for the next interview:

1. She feared the interview committee would think she was disorganized.

2. She feared she wouldn't be thought of as sharp and fast on her feet in responding to questions.

3. She feared the committee wouldn't get a sense of who she was.

4. She feared she would be turned down again.

Identifying these fears was a good beginning. Judy learned that these fears couldn't be directly transformed into goals because they weren't under her control. She had no control over the committee's evaluation. So, her next step was to translate her fear-provoking thoughts into specific actions she could take to improve her presentation. When taken, each of these actions would reduce her fears and help bring about what she wanted. The following became her list of goals.

• **Take steps to appear more organized.** Judy identified several steps she could take to give the interview committee the impression she was organized and to reduce her worries about not appearing organized. She would prepare and edit a concise outline of her relevant past experiences and qualifications for the position. With this concise outline fresh in her mind, she would be able to walk into the interview confident that when questioned about her background, she could deliver a clear, well-organized response.

To help meet this goal, Judy created two specific tasks, or subgoals: 1) Show her outline to three colleagues who had served on interviewing committees and use their comments to revise her outline, and 2) Practice saying her outline aloud while driving to and from work, until she was confident she could deliver it smoothly.

• **Practice responding to possible interview questions.** Judy couldn't guarantee she would respond well to questions, but she could certainly practice responding to questions. To simulate the question-and-answer part of the interview, she would gather sample questions from three experienced colleagues and prepare and practice her answers.

Again, she added two subgoals here. Her first goal was to work out a format for responding to questions. What Judy eventually came up with was that if she had a ready answer, she would pause for a few seconds to organize her thoughts, then respond. If it was a difficult question for which she did not have a prepared answer, she would first compliment the interviewer for posing such a challenging question, then try to relate it to something she did have prepared. If all else failed, she would admit to not knowing the answer, but outline how she would go about getting it. This would show command of her professional resources. Her second goal was to approach a group of experienced colleagues and request that they give her a mock interview so she could practice responding "under fire."

• **Attempt to reveal my personality to the interviewers.** There is certainly no way Judy could be certain that the interviewers would get to know her personally and recognize her good qualities, but there were a few things she could do in the event the opportunity presented itself during the interview. She set a goal of preparing and practicing five anecdotes that would reveal something appropriately personal to the committee. Having this material prepared would give her more confidence, because she could now focus on the conversation, looking for an opportunity to insert one of her anecdotes. She believed that through sharing these anecdotes, she'd be able to present an accurate view of herself to the committee.

• **Make the best effort I can to get the position.** Judy concluded that if she could achieve her first three goals, she would have done as much as she could possibly do to get the job.

Achieving specific goals that were under her direct control helped Judy complete her second interview with less anxiety. She didn't get the job, but was complimented by two of the interviewers on her performance. She later found out that the position was filled by a board member's relative. The next interview she went on landed her the position of CFO.

The Case of Bill H.

Bill H., an investment analyst, was preparing to make a PowerPoint presentation to a group of investment counselors and accountants. He believed that if he made a successful presentation, he would earn a great deal of money. He feared that if he failed, his colleagues and clients would spread the word about his ineffectiveness, which could lead to his financial ruin. He worried about the presentation for weeks. He arranged and rearranged the order of his PowerPoint slides, and kept on stressing over which suit and tie to wear to the meeting. He got very little sleep for several nights before the presentation.

Bill's presentation started out well enough, but by the third PowerPoint slide, he had forgotten the order of the slides. He announced the wrong slide several times, drawing snickers from his audience. He grew more nervous, lost his place, and began tripping over his words. Each time someone interrupted the presentation with a question, he lost his place again. As the talk went on, he got progressively more nervous.

When Bill came to see me, he fondly referred to this presentation as one of the worst afternoons of his life. When I asked Bill what his goals had been, he said they were to inform and impress his audience. When I asked how he had prepared to meet these goals, he said he spent a lot of time thinking about what he would say.

Bill had a similar talk scheduled in a couple of weeks. It was easy to get him to identify the following fear-provoking thoughts:

1. He feared he would appear disorganized—for example, he'd mix up the order of the slides and lose his place again.

2. He feared he wouldn't be able to answer the questions put to him by the audience, making him seem unintelligent.

3. He feared he would trip over his own words and come off sounding inarticulate.

4. He feared he'd appear so useless to his company that he'd be fired.

Next, I had Bill set some realistic goals for himself, goals that were directly under his control. The following became his list of goals:

• **Take steps to appear more organized.** Bill decided to set some very concrete goals that involved organizing his presentation on paper, so that he could refer to it if he got flustered during the presentation. This would ensure that he would not get *too* disorganized during the presentation, because the outline would be available to him. He planned to do the following: 1) prepare a list of the slides and review it several times so he wouldn't forget the order. In the event he did forget which slide was up next, he could simply glance down at his notes, and 2) prepare an outline of his presentation. If someone interrupted with a question, a glance at

"It is not enough to take steps which may someday lead to a goal; each step must be itself a goal and a step likewise."

—*Goethe*

his outline would tell him where to pick up. He also made a list of key words to help him recall important topics, anecdotes, and examples.

• **Prepare answers to common questions so that I can answer any questions posed to me during the presentation to the best of my ability.** Being able to answer every question put to him by the audience was clearly something Bill could not guarantee, no matter how much he prepared. However, he could consult with his boss and colleagues in an effort to reduce the fear-provoking thoughts of not being able to answer the audience's questions. He set a goal to ask his boss and several veteran colleagues to prepare a list of questions that were likely to be asked by this type of audience. In particular, he asked for two types of questions: hostile questions and difficult questions people might ask just to stump him.

He would also ask his boss and colleagues for their opinions about how to handle questions he didn't have an answer for. When he did this, he was given the following tips: 1) Admit that you do not know the answer; 2) Ask if anyone in the audience can answer the question. If so, thank the person and offer him or her a job (or use some other suitable joke to lighten the situation); 3) If no one in the audience knows the answer, tell the person who posed the question that it was a good one. Assure the person you will research it. Then ask the audience to leave their business cards or e-mail addresses with you if they wish to be contacted with the answer.

• **Make every effort to sound articulate.** Bill also feared he would trip over his words and sound inarticulate. Again, there is no way to ensure smooth speech in front of an audience, but there were things Bill could do to make it more likely that his words would flow freely. Bill planned to put the finishing touches on his speech several days before the actual presentation. This would give him time to practice his speech aloud.

Bill used this time to get used to saying difficult words or phrases, and get into the flow of the talk. He recorded his speech so he could get some feedback. By listening carefully, he was able to identify rough spots that needed more practice. Listening to himself give the presentation also made him more familiar with what he planned to say. He resolved to practice until he could go through it smoothly every time.

• **To illustrate my usefulness to the company with my knowledge and actions.** By the time we arrived at this final goal to alleviate Bill's last fear-provoking thought of getting fired, he realized that whether or not he kept his job wasn't directly under his control. Moreover, he realized that if he met his first three goals, the likelihood of being fired was not great enough to worry about. He got *fired up* not fired.

Hopefully, Judy's and Bill's examples have given you some ideas about how to set goals that are under your control. If it's still a little unclear, Exercise 5.1 will help you distinguish between goals that are controllable and those that are not.

Exercise 5.1. Identifying Controllable Goals

A young man is about to be interviewed for a job. He has set the six goals listed below. Identify each as an example of a goal that is either *directly under his control* by placing a "C" in the space provided or *not directly under his control* by placing an "N" in the space provided.

Goals

_____ 1. To make sure I am not misunderstood on key points during the interview.

_____ 2. To ask at least three knowledgeable friends or colleagues to make comments on the appropriateness of the outfit I intend to wear on the job interview.

_____ 3. To keep my voice from quavering during the interview.

_____ 4. To get the job.

_____ 5. To impress the interviewers with my ability to "think on my feet."

_____ 6. To get and review information about the company before the interview.

Feedback for Exercise 5.1

1. **N** Although you can do a variety of things to make being misunderstood less likely, you cannot control how well your audience will understand you.

2. **C** You cannot control whether an interviewer will think that you have dressed appropriately, but you can get good advice from informed friends and colleagues. Such advice will make dressing appropriately more likely.

3. **N** You cannot directly control how much your voice quavers when you are anxious. However, you can practice relaxation exercises and throat-opening exercises (see Chapter 6) so that you are less likely to present this symptom of anxiety.

4. **N** Getting the job is not under your control. You may give a dazzling interview, but the job might have already been promised to the boss's prospective son-in-law (if he goes through with the wedding).

5. **N** You cannot control what others think of your performance.

6. **C** You can totally control whether or not you do your "homework." Most prospective employers are impressed when it's clear that a candidate has made an effort to familiarize him- or herself with the company. By doing this, you are showing that you're sincerely interested in a career with the company rather than just getting a job. It also shows that you prepare well.

Now that you've had some practice discriminating between goals that are under your control and those that are not, Exercise 5.2 will provide you with the opportunity to set some goals for yourself based on the fears you identified in Chapter 2.

Exercise 5.2. Setting Your Own Goals

Use two of the fear-provoking thoughts you identified in Chapter 2 to set a realistic goal you can accomplish to reduce each particular worry.

Fear-provoking thought: _____

_____

_____

Goals: _____

_____

_____

_____

Fear-provoking thought: _____

_____

_____

Goals: _____

_____

_____

_____

Feedback for Exercise 5.2

Examine your goals to determine if they are completely under your control. Make sure you can completely manage every aspect of them. Then, be sure to come up with a way to judge whether or not you've met each goal. For example, identify specific benchmarks, such as a date by which you've completed an action or the number of times you practiced a talk.

If you are satisfied that the goals are under your control, examine the relationship between each goal and the fear that it is related to. If you achieve the goal, will it reduce the fear? If it doesn't, try to determine if there is a better action you can take that will help reduce the fear.

WHAT IF I DON'T GET WHAT I WANT?

There will certainly be times when you do everything right and still not achieve the desired outcome. When this happens, you must learn to feel good about having met your goals. I've heard people say, "I did everything I could . . . but I should have done more!" That makes no sense. You can't really do more than *all you can do*. Unfortunately, there will always be factors that are out of your control. Here are just a few of the possibilities: You give a talk on a very hot day and the air conditioner is not working. You and the audience are uncomfortably warm, and it's hard for anyone—including you—to focus on what you have to say. Your talk is scheduled for 4:00 PM (the drowsy hour), the room is dimly lit, and the chairs are padded (perfect for an afternoon nap). Two minutes into your talk, a baby starts crying, a cell phone rings, the soundtrack from the film being shown in the next room bleeds into your room, latecomers drift in one by one . . . you get the idea. Every one of these things—alone or combined—can wreck a presentation. You cannot control these things, but if you met your goals, congratulate yourself on having carried them out successfully no matter how your presentation turned out. If you continue to meet your goals, there's a good chance you'll eventually achieve the success you deserve.

WHAT YOU HAVE LEARNED
AND WHERE YOU ARE GOING

In this chapter, you learned a helpful approach for setting and achieving your goals. By setting goals that are clearly under your control, you have a better chance of reaching them. Also, having a way to evaluate when you've reached your goals helps you develop a clearer picture of how well you are succeeding. Be sure to analyze situations in which you didn't succeed so you can set goals that will help you achieve success in similar situations.

In the next chapter, you'll learn how to better manage your symptoms of anxiety through relaxation exercises. This is just one of the things you can do to help you achieve your goals. It also feels great!

6

The BIG Idea

Relaxation exercises can help you combat anxiety—your internal response to danger—by lowering it to more manageable levels while making you more alert.

LEARNING TO RELAX

Although the *thought* of having a bad experience when giving a speech is unpleasant, it is the symptoms of anxiety that make most people fear the task so much—this can be thought of as "being afraid of being afraid." What makes it worse is that anxiety is not voluntary; you can't turn it off like a light switch. However, you can learn to work with it to get it more under your control. That's what this chapter is all about—managing your anxiety, physically and mentally, to lessen its effects through relaxation. Sometimes people actually have the skills they need to cope with anxiety-producing situations, but forget to use them when they are under stress. Therefore, you'll also learn some strategies for engaging the relaxation techniques described in this chapter. Let's begin at the heart of the matter—your emotions.

THE EMOTIONAL BATTLEGROUND

Psychologists like myself have learned to attack fear from three directions—emotions, thoughts, and actions. Since we can't attack the fear from all three directions at the same time, which should we attack first? Clearly, if you've read this far into the book or skipped to this chapter first, public speaking makes you *emotionally* uncomfortable. So, with my guidance, this chapter will take you straight to the heart of the problem where you can start attacking your fear on the emotional front.

Because dealing with your fears emotionally is both a direct and indirect form of attack, this approach presents an interesting puzzle. You can't voluntarily control your emotions. If you could control your emotions, why would you ever *choose* to feel frightened or sad? On the other hand, you can *choose* to calm the effects or results of your emotions by using the

"Take rest; a field that has rested gives a bountiful crop."

—*Ovid*

relaxation exercises in this chapter. The only downside of this approach is that you won't remove the cause of the problem, only the results. This is because your emotions are produced by your thoughts.

It is very difficult to change your thoughts. If you were just turned down for a raise, you can't simply tell yourself, "That's okay. I won't let it bother me." (Well, you *can* tell yourself this, but it is very unlikely you'll believe it.) Although it's difficult to control your thinking, you've already been examining how you think yourself into fearful emotions. As you learn to control the way you think through the various exercises I present throughout this book, you will likely find that you have fewer painful emotions.

As you know, there is only one area you can control directly—your actions. When you battle from this direction, you essentially become a scientist. You try something out and evaluate the results to see if it works. When you see it work, it will change how you think, which will change the way you feel.

While this chapter focuses on the emotional front, actually partaking in the exercises in this chapter can be considered taking action. And, in turn, taking action can help you develop more positive thoughts. With that said, let's take a close look at anxiety and how you will benefit overall by learning to relax in anxiety-provoking situations.

THE BENEFITS OF SYMPTOM RELIEF

Working with your emotions is really about providing you with symptom relief. Symptom relief means reducing your discomfort without doing anything about the cause of your discomfort. Does it make sense to deal with the symptoms, perhaps even before the causes? There are a few good reasons for this.

First of all, it makes you feel better! Getting rid of pain and discomfort is worthwhile for its own sake. If these symptoms were not so unpleasant, a fear of public speaking wouldn't be such a problem. Moreover, symptom relief keeps your fear from growing. As you may recall, your rising level of anxiety gives you evidence that things are as bad as you had feared, or even worse. Once you learn how to keep your anxiety in check, you'll be less likely to experience feelings of runaway anxiety and panic. Take the case of William H., for example. When I met with him, he referred to the few minutes before being called up to the podium as "foreplay to hell." I taught him how to do a simple relaxation exercise that focuses on breathing. Using this breathing technique while waiting to be introduced allowed him to relax just before giving his speech. He was no longer frightening himself with predictions of doom during those few crucial moments. Moreover, the breathing exercise increased the amount of oxygen available to his brain, making him more alert and better able to focus on his talk.

Reducing the symptoms of anxiety can also help you overcome avoidance and procrastination (see Chapter 7). Both putting off preparing for a speech and avoiding the situation entirely make stage fright much worse. Even simply thinking about the preparations you'll need to make can cause your anxiety levels to rise, and so you avoid even thinking about it. Relaxation exercises can help calm your nerves and get you focused on your tasks.

Before I provide you with some concrete ways to reduce your anxiety, let's try to get a better understanding of what anxiety is. I want you to know as much about your enemy as possible!

WHAT IS ANXIETY ALL ABOUT?

Anxiety is how your brain and the rest of your body team up to protect you from danger. As mentioned in Chapter 1, you will often hear anxiety being referred to as the "fight-or-flight response." When you are in danger, your brain prepares your body to run away or fight. Your heart beats faster, you begin to sweat, and your breathing speeds up. These are the same changes that occur when you are engaging in physical activity. As uncomfortable as these symptoms are, anxiety is designed to protect you from harm. In the following sections, we'll take a look at both the physical and mental sides of anxiety.

When you are in danger, your brain prepares your body to run away or fight. Your heart beats faster, you begin to sweat, and your breathing speeds up.

The Physical Side of Anxiety

When you perceive danger, your brain sends signals to two parts of your nervous system. One part is the sympathetic nervous system. Its job is to arouse your senses and mobilize you for action. The other part is the parasympathetic nervous system. Its job is to bring you back to the way you felt before you thought you were in danger. It is the parasympathetic nervous system that helps you relax.

It's important to understand that the sympathetic nervous system tends to be an all-or-nothing system. Once it's called to action, all of its effects are turned on. You either experience all of the symptoms of anxiety or no symptoms at all. You will rarely feel symptoms in only one part of your body. This explains why panic attacks involve so many different sensations, not just one or two. The only thing that tends to change is how drastic the symptoms are—and this depends on how dangerous you think the situation is.

The sympathetic nervous system releases two chemicals called *adrenaline* and *noradrenaline* from your adrenal glands. These chemicals are messengers that tell your sympathetic nervous system to keep you revved up until the danger has passed.

Eventually, the parasympathetic nervous system will reactivate and restore a relaxed feeling. It is built to protect you from letting the sympathetic nervous system get too carried away. Unfortunately, adrenaline and noradrenaline take some time to be destroyed by the body, so even after the danger has passed and your sympathetic nervous system has stopped responding, you are likely to feel anxious because the chemicals are still floating around in your body. You must remind yourself that this is perfectly natural and harmless. This realization will also help you relax sooner.

Let's take a quick look at some specific physical effects of anxiety so they don't come as such a shock the next time you experience them.

Anxiety's Effects on Blood Flow

Adrenaline increases your heart rate and the strength of your heartbeat to prepare you for activity. It speeds blood flow through the body, sending more oxygen to your tissues, and removes waste products from those tissues to make them more efficient. Blood is redirected from parts of the body where it's currently not needed, like the skin, fingers, and toes, to the parts of the body that need more, like the legs and arms.

Less blood in your skin is helpful because if you were to be slashed in an attack, you would be less likely to bleed to death. This redirected blood flow also explains some of the symptoms of anxiety such as pale, cold skin and clammy fingers and toes, which may also feel numb or tingly.

More important, if you are not very active at this time, the blood supply to your head can actually decrease. While this is not at all dangerous, it can produce some unpleasant symptoms such as dizziness, blurred vision, confusion, and hot flashes.

Anxiety's Effects on Breathing

Anxiety also increases the speed and depth of your breathing. In a dangerous situation, your tissues require more oxygen to prepare you for action. Unfortunately, this results in a feeling of breathlessness. You may even feel pains or tightness in your chest. Some people report that they feel like they are choking.

Other Physical Symptoms of Anxiety

When you're anxious, it's not uncommon to start sweating. The original purpose of this symptom of anxiety was probably to make your skin slippery so that a predator has more difficulty grabbing you. Also, the sweat cools your body to keep it from overheating. Also, your pupils widen to let in more light; this may result in blurred vision and "spots" in front of your eyes. You salivate less, resulting in a dry mouth. There is decreased activity in your digestive system, which can produce nausea or a heavy feeling in your stomach. Your muscles tense up to prepare you to respond to danger, and this results in feeling tense, which can lead to trembling and shaking. Since you notice all of these symptoms, they have quite an effect on your thoughts, which brings us to the mental side of anxiety.

The Mental Side of Anxiety

As you know, anxiety's main purpose is to alert you to danger. It focuses all your attention on your surroundings. Assuming no real danger exists, anxiety distracts you from the task or tasks at hand, making it very difficult to concentrate on whatever you should be doing or to remember things you need to recall at that moment. Sure, feeling anxious would be helpful if you were in real danger because it would keep you from being distracted by unimportant things. However, if the perception of danger is only in your head, feeling anxious can keep you from focusing on your presentation.

When you mentally review all of your fear-provoking thoughts and add to that your awareness of your unpleasant symptoms as well as the input you are receiving by monitoring the audience's behavior, you have a symphony of distractions to deal with. The likelihood these distractions will decrease your effectiveness in making your presentations is very high. That is why it is essential to learn to differentiate between real and imagined danger. In any event, whether your anxiety is a result of an actual threat or an imagined one, you can learn to relax to reduce your anxiety symptoms, so let's move on.

LEARNING TO RELAX TO REDUCE
THE SYMPTOMS OF ANXIETY

Herbert Benson, M.D.—a pioneer of mind/body medicine and best-selling author of *The Relaxation Response*—has spent decades researching the relaxation response and has synthesized many relaxation-training methods. While there are many different types of relaxation techniques developed by various experts, I selected Benson's method because of its simplicity and proven effectiveness.

Virtually all forms of relaxation training achieve the same end: they reduce the amount of stimulation sent to your brain. This produces slower heart and breathing rates, decreases oxygen requirements, and reduces muscular tension. All of this, taken together, leads to a feeling of well-being and relaxation throughout the body.

There is perhaps an easier way to explain what happens during relaxation training. The French satirist Voltaire said, "The art of medicine consists in amusing the patient while nature cures the disease." Likewise, your body will relax itself if you can distract yourself from your fear-provoking thoughts. During relaxation training, you are so busy concentrating on relaxing that you can't think about your problems. Your body is smart enough to do the rest for you.

There are four components involved in practicing Benson's relaxation response described in Exercise 6.1 on page 101—a quiet environment, a comfortable position, a mental device, and a passive attitude—each of which is discussed below. You should make every attempt to provide them all to get the greatest benefit from this technique. At the end of this chapter, there is a longer, more detailed relaxation routine that uses several of these components (see Exercise 6.4 on page 109). Relaxation skills are no different from any other skills you acquire. They must be practiced to be effective. Fortunately, it feels great to practice them.

If you have high blood pressure, diabetes, or any other health problem that requires medication, consult your physician before partaking in the exercises described in this chapter.

A Quiet Environment

When you are first learning to relax, practice in a quiet environment. Choose a quiet place without background noise where you can be alone and free of distractions and interruptions. Later, when you become more adept at it, you'll find that you can you perform your relaxation techniques in virtually any situation.

A Comfortable Position

Wear comfortable clothing or loosen any tight-fitting clothes you're wearing. For instance, if you happen to be wearing a belt, loosen it a few notches. Lie down on a bed or couch, or sit in a comfortable chair. Position yourself so that your body feels totally supported. This is key so that you don't have to work at holding your body in place by tensing your muscles. Let go completely so that all your muscles loosen and your body feels like "dead weight."

A Mental Device

The purpose of a mental device is to distract you from thinking your fear-provoking thoughts. Dr. Benson suggests mentally repeating a one-syllable word, such as "peace" or "calm." Dr. Benson's preferred word for this exercise is "one." He suggests that this word be repeated each time you exhale. (Make each exhalation long and slow.) While you are focusing your attention on whatever one-syllable word you choose, your thoughts won't turn to the hostile questions your audience might ask during the next sales meeting, for instance.

A Passive Attitude

Relaxation is not something you can make happen. You need to allow it happen. Ironically, the harder you work at trying to relax, the more difficult it becomes. Therefore, if you find your mind wandering and you fail to repeat your word, don't criticize yourself and become frustrated. Simply start repeating the word again when you realize you've stopped. This experience should be as pleasurable as possible.

Exercise 6.1. Eliciting the Relaxation Response

Familiarize yourself once again with the four components involved in practicing the relaxation response. Once you have all of the conditions in place, you're ready to begin.

1. Get comfortable and relax your muscles. Close your eyes.

2. Tune in to your breathing and concentrate on slowing it down. Breathe in and out through your nose. Since there's always a little tension involved in inhaling, inhale as softly and gently as possible. Also, make your exhalations longer than your inhalations. Since the exhalations are the most relaxing part of this exercise, try to make them as pleasurable as possible.

3. To further relax your muscles, focus your attention on each part your body and feel how it is being fully supported by whatever surface you're on.

4. Search your body for any signs of tension. Start with your feet and then work your way up your body—your ankles, calves, legs, pelvis, and so on. If you identify a tense muscle, focus your attention on it, and as you exhale, allow the muscle to relax.

5. Continue to breathe slowly through your nose, but now think the word "one" to yourself. Do this for five to ten minutes. If you become distracted by stray thoughts, simply pick up where you left off. (After doing this exercise a few times, you may want to substitute a word that you feel is more conducive to relaxation, such as "calm.")

6. When you are ready to end your session, open your eyes. If you are lying down, sit up slowly. Take one or two more deep, slow breaths before standing.

Feedback for Exercise 6.1

When you've completed this exercise, you should notice that you feel both relaxed and alert. If so, the training session was successful. After waking up from a midday nap, you're probably used to feeling groggy, but this is a very different feeling. You've given your body a chance to relax, while at the same time you increased the amount of oxygen to your brain, making you more alert.

If you have difficulty relaxing with this exercise, here are a couple of variations to try:

• Once you've gotten into a comfortable position, look straight ahead and select a single place or object to focus on. Continue to gaze at that point throughout the exercise. Staying focused on this one spot decreases the arousal of your central nervous system. (If your eyes become tired, it's okay to close them.)

• If you find that repeating a calming word doesn't help, simply tune in to the stream of breath as you inhale and exhale. Feel the breath filling up your stomach and follow it as it fills your chest, then follow it back down. Doing this should absorb your attention and keep out unwanted thoughts.

• Do not practice for at least two hours after a large meal. It is always best to practice your relaxation techniques before you eat. Many foods affect your activity level and may make it more difficult to relax. Foods containing a great deal of sugar or caffeine are obvious examples.

• To determine the most successful time of day for your practice, schedule your relaxation-training sessions at different times for a few days. Some people prefer to do these techniques in the morning, before the day introduces new upsets. Many others find that after work, before dinner, or even during coffee breaks are good times.

DOES YOUR ANXIETY SURPRISE YOU EVERY TIME?

During sessions with my clients, I often hold up a pen and ask, "What will happen if I drop this pen?" After the usual dubious look, they say, "The pen will fall to the floor." Then, I ask, "So, it wouldn't surprise you if the pen falls?" They all reply, "Of course not." Next, I ask how they can be so sure. This is usually followed by a brief explanation of the law of gravity. Now, I turn the tables and ask if speaking in public makes their hearts beat faster. "Yes," they reply. "Then why," I ask, "are you always caught by surprise when it happens?!" This is when my clients begin to understand the concept of surprise. After the first dozen or so times a person becomes nervous in a certain situation, he or she really should catch on and actually prepare ahead of time to deal with the symptoms.

It's important for you to be fully aware that your adrenaline pump will start working while you are waiting to perform, while you are performing, and often just when you're thinking about performing. The best way to deal with this feeling is to make use of your previous experiences. You know what being afraid feels like and which situations tend to bring it on: So don't let your anxiety jump out at you during a presentation, shouting "Surprise!" If you expect anxiety, you won't be caught off guard and you'll be in a better position to counter its attack. Learn to "yawn" inwardly and say, "Oh, here's that heart-pounding adrenaline again just like I expected." If you are prepared for it, you will undoubtedly feel less anxious. Exercise 6.2 will help you prepare to meet your particular symptoms of anxiety head-on. Then, knowing what to expect, you can use those symptoms as a signal to relax, which is discussed in the next section.

Exercise 6.2. Eliminating a "Surprise" Anxiety Attack

Bring to mind a nerve-wracking scene in which you must speak in front of an audience or use a past experience. Imagine all of the stages—waiting to be announced, walking up to the podium, greeting your audience, beginning your speech, and so on. Answer each of the questions below as fully as possible in the space provided.

1. How is this situation similar to past anxiety-provoking situations?

_____

_____

_____

2. How are your thoughts similar to the fear-provoking thoughts you've had in the past?

_____

_____

_____

3. On a scale of one to four, indicate how anxious you are.

   Not anxious   1   2   3   4   Very anxious

4. On a scale of one to four, indicate the highest level of anxiety you expect to reach.

   Not anxious   1   2   3   4   Very anxious

5. What are your physical symptoms of anxiety?

_____

_____

_____

_____

6. What are your mental symptoms of anxiety?

_____

_____

_____

_____

Feedback for Exercise 6.2

By now, you probably realize that you keep experiencing the same symptoms of anxiety over and over again. Make the fear they've invoked in you in the past pay off by using them to eliminate the element of surprise. As soon as you notice that you're experiencing the symptoms, put your relaxation skills in full swing. This is discussed in the section "Using the Symptoms of Anxiety as a Signal to Relax" below.

Repeat this exercise each time you are faced with an anxiety-provoking situation. You'll soon see that your level of fear is reduced more and more as you learn to keep the element of surprise at bay.

USING THE SYMPTOMS OF ANXIETY AS A SIGNAL TO RELAX

When you are paying attention to your physical and mental symptoms of anxiety as well as assessing how you think you are doing and how your audience is receiving you, you are "self-monitoring." This bad habit takes your attention away from your most important task—your speech or presentation. An important benefit of developing your relaxation skills is the ability to focus on the task at hand by eliminating distracting thoughts. The more you practice your relaxation exercises, the more you will learn to avoid your tendency to self-monitor. However, if you do find yourself self-monitoring and notice physical and/or mental signs of anxiety, use this as a reminder to put your relaxation training to work for you. As soon as you feel any symptom of anxiety, say the word "relax" to yourself, and refocus your attention on your breath. Whenever you encounter anxiety, if you are able, take ten minutes out to practice the relaxation technique in Exercise 6.1, or simply breathe in and out in a steady manner and focus your attention away from your symptoms. Doing this often will help you break your harmful old habit of self-monitoring by replacing it with a new, productive one. It's true, however, that sometimes you won't be able to take a break from what you're doing to practice your relaxation techniques—let's say you're right smack in the middle of a speech when you notice your anxiety. For some helpful advice, see "Take a Breather" on page 106. In the meantime, let's take a look at the Case of Alice H. for an example of how a person can use anxiety as a cue to remember to relax.

The Case of Alice H.

Alice H., a biology teacher, had just returned to school to earn her master's degree. She told me that she'd get extremely nervous before giving a seminar presentation. Like many other people who have a fear of public speaking, her thoughts would focus on what might go wrong. When she noticed how tense these negative thoughts were making her, she'd use the tension as proof that there really was something to worry about.

During Alice's first session, I taught her a relaxation technique along with the instruction to put the technique into practice whenever she becomes anxious. I reminded her to use her symptoms of anxiety as a cue to relax. Because Alice couldn't stand feeling anxious, she practiced the relaxation technique a great deal.

The next time Alice was about to give a seminar presentation, she had a fear-provoking thought that she'd be unable to answer one of her professor's questions. As a result, she began to panic and experience the symptoms of anxiety—a pounding heart and shaking knees. On cue, she focused her attention on her breath and told herself to relax. With her attention focused on relaxing, she stopped thinking her fear-provoking thought.

At her next session, Alice reported that she'd given a successful seminar presentation and had experienced only a minimal level of anxiety. Like Alice, once you have learned to relax, you need to practice reminding yourself to use it when a situation calls for it.

Relaxation skills are physical skills that improve with practice. Physical relaxation exercises increase your alertness and intake of oxygen. In the next section, you'll learn how to create a state of relaxation by using imagery. By directing your thoughts, you can keep fear-producing thoughts out while focusing on calming thoughts that make it easier for you to perform.

Take a Breather

Once you've practiced the relaxation exercises in this chapter on a regular basis, you should be able to invoke the relaxation response anywhere—on checkout lines, in doctors' offices, and while waiting to be called up to the podium. But what if you suddenly notice feelings of anxiety creeping up on you as you are giving a speech? First of all, quickly remind yourself to focus. Then, pause a moment after each sentence to take a deep, steady breath.

To be able to do this on the spot, I suggest you practice breathing deeply between sentences until it feels natural to you. While you are rehearsing your speech, put this breathing exercise into practice. This will do two important things for you: First, as you would expect, breathing will help you to relax during your speech. And second, breathing deeply will give your voice more power as you deliver your words, an excellent side benefit. (If you want to see what I mean by "more power," try this little experiment: Exhale until you have almost no air left and then say, "I want a piece of apple pie." Now, take a deep breath and repeat the statement. You should notice that the second sentence felt way more powerful—and you just might get that piece of apple pie.)

With just a little practice, you'll be surprised by how much air you can take in between sentences without it seeming like you're taking too long. Also, an occasional pause during a speech can make you seem more thoughtful. So don't worry about on-the-spot anxiety symptoms; you can counteract them just by taking a "breather."

RELAXING WITH IMAGERY

Total Recall
Your memory stores more than just words. If you evoke images, your memory can actually affect you physically.

Your brain stores a lot of information in the form of images. These images have a more profound effect on you than most of the information you store as words. Try this simple demonstration: Close your eyes and imagine that you are picking up a fresh, juicy lemon. See its bright yellow color, and take note of its texture and weight in your hand. Now, slice it open and see juice squirt out. Smell its tart aroma. Put a slice of the lemon in your mouth and roll your tongue over it. Taste its sour juice. Your body probably reacted to the image as if it were real. As you can see, your memory stores more than just words. If you evoke images, your memory can actually affect you physically. The language of imagery allows your brain to communicate with your body. This is why positive imagery is so valuable in helping you relax.

In clinical research studies, imagery has been shown to slow down heart and breathing rates and lower blood pressure. It also increases alpha brainwave activity, which is associated with a relaxed state of mind. Positive imagery increases your body's production of the hormone melatonin, which is needed for healthy sleep. There is evidence that imagery can even boost immune-system activity.

The goal of positive imagery is to calm your mind by focusing on scenes that relax you. Here's a quick example: Imagine that your mind is a glass of muddy water. When you shake it up, particles swirl around the glass and cloud the water. If you let the glass sit for twenty minutes, all of the particles floating around in the water settle, leaving the water clear. Use imagery to quiet the "debris" swirling around your head. This should leave you feeling calm and peaceful. Now try Exercise 6.3, which takes imagery a bit further.

Exercise 6.3. Using Imagery

Perform the relaxation exercise described in Exercise 6.1 for several minutes. Then, with your eyes closed, clear your mind and surround yourself with peaceful and calming images. Focus on being "in the moment"; stay in the here and now. Tune out any thoughts or ideas that may be racing through your mind and remain focused on your breath.

Now, select a "special place" in your imagination and visualize being there. Be sure to choose a place that is special for you—for example, a secluded beach, a brook at the base of a mountain, a cascading waterfall, or a meadow filled with lush vegetation. Be sure it is a place where you feel safe and free of distractions. Focus on the vivid details of the scene, including sights, sounds, and smells, and the overall feeling of being in this peaceful place. Alternatively, you can create a mental connection with close friends or loved ones. These connections may be from your present or your past. You can also select a pet from the present or past. The only important criterion is that your selection makes you feel good.

Practice this routine until you can go directly to the peaceful imagery state without having to first perform the relaxation exercise.

Feedback for Exercise 6.3

The key to this exercise is to extend the relaxing effects of Exercise 6.1 by focusing on the pleasant scene you have chosen. Did you have a vivid picture in your mind's eye? Were you free of distractions? Were you able to deeply immerse yourself in the image? If you can lose yourself in the imagery, you have succeeded. If you are not immersed and can't find an image to lose yourself in, try a different approach. For example, create a pleasant image by describing it on paper. Then, try to convert the words into mental pictures, or images, until you find something that works. Photographs and lifelike painting may also help you visualize a relaxing scene in your mind's eye.

No matter how relaxed you manage to become, sometimes you'll find that just before you are ready to speak, your throat feels very tight. Therefore, before we get to the really good stuff, let's take a look at a technique to help you "open your throat" and make your voice sound a lot stronger. This is a skill that will improve with practice, but as you will see, it should be done in private.

THROAT-OPENING EXERCISE

One evening, I was standing outside a club where I'd be singing in an hour. I suddenly felt like I had gotten a terrible sore throat, and I could hardly speak. My yoga teacher, who had come to watch my performance that night, approached to say hello. I told her about my sore throat, and she asked when it started.

When I told her it had just come on suddenly, she laughed and said, "You don't have a sore throat, you're just nervous. Do the throat-opening exercise I taught you."

I did as she instructed and within minutes my throat felt fine. This same exercise has helped countless other public speakers and singers who I've shared it with, and I want to share it with you.

Before you begin the exercise, read the following statement out loud: "I want to say a few words to you." Pay close attention to the sound of your voice. Now, inhale through your mouth as you roll your tongue backward. The tip of your tongue should move past your upper teeth and the bottom of your tongue should be resting on the roof of your mouth. Then, as you exhale through your mouth, extend your tongue out and down as far as it will go—try to touch your chin with the tip of your tongue. It's essential to put pressure on your tongue as you move it out and down. Repeat this cycle five times.

When you've completed the exercise, read the statement again. Once again, pay close attention to the sound of your voice. You should notice that your voice sounds considerably stronger.

It's a good idea to do this exercise a few minutes before speaking. It's an even better idea to do it in a private place such as a restroom.

THE FULL RELAXATION EXPERIENCE

I've saved the best for last! I want you to feel the very best you can as this chapter comes to a close. I also want you to be able to head out into the world with fewer anxiety symptoms when faced with the prospect of speaking in public. Exercise 6.4 is designed to induce a full state of relaxation. If you have a background in yoga or sports psychology, you may already be familiar with some of the concepts this exercise introduces. This is an excellent exercise to do the night before, or the morning of, a presentation—and certainly anytime you want to reach this calming state. In fact, I recommend that you do it every day! But before you get started, you'll need to prepare a relaxation recording, which you will play while resting in a comfortable position. Read the Relaxation Transcript on page 273 in Appendix B into a recorder. Be sure to pause for a moment between lines so that you have time to follow the instructions when you listen to it later.

Exercise 6.4. The Full Relaxation Experience

You will begin this exercise by focusing on your breath to maximize relaxation. You will be breathing in a slightly different manner than you might normally breathe, so it will take some time to get used to. Throughout the entire exercise, breathe only through your nose.

Step 1. Learning to Breathe

1. To begin, lie down or sit with your neck, back, and legs supported.

2. Place your hands on your stomach, and feel its movement as you gently inhale and exhale through your nose for a few moments.

3. Now, exhale all of the air from your lungs—pulling, or sucking, your stomach in as much as it will go. Engage your diaphragm to push out the air.

4. Next, using only your diaphragm, inhale through your nose. As you breathe in, allow your stomach to fill up and balloon out, while keeping your chest and shoulders still. Only your stomach should be moving, and you should be able to feel it rising under your hands. (If you are sitting and having some difficulty filling up your stomach, try this exercise lying down.)

5. When you feel you have taken enough air into your diaphragm, draw a second breath—this time into your chest. You should be able to feel two distinct breaths—one into your diaphragm and the other into your chest. At this point, you should feel your chest rising and expanding as you inhale. (This feeling of breathing into separate chambers—the diaphragm and chest—will take some getting used to.)

6. When you have completely filled up your diaphragm and chest, slowly exhale. First breathe out from your chest, and then out from your diaphragm.

As you become more comfortable with this "two-chambered breathing," you can begin concentrating on "softening" the muscles you use during your inhalations. Practice this breathing method until it starts to feel natural.

Step 2. Guided Two-Chambered Breathing

Now that you have become familiar with two-chambered breathing, you are ready to listen to your relaxation recording. (If you haven't done so already, read the Relaxation Transcript in Appendix B into a recorder.) Listen to your recording in private where you will not be disturbed. Get comfortable, and follow your prerecorded instructions. Relax and enjoy....

Feedback for Exercise 6.4

In order to fully benefit from this exercise, the experience should be as relaxing and pleasant as possible. So, eliminate unwanted noises from your recording and from your environment. You may even want to listen to the recording through a headset to block out other sounds.

Your final recording shouldn't be any longer than eight or so minutes, so doing the exercise won't take up much of your time. Therefore, I recommend you do it every day. You'll find that each time you partake in this exercise, you will feel even better than you did the last time. And, when you've mastered two-chambered breathing, it'll just feel great every time.

Don't be alarmed if you feel a bit lightheaded at any time during this exercise. This lightheadedness is a result of increasing your oxygen intake. This is a good thing. It will make you more alert.

WHAT YOU HAVE LEARNED
AND WHERE YOU ARE GOING

Relaxed? I hope so. The techniques you learned in this chapter should help you relax in any anxiety-provoking situation. Invoking the relaxation response just before beginning a talk can be a great source of comfort. And getting yourself to relax as soon as you notice your symptoms of anxiety—which will no longer come as a surprise to you—can do a lot to reduce your fear of public speaking.

You know what else can do a lot to reduce your fear of public speaking? Learning how to curtail avoidance and procrastination, the topics of the next chapter.

7

The BIG Idea

Avoidance can lead to missed opportunities in your career and personal life, and procrastination reduces your chances of adequately preparing for a presentation or speech.

Dealing With Avoidance and Procrastination

Years ago, while writing a book on the use of technology, I came to a place around page ten where I needed to provide a powerful example to make an important point. I thought about it for a few minutes, but I came up dry. By reflex, I reached for a yellow legal pad to jot down my ideas so I could return to that part at some later time and keep writing. That was when I really came to understand the sinister nature of procrastination. I realized that I would end up writing all the fun, easy parts of the book, and my big yellow pad would be waiting for me with pages of all the difficult tasks I'd put off. Then, when faced with such a list of anxiety-provoking tasks, I'd likely avoid it entirely and busy myself with other things to ease my mind. Fortunately, I realized I'd never finish the book that way. So I made a decision to put down the legal pad, and I worked on the example until I came up with something I liked. I finished the book and, in the process, had beaten a pair of dangerous opponents—procrastination and avoidance.

In this chapter, you'll learn that although avoiding the act of public speaking or a similar performance can reduce your anxiety in the short run, it can cause you even greater harm in the long run. You'll also learn how procrastination has a similar, but sometimes even more harmful, result. Then, you'll learn some techniques for overcoming these powerful hurdles.

> "Procrastination is the art of keeping up with yesterday and avoiding today."
>
> —*Wayne Dyer*

THE DIFFERENCE BETWEEN AVOIDANCE AND PROCRASTINATION

Because avoidance and procrastination are similar in nature, they are often confused. In general, they both reduce short-term anxiety by putting things off, but there are two big differences between them. With avoidance, a task *never* gets completed. Procrastination puts off a task, but it finally gets done, perhaps poorly.

There are many consequences of avoidance that range from being considered unreliable to passing up promotions and even careers because they involve public speaking. The consequences of procrastination are poor preparation and limited practice time. The results of procrastination are generally a poor performance. In the following sections, we'll take a close look at both of these foes.

AVOIDANCE: HOW IT IS REWARDED AND PUNISHED

Strap Yourself In!
When fear controls you and keeps you from achieving your goals, you can expect your self-esteem to take a nosedive.

If you have to do something that makes you anxious, what's the best way to feel better fast? Don't do it. The most common way to eliminate your anxiety about speaking in public is to just say no; don't give the speech or presentation. Avoid the situation completely. However, while this will make you feel better in the short run, you'll feel worse in the long run. True, avoidance will reduce your feelings of anxiety, but it won't help you feel better if you pass up the opportunity to interview for a better job, decline a nomination to an office in some organization, or miss out on an opportunity to assume a leadership role because the position requires you to present your views to others. When fear controls you this way and keeps you from achieving your goals, you can expect your self-esteem to take a nosedive. What's more, avoidance feeds on itself. When you avoid something, you are rewarded with the loss of fear. This short-term "reward" strengthens your tendency to avoid things in the future. And why shouldn't it? It works—or at least it seems to. The Case of Rod R. is a good example of how avoidance gets rewarded, at first. Let's take a look.

The Case of Rod R.

Rod R., an attorney, came to see me because he was afraid to appear in court. It turned out that, due to his shyness, he was also afraid to strike up a conversation with an attractive woman. When he would have to prepare a case, he would imagine the opposing attorney finding holes in his work. He would describe it as "getting pants" in court. This would make him so anxious that he would stop preparing. Then, when he did go into court, his diminished preparation would result in poorer performances. After a few weeks of working together, Rod came to see how he was putting off his preparations. He began to prepare more thoroughly and found that he was performing much better. As his confidence increased, so did his preparation time. He now looks forward to litigating. Given my view of attorneys and litigation, I sometimes wonder if sending another confident litigator into the system is a good thing or not. In this case, Rod was a very ethical attorney.

As for his shyness around women, whenever Rod considered approaching a woman for a date, he'd think about what he would say and how he'd say it, and then imagine her reaction. The only response he could ever think up was a rejection. Just thinking about being rejected quickly increased his anxiety level. To calm himself, Rod would turn away to avoid the woman he had considered approaching. This calmed his nerves immediately, but later he'd get down on himself because he realized he would be lonely forever if he kept avoiding this type of situation. The good news is that Rod finally used some of the strategies discussed in this chapter. He made me very proud at his wedding when he pulled me aside and said, "You know, without our work together, this would never have happened."

The reason so many people avoid public speaking is because avoidance works. As it did in Rod's case, it immediately reduces uncomfortable feelings. Unfortunately, each time it works, the habit of avoiding fear-provoking situations gets a little more ingrained. Lost are the rewards one could gain by doing the presentation or giving a speech. In general, the longer a person has had the fear, the more he or she has probably avoided it, and the longer it will probably take to overcome. Rest assured, however, it can be overcome with a little work.

When you have a fear of public speaking and are faced with the prospect of having to give a talk, you are in conflict. Should you do it or should you try to avoid it? You may take the safest route and decide not to make a decision, but this leaves you in a state of conflict because you know a decision will have to be made. A state of conflict is uncomfortable, but it does delay the greater discomfort that would be brought on by the consequences of making a decision. There are several type of conflicts, which are discussed in the sections to follow.

Avoidance and the Nature of Conflict

A conflict is a mental struggle in which you must make a choice between two or more alternatives. For example, do I stay in my current job or interview for a better position? Not all conflicts are fear-producing. In fact, there are three types of conflict: the double-approach conflict, the double-avoidance conflict, and the approach-avoidance conflict. Let's take a look at each type of conflict. We will focus on the last of the three as this is the type of conflict you will most often have to face when dealing with your fear of public speaking.

The Double-Approach Conflict

The double-approach conflict is the best type of conflict to be in. You have to choose between two favorable things because you can have only

If you must make a choice between two unfavorable things, you'll probably try to choose the one you think will be less bad.

one of them. Any restaurant diner who sees more than one dish that he or she likes on the menu is faced with a double-approach conflict. If this is you, the good news is that you'll end up with something you like. On the other hand, if you're a bit of a pessimist, you might be left wondering if you should have gone with the other choice. People who tend to dwell on the negative often experience "buyer's remorse"—they are always sure that the other choice would have been a better one. When it comes to public speaking, you probably won't find yourself in a double-approach conflict all that often.

The Double-Avoidance Conflict

The double-avoidance conflict is the "lesser of two evils" conflict. Anyone who has ever voted in a presidential election surely understands this type of conflict. You must make a choice between two unfavorable things, so you try to choose the one you think will be less bad. Here's an example of a double-avoidance conflict: Your boss informs you that you must either go to Chicago to address the board of directors of your company or you must be a keynote speaker at the annual company retreat. Each of these speaking engagements seems risky and even terrifying, and you feel that you will lose out either way. Therefore, you'll avoid the more stressful, riskier choice and will probably choose the company retreat.

The Approach-Avoidance Conflict

The approach-avoidance conflict is the most difficult of the conflicts. Whenever you have to make a choice that involves both getting something you want *and* having to accept something negative as a result, you are in an approach-avoidance conflict. For example, consider Rod R.'s predicament. He wanted to talk to women (approach), but he feared the anxiety and potential rejection (avoidance).

In approach-avoidance conflicts, the desire to avoid the unpleasant part of a situation is usually stronger than the desire to approach the pleasant part. Most people choose to avoid pain before seeking pleasure. This leads to an interesting problem: Because we always want to avoid pain, the rewards for making a successful presentation or giving a speech are obscured by our fear-provoking thoughts and the accompanying anxiety. The relief we get by avoiding the situation seems so wonderful that, for the time being, we lose sight of all we are giving up by not facing the situation head-on.

An example of an approach-avoidance conflict would come if you had to give a talk to a local church or civic group. The approach part would be that you were doing something that was valuable for your community. The avoidance side would be the fear of presenting badly and being disgraced.

One way to overcome the approach-avoidance conflict is to focus on the rewards for a successful outcome. You must conquer your tendency to dwell on your fear-provoking thoughts and forgetting or ignoring the possible rewards of moving forward.

Exercise 7.1 can help you identify and evaluate the potential rewards of going through with your performance or avoiding it. If you want to overcome your tendency to avoid uncomfortable situations, keeping in mind the benefits of facing that situation can be very motivating. By focusing your attention on the positive aspects of how you will present yourself to your audience and what benefits may occur as a result of it, you will weaken your tendency to avoid the situation.

Exercise 7.1. Identifying Rewards

Think of something you've been avoiding—for example, giving a speech, going on an interview, or even asking someone for a date. Record a brief description of this situation in the space provided. Then, below each heading, list the benefits, or rewards, of carrying out that task. Do the same for avoiding it completely. Be sure to include both the short-term and long-term benefits of each.

Task: _____

Rewards for Doing the Task: _____

_____

_____

_____

_____

Rewards for Avoiding the Task: _____

_____

_____

_____

_____

Feedback for Exercise 7.1

As you examine the potential rewards, think about how both sets of reasons will affect the quality of your life. Weighing the alternatives generally turns out to be a good motivator to overcome avoidance. For some help with this exercise, let's take a look at one of my client's responses:

Task: Giving a presentation to the youth sports league about my views on competition.

Rewards for Doing the Task

I will feel proud of myself for having the courage to do something difficult.

I will feel good about trying to decrease the league's emphasis on "winning" and move it toward kids' personal growth and skill development.

I will feel good about being able to express my views and get support from like-minded people.

My kids will begin to like competing more in the sports leagues and get more exercise.

Rewards for Avoiding the Task

People won't look at me as someone who just wants to complain about something.

I won't be nervous about having to speak at the league meeting.

I will remain that mysterious, intelligent-looking guy on the sidelines.

If this guy doesn't speak at the league meeting, he'll probably feel guilty for "abandoning" his child's welfare. He'll probably also feel weak for backing down from a challenge. On the other hand, he will be rewarded with reduced anxiety. Unfortunately, his lowered anxiety level will be tempered by the negative feelings of having backed away from a challenge. Fortunately, he saw that the rewards for doing the task outweighed the rewards for not doing it.

PROCRASTINATION: HOW IT IS REWARDED AND PUNISHED

There's an old saying, "The problem with being a procrastinator is that you're never quite sure when you're done." Procrastination is a nice word for "stalling" or "putting things off." Sometimes, you'll find yourself forced into making a speech or giving a presentation. Even here you can *almost avoid* the situation by procrastinating. When you finally do perform, however, procrastination actually makes your performance worse. This is because procrastination doesn't give you the opportunity to prepare adequately. It also gives you an excuse for a poor performance—*I'm not incompetent; I just didn't have time to prepare*. This is a bizarre type of reward that seems to work on the surface. You can always maintain the fiction that you would have been great if you had prepared enough, and if you never test it out, you can just go on believing it. But poor presentations will catch up with you, and your reputation will suffer. The Case of Gerald M. is a common example of procrastination.

The Case of Gerald M.

Gerald M. was a graduate student at a local university who was enrolled in a seminar class. In a seminar class, each graduate student is expected to select a research area and thoroughly investigate it. The student must then present the results of the investigation to the class in a talk that typically lasts for at least an hour. The graduate student giving the talk must also be prepared to answer a series of questions from other students in the class and from the professor. The student is expected to have become an *expert* on the topic.

Gerald, like many students, found this situation very intimidating. He could not avoid it if he wanted to earn his master's degree. Whenever he thought about presenting his topic, he'd get very tense. To calm himself down, he simply put off preparing the speech—out of sight, out of mind.

Unfortunately for Gerald, when the time came for him to present his seminar paper, he ended up with a great deal of anxiety and gave a terrible speech. By putting off his preparation, he had less time to get ready and, therefore, did a poor job.

If you are a procrastinator, I have a way for you to deal with and overcome procrastination so that you can adequately prepare for your performance. It involves investigating how influential your reasons are for putting things off. It takes you deeper than the surface so you can identify the power of your reasons.

"Why Do I Procrastinate?"—Creating Your Con List

Whenever you have to make a crucial decision to either prepare for or put off preparing for a speech or presentation, you engage in an internal dialogue about it. You identify the pros and cons, and, at the end of the dialogue, you either begin working on it or you don't. The next time you are faced with this decision and choose not to prepare, you must record your reasons for not doing it, as discussed in Exercise 7.2 on the next page.

Identifying your reasons for procrastinating is like taking an internal scan of your particular case of procrastination. Your reasons for not making the necessary preparations can be very revealing, and hopefully, when you discover that you are running out of good reasons or realize that your reasons are not so solid, you will overcome your tendency to procrastinate. By taking note of why you are putting something off, you are giving yourself the opportunity to closely observe your actual reasoning processes, and perhaps see some flaws in your arguments.

If you are successful, when you think of one of these arguments, you will remember the data behind it. Then you will assume a form of self-talk that drips with sarcasm, and you'll find yourself saying things like, "Oh sure, I'm going to start researching the material for my talk as soon as this show is over—yeah, right!" And that sarcasm just might get you up and going!

Exercise 7.2. Creating Your Personal Con List

This exercise is most valuable if you are currently putting off preparing for an actual presentation. If you are not, select any task you have been putting off, such as exercising, dieting, or asking for a promotion.

Whenever you recognize that you have the opportunity to prepare for the situation but choose not to, record your reason for putting it off in the space provide below. For example, *I have to do the laundry,* or *I have to walk the dog,* or whatever. Then, the next time you put off the same task, review your list and then add your reason for putting it off this time.

_____

_____

_____

_____

_____

_____

_____

_____

_____

_____

Feedback for Exercise 7.2

Once you've kept this list for a while, you'll be surprised at how difficult it is to use a reason or a closely related reason once you've used it a few times already. Imagine how difficult it will be to say over and over again: "It's too late when I get home from work," or "I have phone calls to make," or "I have housework to do," or "I need to unwind by watching some television."

The key to this exercise is, of course, to be an advocate for actually doing the task. Don't bother trying to come up with additional reasons to put off the task. Be sure to make a real effort to get yourself to prepare by minimizing the importance of the items on your con list.

THE ROLE OF EXAGGERATION
IN AVOIDANCE AND PROCRASTINATION

The thought process you go through when you avoid or procrastinate is fascinating. You don't just avoid the actual task or put off preparing for it; in most cases, you also exaggerate its difficulty to justify your behavior. The closer you get to actually performing the task, the more difficult, dangerous, or unpleasant you make it out to be. For example, I joined a gym years ago and planned to use the machines to build my muscles. The machines were quite intimidating. I started noticing that the closer I got to the gym, the weaker I'd feel and the more ominous the gym equipment seemed. I'd be so exhausted by the time I parked my car in the gym lot that, on a couple of occasions, I actually turned around and went home without stepping foot in the club.

The Case of Barry R. is an example of a procrastinator who kept postponing a task because he kept building up how much work it would take until it seemed almost impossible. Notice the difference between his predicted assessment and the actual time it took to complete his goal. Exaggeration is one of the fundamental reasons why people procrastinate.

The Case of Barry R.

Barry R., an attorney, complained to me about how disorganized he kept his files. Being the direct type, I asked him why he didn't just organize them. With a weary look, he said he just didn't have that much time available. I asked him to estimate how long he thought it would take, and he said, "At least forty man-hours." So, we tried an experiment. I asked him to work on organizing his files for fifteen minutes a day. He laughed and said that fifteen minutes a day would never even make a dent in his files, but he agreed to try it anyway. The following week, he came swaggering back into my office and said that had finished reorganizing his files. He told me that once he got into doing it, the whole job took under five hours.

There are two interesting styles of behavior shown by people who procrastinate. They either can't get themselves started or they can start but don't stay with it. The "fifteen-minute miracle," as Barry kept referring to it, is very effective for both types of people. For Barry, who had trouble getting started, it is ideal. Once a person like Barry gets started and realizes that the task isn't as bad as he or she thought, it becomes possible to power right through it. For a person who just can't stay with the task, fifteen minutes at a time is a way to make slow and steady progress. There are further ways to deal with procrastination as well as avoidance. Let's take a look in the next section.

AVOIDANCE BEHAVIOR
AND STRESS INOCULATION

By now it should be abundantly clear why people avoid and procrastinate—to reduce their anxiety-provoking thoughts. The fear of actually
giving a speech, going on an interview, asking someone out for a date, or
any number of other things that invoke stage fright is just too much to
even think about. So they avoid thinking about it or put off preparing for
the task. An excellent way to go about reducing this tendency to avoid or
procrastinate is to go straight to the heart of the problem and reduce the
fear. In other words, reduce the avoidance behavior. For many years,
psychologists have been developing ways to deal with this type of
behavior. We refer to it as "stress inoculation."

Here's how stress inoculation works: When you are vaccinated
against a disease, you receive a small dose of that same disease. This
allows your body to build up antibodies against that particular malady
to protect you from a full-blown attack. Stress inoculation works on the
same principle. You immerse yourself in a fear-provoking situation gradually, and then adapt to it with repeated exposure. It's as if your body is
building *anxiety antibodies.*

"You may delay,
but time will not."
—*Benjamin Franklin*

The more closely you simulate the actual conditions under which
you will eventually perform, the more secure you will feel when it is
time to give your speech or make your presentation. The reasoning here
is that if you learn and practice a skill only in a safe environment, it will
be very difficult for you to perform that same skill when things are tense
or dangerous. For example, George M. learned how to do an "Eskimo
roll" in a kayak—that is, how to right himself if the boat capsizes. He
acquired this skill while training in a large swimming pool. However,
when his kayak capsized in rough river rapids, he was unable to perform
this maneuver. Fortunately, he did survive, although his kayak wasn't as
lucky. Similarly, relaxation skills that are practiced only in safe environments are frequently ineffective under stress. That's why I urge my
clients to practice their relaxation skills during an argument or a difficult
business meeting—and just before "road rage" sets in.

There are three major forms of stress inoculation—systematic desensitization, flooding, and implosion. I use the technical terms so you can
"sound like an expert" when you discuss them with your friends. With
systematic desensitization (the gradual approach), you sneak up on your
fear in small steps so that you get more and more used to it. For example,
if you want to overcome your fear of water and learn to swim, you could
start with one toe in the shallow end of the pool and proceed in very

slowly. You would keep going in deeper and deeper as you became more comfortable with the situation.

In the flooding (comparable practice) method, you confront your fear head on. You would dive right into the pool. In fact, the term "flooding" came about from the use of the technique for overcoming water phobia. Instead of gradually acclimating a person to water, you'd toss him right into the pool.

In the implosion (going beyond) method, you perform a more difficult task than the one you will eventually have to face. Then, by the time you're ready to perform, the task will seem easy by comparison. In this case, you'd dive into the ocean, and save the pool for later. This is *trial by fire*.

Let's say you have to present a talk to an audience of seventy-five people. The following sections will take a look at how you could use each of these stress-inoculation techniques in this situation.

Systematic Desensitization (The Gradual Approach)

The idea behind desensitization is to start with a mild aspect of your fear and then keep having it presented to you until you just get tired of being afraid of it. Then, you face closer and closer versions of what makes you afraid until your fear is gone. This method can take a while, but it does work. How long you've had the fear, how intense it is, and how much you want to overcome it are three key factors in how long it will take.

Using our example of speaking in front of seventy-five people, here are the steps you might go through. Do not go to the next step until you feel completely comfortable with the current step.

1. Identify a list of actions you can take to reach your goal of speaking in front of a group of seventy-five people. Rank the order of the tasks by how anxious they make you—from least to most frightening (your goal). With this method, you will approach your goal slowly, beginning with a task or situation that is far removed from the final goal itself. For example, your first and least frightening task may be presenting your talk into a recorder. You will be surprised to find out how much pressure a recorder will put on you as you practice your talk into it. When you do such practicing, however, you must make a commitment not to stop. Perform just as if you had a real audience. Using a recorder has a few other advantages. It gives you excellent feedback on what your talk sounds like. It lets you play the tape back so that you can use it to learn the material better. You can practice again and again in the tape recorder until you feel comfortable. Then, you might want to graduate to a video recorder.

2. Use the relaxation skills you learned in Chapter 6 so that you are in a state of relaxation before you begin this process. Then give your talk to an audience of a couple of your friends or family members. Keep in mind that your family or friends may be bored by your presentation if they have little interest in the topic, but your intended audience, who is there to hear what you have to say, will recognize its value.

If you become tense during this practice presentation, stop for a moment and get yourself to relax. Then, start again when you feel better. Your family and friends will understand. The more often you do this, the more comfortable you will become.

3. Once again, use your relaxation techniques and try taking it a step further. Remember, the more your small audience resembles the intended audience, the better. For example, try giving your presentation to a few colleagues, who may be more familiar with the topic. This gets you still closer to your future audience. If you are feeling brave, ask them for feedback. If you are feeling even braver, listen to their feedback.

4. As you master each step, proceed to the next one until you arrive at your goal. For example, you can now try your talk out on a group of people who are very similar to your intended audience. Various organizations are often looking for people to speak at one of their events without having to pay them. Sometimes you may find similar groups in related organizations. Remember, the closer you can get to the actual situation of talking to those seventy-five people, the better.

5. The last step in systematic desensitization is always performing the actual task. Go ahead and give the talk to your audience of seventy-five.

In Exercise 7.3 on page 123, you will have the opportunity to try desensitization for yourself. Try to use your visual imagery to place yourself in the speaking situation you will find yourself in and note what aspects are making you anxious. You will be asked to identify four of them and place them in order.

Flooding (Comparable Practice)

The flooding technique differs from systematic desensitization in a big way: you don't look for an easier version of the problem; you begin with an identical one. You'd jump right to step five and speak to the audience of seventy-five. This is obviously a much quicker procedure, but it's usually only taken by people who are very motivated or very brave. You basically act as if you are not afraid to give a talk and prepare the way you normally would, if you weren't afraid. Then, you just give the talk.

Exercise 7.3. Systematic Desensitization

Bring to mind the next time that you will have to speak in front of a large group. Go through each of the steps presented on pages 121–122. If your particular type of stage fright is not related to speaking in front of a large group of people—perhaps it is a small group—design your own series of gradual steps toward whatever task you must confront. Write down each of the steps you will take below:

Step One

_____

_____

_____

Step Two

_____

_____

_____

Step Three

_____

_____

_____

Step Four

_____

_____

_____

GOAL

_____

_____

_____

Feedback for Exercise 7.3

Make sure that the least frightening step is far enough removed from the fear-provoking goal that you will be willing to try it out. If you start too close to the task itself, you may become too frightened to do it. Make sure that you don't go to the next step until the current one is truly comfortable.

Implosion (Going Beyond)

With this technique, you'd make a presentation to an audience that's larger than the intended audience. As explained before, the idea behind implosion is to go so far beyond what you have to do that the actual task pales in comparison. I once used this technique on myself, although not intentionally; it just sort of happened. My friends and I had formed a musical trio, and we'd practice weekly. When we began to think we were getting pretty good, we decided we'd like to appear at a few local nightclubs. We were pretty sure a public appearance would make us nervous at first, so we invited a few close friends over for the following Saturday night to try out our act on a very small audience. Other friends heard about this invitation and asked if they could also come to the "party." Within a week, we had eighty of our "closest" friends coming to the "party." Somehow, our trio survived the night, and we began playing in local clubs. Performing at those clubs was nothing compared to that Saturday night with eighty close friends looking on.

WHAT YOU HAVE LEARNED AND WHERE YOU ARE GOING

In this chapter, you learned to identify your avoidance and procrastination behaviors. You've also taken a close look at how you've fooled yourself into thinking these behaviors will work in the long run. Overcoming these tendencies begins with examining the reasoning you use to support them and then to discount those reasons. Finally, you learned that you can take some concrete steps to overcome avoidance and procrastination by practicing the stress-inoculation techniques described in this chapter.

In the following chapter, you'll learn some excellent methods for improving your memory to make it unlikely you'll forget the content of your presentation or speech. And maybe this will even make you less likely to avoid the task in the first place!

8

The BIG Idea

Organized information is much easier to remember, especially when the information is personally meaningful to you— and your audience.

IMPROVING YOUR MEMORY

O ne of the most common fears people have when it comes to public speaking is that their memories will fail them during their presentation. I can't think of anything more humiliating than being in front of an attentive audience and not knowing what I'm supposed to say or do next. Fortunately, forgetfulness is fairly easy to overcome. Being able to recall the key points of your speech will make you less afraid of speaking in public and will improve your presentation. And, as you recognize your ability to recall your information, you can use it to revise your fear-provoking thoughts and predictions. For example, remember Barbara G. (see page 10)? She was afraid she'd forget important information during her talk. Once I taught her a few memory-improvement techniques, which she practiced regularly, she noticed an obvious improvement in her ability to recall her material. This led to a new, positive prediction that her memory would not desert her when she most needed it.

There are many techniques designed to help improve your memory, many of which are described later in this chapter. First, let's first take a look at how your memory works in general. Armed with this information, you'll be better able to put the memory techniques to good use.

"The secret of a good memory is attention, and attention to a subject depends upon our interest in it. We rarely forget that which has made a deep impression on our minds."

—*Tyron Edwards*

HOW YOUR MEMORY WORKS

The process of remembering *and* forgetting exists to make your life bearable. Without a working memory, every single experience—regardless of whether you've done it a thousand times over—would seem like a new one, and your life would be hopelessly complicated. Therefore, it's essential to remember certain basic things, like how and why to brush your teeth. On the other hand, it's essential that you forget much of what happens day in and day out. Would you really want to be able to recall what you had for lunch on August 2, 1994? Would you want to be able to remember what size portions you had during that lunch? If you could remember every single occurrence and every tidbit of information you receive daily, your brain would be cluttered with useless details, and you'd be unable to focus on matters of importance.

Years ago, during a martial arts class, the instructor said to us, "It's time to learn how to defend yourself against a knife attack. But first, you must learn how to use a knife so that you know how your opponent thinks and acts with his knife." In the same way, the best way to understand the process of forgetting is to first understand the process of remembering.

There are four mental operations involved in memorization: 1) paying attention to the information, 2) processing the information, 3) storing the information, and 4) retrieving the information. Here's an example of how this works: You are introduced to Mr. Ferry. First, you listen to his name as you are being introduced. If something distracts you while you are being introduced, the name is gone. Once you hear it, you process it by repeating it to yourself or by making an association with the name. This stores it in your memory. If you fail to process it by repeating it or by making an association, once again the name is gone. The better you processed it, the more efficiently it will be stored. If you don't store it carefully, it's as difficult to find as those keys you misplaced when you got home and rushed to the ringing telephone. Finally, when you meet Mr. Ferry again, you must retrieve his name from your memory. This should be relatively easy if the other three operations all went well. If not, Mr. Ferry's name may be on the tip of your tongue, but you can't quite recall it.

We'll revisit these four mental operations in more detail shortly, but first let's take a look at the three stages of memory so you can better understand how the four mental operations work within that structure.

The Three Stages of Memory

When you have an experience, like meeting Mr. Ferry for instance, the information you receive and eventually are able to recall goes through three stages: sensory memory, working memory, and long-term memory. You receive the information through your senses, and the information gets stored in your sensory memory. This is where you must pay attention to it. Next, the information moves forward to your working memory where you must process it. Here, you decide whether it's worth keeping or discarding. If it is worth keeping, you must do something with it to move it along. The most common way to do this is to repeat the information to yourself. You may also try to think of a way to make the information personally meaningful. If it makes the cut, the information gets stored in your long-term memory.

The three stages of memory are not real places in your brain, but rather a model of how your memory works. Take a look at Figure 8.1 below for a visual example, then read on for a discussion of each.

Figure 8.1.
The Three Stages
of Memory

Sensory Memory

All of the information you receive is taken in through your senses. Pictures and text come in visually, and words and music come in auditorily. All of this sensory information is stored in your sensory memory, which holds information for only about one-tenth of a second.

To get an idea of how sensory memory works, look at any object in the room for a moment or two, and then quickly close your eyes. You will see a brief trace of the object for a fraction of a second, and then it is gone. If you want to keep this information moving through the system so you can remember it, you must pay close attention to it. If you don't pay attention to it, it goes away very quickly, to be replaced by the next sensation that comes in. If you do pay attention to the information, it gets passed on to the next stage—working memory.

Sensory memory takes in information through your senses and holds it for a fraction of a second. If you pay attention to it, you can move it into your working memory. If you don't pay attention to it, it is lost in the void forever.

Working Memory

Working memory is like a clearinghouse where you have fewer than thirty seconds to decide if the information is worth keeping. If it is not encoded or processed, it is discarded. If information is rehearsed through repetition or recognized as related to something you already know, it can get transferred to long-term memory. That reminds me of my first visit to the Comedy Store, a club in Los Angeles. Hanging inside was a sign that read: NO TAPE RECORDERS OR PADS AND PENCILS PLEASE! *How silly,* I thought, *that won't protect the comics' material!* I thought that if I heard a joke I liked, I'd simply remember it. However, at the end of an evening of uproarious

Working memory holds information for fewer than thirty seconds. You must find a way to process it so you can send it into long-term memory or you will lose it forever.

laughter, I could remember only two or three jokes, and they weren't even the ones I liked best. That's because I'd laugh at the jokes, then listen for the next. I didn't have the opportunity to transfer anything to long-term memory because I was distracted.

Long-Term Memory

Long-term memory is where you permanently store information that has successfully been transferred from your working memory. Research seems to support the belief that once information goes into long-term memory, it is there for the duration of your life—although you may not always be able to retrieve the information at will. In a well-known experiment, a man whose brain was electrically stimulated during brain surgery began singing a song he'd learned as a three-year-old, even though he hadn't thought about the song for several decades!

Long-term memory stores information forever. This doesn't mean you can always retrieve it when you want it, but it's comforting to know it's in there somewhere.

The Four Mental Operations Involved in Memory

To get information through the three stages of memory so that it will be stored permanently in your long-term memory, you go through the four mental operations mentioned earlier: 1) paying attention to the information, 2) processing the information, or encoding, 3) storing the information, and 4) retrieving the information. Figure 8.2 below illustrates the four operations overlaid on the three stages of memory. As you'll learn in the sections to follow, each stage has specific operations that guide how information enters and gets processed.

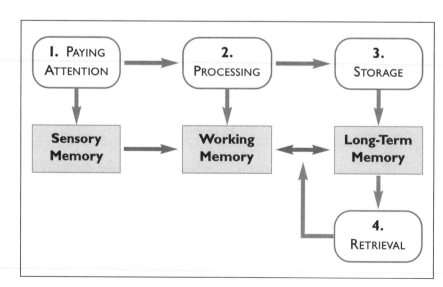

Figure 8.2.
The relationship between the four mental operations and the three stages of memory.

1. Paying Attention to the Information

There is far too much going on in the environment to take it all in at any one time. Many people believe it's the eyes that tell the brain what they see, but that's not how it works. It's the brain that tells the eyes what to look for. Your brain will have you pay attention to what interests you, to what startles you, or to what you've already learned to recognize.

Here is an example of how paying attention might work differently for different people. A newlywed couple is on their honeymoon. The husband is a writer, and the wife is a musician. They're taking their first walk through the downtown section of a city. A stranger approaches and asks if the couple knows of a nearby bookstore. The young wife shrugs her shoulders; she has no idea. But the young man points out the location of two bookstores. Later, another stranger approaches the couple and asks if they know of a music store in the neighborhood. This time, it's the husband's turn to shrug and the wife's turn to point out the location of two music stores. Although the newlyweds took the same walk, they had paid attention to different sights based on their personal interests.

So, the first step in putting information into your long-term memory is to pay attention to it. When it comes to public speaking, if you allow your fears to distract you and, as a result, do not pay close attention to the material while you are preparing for your presentation, you are on the road to forgetting what you want to say to the audience.

Who's in Charge?
Many people believe it's the eyes that tell the brain what they see, but that's not how it works. It's the brain that tells the eyes what to look for.

2. Processing the Information (Encoding)

Next, the sensory information you receive is translated into a mental idea or image your brain can comprehend. In some cases, you must make a conscious effort to understand what you have heard or seen in order to encode the information. This mental idea or image is then placed into your working memory. Identical information can be encoded, or processed, in several different ways. For example, when you meet Mr. Ferry, you might store his name as a sound. Saying his name aloud or in your head would reinforce this auditory memory. Jotting his name down or closing your eyes and picturing his face would reinforce your visual memory. You could also use a mnemonic device—for example, imagine Mr. Ferry as the captain of a ferryboat in New York Harbor.

The way you encode information determines how it will be stored and later retrieved. Your first encounter with new information determines how you will store it. If you hear a joke and say to yourself, "Joe will think this is hysterical," you will be more inclined to remember it than if you didn't think the joke was funny. If you hear about a timesaving shortcut in a computer program you use often, you're more likely to remember it than if the shortcut were for a computer program you know little about. This is because the manner in which you encode and organize new information and how it is ultimately stored depend a good deal on your background knowledge and your particular needs at the time.

It is during the encoding process that you have the chance to recognize patterns and order, which is the key to being able to store it efficiently. When you encode, you use all of your previously stored memories to relate the new information to your prior knowledge. Your prior knowledge makes it easier for you to see the purpose or meaning of this new information, and allows you to organize it more efficiently in your memory and to recall it more readily.

Here is an example of how prior knowledge comes into play during the encoding process: Two people go to the same concert. The first is a talented music composer, and the second simply likes to listen to music, but has never studied it formally. When asked about the concert, they will recall it very differently. The untrained listener may recall the slow, dreamy movement of the music during the first set and the faster-paced beat of the second set. The composer, however, will recall the patterns in rhythm, harmony, structure, and counterpoint and could give specific examples of each. He has a vocabulary to help him classify what he heard. The one who simply liked the music would be limited to an organizational structure such as "fast and slow, loud and soft."

When you have little background in a certain area, you will miss a lot of information as it is being presented because you have nothing to relate it to. This will greatly affect how much you will remember the material later on. One way to deal with this situation is to prepare. For example, if you were the untrained listener going to a concert and you wanted to be able to recall certain details of what you heard, you could train yourself ahead of time by listening to pieces in advance, taking lessons from a trained musician, or researching the pieces you will hear. The more you know, the better you can organize, and remember, what you will hear at the concert.

3. Storing the Information

Storing is the process of placing and holding information in your long-term memory for later recall. While the term "encoding" refers to how the information is taken in, the term "storing" refers to how that information is remembered. Obviously, the more clearly it is taken in, the better it is remembered. The key to how information is stored in your

What Do You Know?
Your prior knowledge makes it easier for you to see the purpose or meaning of new information, and allows you to organize it more efficiently and recall it more readily.

long-term memory is how efficiently it is organized. If it is well organized and encoded in several different ways, it will be easy to retrieve it when you want it. The organization must be done when the information is first encoded. This means that you must be aware of the organization when you first process it.

Here is an example. Two men watch a football game on television. The first is a high-school football coach; the other is his Australian cousin, who had never before seen an American football game. If the Australian were to describe the game from what he had stored in his memory, he'd say something like, "A bloke in a striped shirt blew a whistle, the players slammed into each other, and they kept at it for hours!" The coach, on the other hand, would probably describe almost every single play like it was some complicated chess match. He would look at a play and see a play-action pass made possible by a fake handoff to the tailback, making it possible to run to his left and throw a pass to the tight end who looked like he was blocking, before he actually ran the pre-planned pattern. The Australian would have missed all of this subtle strategy. But because the coach understood how the play was organized, he'd be able to store it in detail. Although the coach and his cousin watched the same game, they did so with different levels of understanding, and this led to very different amounts of organization during the storage process.

4. Retrieving the Information

Retrieving information is a process in which you pull data out of your long-term memory when necessary. It's easy to think of instances when you knew that you knew something—it was on the "tip of your tongue"—but you couldn't quite remember it. At that moment, you became intricately involved with the retrieval process. Surely you can see how retrieving information is very different from storing it. When you find yourself saying, "I know him, but I just can't think of his name," you know that you have stored something but are unable to retrieve it.

Psychologist Richard Anderson, a leading memory scientist, has a great analogy for how the storage and retrieval systems work. Imagine your long-term memory as a dark attic and your retrieval system as a flashlight with a narrow beam of light. In a well-organized attic, you can pretty much find anything you want. However, if it's cluttered and unorganized, trying to find something can be a chaotic task.

The way you encode information relates to both how you store it and how you retrieve it. If you encode something visually, it may be easy to

Imagine your long-term memory as a dark attic and your retrieval system as a flashlight with a narrow beam of light. In a well-organized attic, you can pretty much find anything you want.

retrieve it in the same manner but difficult to retrieve it verbally. If you can encode something visually *and* verbally, it is much easier to remember. The more paths you have available in your retrieval system, the easier the process of remembering the information becomes.

Although we've been focusing specifically on your ability to remember information, you also want your audience to remember you and to be able to retrieve the information you present to them. For more on this, see "Creating a Memorable Impression" below.

THE FACTORS INVOLVED IN FORGETTING

Now that you have a better understanding of how memory works, you're ready to take a look at what happens when it doesn't. The better you can understand the process of forgetting, the easier it will be for you to guard against it and improve your retention. There are several factors that either alone or in combination will cause you to forget important information. These include physical issues, such as fatigue, failure to pay attention, interference, faulty storage and retrieval, as well as psychological issues, such as depression. Let's take a look at each of these factors.

Creating a Memorable Impression

To make yourself and the information you present as memorable as possible, plan your presentation with the four memory processes in mind. Here are some tips:

1. **Attention**—You will maintain the audience's attention by holding their interest with vivid examples and interesting stories.

2. **Encoding**—Make your points easy to grasp by relating them to the background and areas of interest to your audience. This will make it easier for your audience to organize the information you present.

3. **Storing**—If your information is well organized, it will be easier for the audience to store it efficiently. Give them many hooks on which to hang the information.

4. **Retrieval**—If your information is stored efficiently and you are able to relate it to your audience in the same manner, it will be easier for them to call up that information when they need it.

When it comes right down to it, you have a great deal of control over how much of the information you present will be remembered by your audience. When a speaker structures his or her presentation so that it is interesting and well organized, the audience will find it easier to remember both the content and the person delivering it. Remember to pay close attention to the context in which your information is presented. The more ways the audience can relate your information to their lives, the more likely they will recall it.

Fatigue

Fatigue often causes memory failure. A few of the factors that cause fatigue include overwork, chronic worry, depression (see page 136), and a lack of restful sleep. You must always try to be well rested before you make a presentation. Waiting until the last minute and staying up late to cram or prepare puts you in a vulnerable position—a good reason to avoid procrastination (see Chapter 7).

Aging

The aging process brings about physiological changes in the brain. Aging slows down the processing of the central nervous system and is a factor in a variety of diseases. These age-related changes decrease a person's ability to recall information. So, whenever possible, try not to age.

On a more serious note, there is evidence that you can keep your mental processes in better condition by increasing your level of physical exercise. The evidence shows that less stressful exercises, such as walking every day for twenty minutes, can make a huge difference in your mental functioning. Research also shows that increasing your level of mental stimulation facilitates memory functioning. Moreover, better nutrition and the use of dietary supplements such as vinpocetine, alpha lipoic acid, and acetyl-l-carnitine also have been shown to improve memory function. Be sure to consult with your healthcare practitioner before embarking on any new lifestyle or dietary regimens.

Also, be wary that the aging process seems to increase the use of medication. The use of certain medications also contributes to making the memory processes less efficient. (For a list of prescription drugs that are most often associated with memory problems, see "Drugs That Interfere With Memory" on page 134.)

Alcohol and Drugs

There are many substances that can affect the transfer of information from working memory to long-term memory, as well as retrieval from long-term memory. Alcohol and drugs—illegal *and* prescription—are obvious examples.

When considering alcohol and illegal drugs, choose Nancy Reagan's advice ("Just say No!") over Nike's advice ("Just do it!"). In any event, if you are in a situation where you know there will be pressure on you to recall information, be sure to avoid these memory busters.

Just Say No!
Avoid substances that can interfere with your memory, especially before giving a speech or presentation.

Drugs That Interfere With Memory

The following prescription drugs are most often associated with memory problems. If you are taking any of these drugs and notice any changes in your mental functioning, consult your physician immediately. Do not discontinue any medication without your doctor's approval. Cleary explain the symptoms you've been experiencing and discuss all the possible alternatives.

Aldomet (methyldopa)	Inderal (propranolol)	Serax (oxazepam)
Asendin (amoxapine)	Mellaril (thioridazine)	Symmetrel (amantadine)
Dalmane (flurazepam)	Miltown (meprobamate)	Tagamet (cimetidine)
Elavil (amitriptyline)	Pamelor (nortriptyline)	Valium (diazepam)
Equanil (meprobamate)	Pepcid (famotidine)	Zantac (ranitidine)
Haldol (haloperidol)		

The above list is not, by any means, exhaustive. There may be other types of medication that can affect your mental functioning as well. When you fill a new prescription, your pharmacist should be able to provide you with a list of side effects associated with that drug. Even if cognitive side effects are not associated with a particular medication, and you suspect your memory is impaired as a result of the new medication, be sure to voice your concerns to your doctor—this is a time when public speaking is a must!

Inattention

Maintaining your focus is key when you are trying to learn or do something. If you don't pay attention to the information you are receiving, you will not be able to encode it. Information you don't encode will never make it into your working memory. Paying attention usually requires effort, but it's not always easy to keep your attention focused on something—especially if you're bored, tired, restless, or distracted. For example, have you ever left your house only to wonder if you'd turned off the oven or shut off the light? You were likely distracted by something on your way out—maybe you were deep in thought or on your cell phone. With experiences like these, you can surely understand the concept of being inattentive to a task and how easily that task is forgotten as a result.

"I sometimes worry about my short attention span, but not for very long."
—*Strange de Jim*

Inattention can disrupt your memory at any time. For example, focusing on either the causes or the symptoms of anxiety can divert your attention and leave it unavailable for the task at hand. The inattention brought about by anxiety can cause you to forget information during any stage of the memory process.

Poor Encoding

One of the ways people try to remember things is by repeating them. However, if you merely repeat things without understanding them, the material will not be stored efficiently. If information is not stored efficiently—in other words, if it's not well organized—retrieving that information becomes very difficult. Avoid learning by rote. Rather, always try to make sense of the information you want to remember in order to be able to store it in an organized fashion.

Interference

Interference is when one thing you have stored in memory is similar to new information and gets confused with the information you are about to store. This can come from old things being confused with incoming information, or incoming information affecting already stored memories. Whenever new material is very similar to and easily confused with stored memories, forgetting is likely to occur. Learn to focus on the features that differentiate the two pieces of information. A common example of interference is trying to memorize telephone numbers. They all sound alike and are very easy to confuse.

Whenever new material is very similar to and easily confused with stored memories, forgetting is likely to occur. Focus on the features that differentiate the two pieces of information.

Faulty Reconstruction

Your memory does not record information like a video recorder. You *reconstruct* memories based on several factors. You piece together events from a few highlights you remember, whether or not that information is accurate. You change events and facts to make them consistent with the way you remember things. There are many court cases where witnesses have been shown to bring in invented memories. They claim to have witnessed or experienced events that never occurred, but since they had been told about them repeatedly, they come to believe them. Rather than recalling facts and experiences detail by detail, we reconstruct and distort them to fit information we already have stored in our memories.

For example, when I was five years old, my family escaped from Hungary. For years, I'd listened to my father retell the story about how I had woken up at a border checkpoint and began to cry, forcing him to take off in the dark, without headlights and with bullets flying over our heads! I can still hear the explosion of the firing guns when I recall the incident. Years later, my mother told me that my father had embellished the story: there were no shots fired at us. Somehow, I had created that memory simply by hearing the tale told so often.

Disuse

There is some truth to the saying, "If you don't use it, you lose it." You will often learn more than you can remember and certainly more than you can retrieve. The greatest amount of forgetting occurs right after you finish learning something. This process continues for about two weeks. Each day you will forget a bit more, partly because you have already forgotten so much. University professors often become discouraged when they read the research on how quickly their students forget the information given in their lectures. You forget more of what you hear than what you have read. Practice is the best antidote to avoid this kind of forgetting.

Depression

Depression often affects concentration, learning, and memory. It decreases the motivation to pay attention and put effort into encoding and retrieval. People who are depressed feel as if any effort is more than a task is worth and they are generally too fatigued to try. If you believe your forgetfulness is due to depression, consider seeing a mental-health specialist.

Repression

Sigmund Freud talked about a concept called "motivated forgetting." He said that certain memories are so painful and traumatic that our unconscious mind keeps us from remembering them. Repressing such memories keeps a person from being in a constant state of panic so that he or she can continue to function. This process is generally limited to the memory of traumatic events. Once again, if you believe your forgetfulness is due to a problem along these lines, consider seeing a mental-health specialist.

SIX WAYS TO IMPROVE YOUR MEMORY

Now that you have a good idea of what's involved in the process of remembering and forgetting, let's focus on what you can do with this knowledge. The key question in this chapter is "What can you do to remember your material when you get up to speak?" You'll be glad to know that with just a little work, remembering the contents of your presentation is well within your control. Based on what you have learned, the following are some suggestions for improving your memory.

1. Reduce Your Anxiety Level

In Chapter 6, we discussed reducing the symptoms of anxiety through relaxation. Before each practice session, and especially before any presentation, do a relaxation exercise to calm yourself down and increase your alertness. This will help you focus on what is happening in real time and help you eliminate distractions caused by your anxiety.

There is a great deal of research demonstrating that high levels of anxiety decrease performance on memory tasks. For example, I performed a simple experiment to demonstrate the effects of social anxiety on short-term memory. I asked the university students in several of my seminar classes to introduce themselves to one another during the first class meeting. At the end of the round of introductions, I asked the students to write down as many names as they could remember. In almost every case, their retention was poorest for the students who sat on either side of them. This effect was clearly due to the social anxiety they experienced immediately before and after the introductions. Just as the introductions began, the students were distracted by thoughts of how they would go about introducing themselves, instead of paying attention to the first student. Then, as the introductions came to a close, they were so busy evaluating how they had done, they were distracted again and failed to pay attention to the last student's name.

Relax and Get Alert! Before each practice session, and especially before any presentation, do a relaxation exercise to calm yourself down and increase your alertness.

2. Reduce Interference

As mentioned earlier, interference occurs when something stored in your memory is similar to the new information you are trying to process. If the material you are learning can be easily confused with things you already know or with other information you are trying to learn at the same time, try to figure out how the two sets of information differ. Look for anything you can use to tell them apart. This may require a very careful examination and some ingenuity.

3. Reduce Your Tendency to Self-Monitor and Overcome Distractions

As you now know, our brains are set up to perform only one difficult task at a time. This is a major problem during a presentation. If you permit yourself to become distracted, you will surely experience problems with your memory. The most common distracters during a presentation are paying too much attention to your symptoms of anxiety or to the audience's reactions. As you may recall, this is referred to as "self-monitoring." Another type of self-monitoring is evaluating how well you are doing during your talk—am I succeeding, failing, boring the audience, or dazzling them? Whatever the case, this type of behavior is very distracting.

As you continue to take notice of how anxious you are—and just how badly you are doing as a result of this anxiety—a good part of your attention is captured in this self-monitoring process. The more attention you give to self-monitoring, the less attention you have left for your presentation. This will certainly weaken your performance, which will make you more anxious, which will continue to weaken your performance, and so on. The whole process just keeps going in a vicious downward cycle.

To understand the damaging effects of self-monitoring a little better, ask a friend to give you a seven-digit telephone number to memorize for thirty seconds. This should be a fairly easy task, but not if you are distracted. While you are being timed, close your eyes and describe your physical features as well as the clothing you are wearing to your friend. When the thirty seconds are up, try to recall the telephone number. It's no surprise if you can't. Not only is this an exercise in humility, but it's also a clear illustration of the power distraction has over memory. If you lose focus by self-monitoring, you cannot transfer the information from your working memory into your long-term memory.

"I can hardly breathe! Can they tell?!"
The most common distracters during a presentation are paying too much attention to your symptoms of anxiety or to the audience's reactions.

Self-monitoring is the biggest cause of a poor performance. It robs you of your concentration and focus. It makes it difficult to perform any complicated task that needs your full attention. Self-monitoring is the most common form of distraction for public speakers and performers of all types. If you have any fears or vulnerabilities, you will easily be seduced into self-monitoring. There are many ways to go about reducing the effects of self-monitoring and other distractions. Here are a few of them.

Overlearn and Overpractice

One of the best ways to reduce the effects of self-monitoring is simply to become so good at whatever you are performing that if you self-monitor, it won't affect you very much. There is good psychological evidence to show that the better you can do one task, the more you can perform another task simultaneously. The more automatic the task becomes, the less it will be affected by your self-monitoring. Overlearning your talk, overpracticing your violin solo, or overpracticing how you will run a meeting will help you cope with distractions, whether they are internal or external.

There is a great deal of psychological research showing that repetition makes memory stronger. Try the "Joke Test." Find a fairly long joke and tell it to ten people.

Notice that you may falter and forget on the first try. You may lose some details on the next telling or two, but by the tenth time, the joke will be rolling off your tongue. Here's a joke you can practice with:

An engineer, a psychologist, and a theologian were hunting in the wilderness of northern Canada when they got caught in a snowstorm. They saw an isolated cabin, far removed from any town. The hunters had heard that the locals in the area were very hospitable, so they knocked on the door to ask permission to rest.

No one answered their knocks, but they discovered the cabin was unlocked and went in. It was a simple place . . . two rooms with a minimum of furniture and household equipment. Nothing was unusual about the cabin except for one thing—a large potbellied cast-iron stove was suspended in midair by wires hanging from the ceiling beams.

"Fascinating," said the psychologist. "It's obvious that this lonely trapper, isolated from humanity, has elevated this stove so that he can curl up under it and vicariously experience a return to the womb."

"Nonsense!" replied the engineer. "The man is practicing the laws of thermodynamics. By elevating the stove, he has discovered a way to distribute heat more evenly throughout the cabin."

"With all due respect," interrupted the theologian, "I'm sure that hanging the stove from the ceiling has religious meaning. 'Fire lifted up' has been a religious symbol for centuries."

The three debated the point for several hours without resolving the issue. When the trapper finally returned, they immediately asked him why he had hung his heavy potbellied stove from the ceiling.

The trapper replied, "I had plenty of wire, not much stove pipe."

Attention Focusing—Dealing with Distractions

Distractions that interfere with your memory can be external, as well as internal. A waiter may drop a few dishes, a baby may begin wailing, your LCD projector or computer may go down, the sound system may feedback, someone in the audience may have multiple sneezing attacks . . . I think you get the picture.

As for internal distractions, self-monitoring, as you now know, is the most common example. The most obvious method for reducing the effects of distractions is to focus your attention back on the task at hand as soon as you sense you are being distracted. Pulling your attention away from distractions—whether they are internal or external—and back to your speech is a situation you can practice. That's what Exercise 8.1 is all about.

Exercise 8.1. Learning to Deal With Distractions

There's one thing you can count on during your speech—distractions. Some will come from the outside and some will come from your head, but they will be there. To counter their effects, the following two steps will help you develop some strategies for getting back your focus.

1. Before you practice your speech or presentation, plan some random distractions. For example, set an alarm clock to go off during your practice or ask someone to call you on the phone or enter the room at random intervals.

External distractions:_____

_____

Once you have a "distraction plan," start your speech without stopping as if you were really performing in front of your audience. Whenever you become distracted, try to regain your focus as quickly as possible. Bring your mind back to your topic and practice picking up where you left off. Also, practice ignoring the distractions completely and continuing with your speech as if nothing had happened.

Practicing your speech with external distractions will make them less likely to come as a surprise, which will make you less likely to become flustered and anxious if they occur during your presentation. The trick is to get used to them and learn how to refocus your attention on the task at hand.

2. When you've mastered working with external distractions, go inward. Once again, practice giving your speech. This time, however, purposely distract yourself by thinking of things such as your tension level or anything else that might break your concentration while you're giving your speech.

Internal distractions:_____

_____

Since a common cause of panic during speech giving is the realization the speaker has lost his or her place, practice losing your place and then resuming the speech where you left off. If you master losing your concentration and then getting it back, you will avoid the anxiety that often accompanies distraction.

Another way to practice dealing with internal distractions is during your guided relaxation exercise (see Chapter 6). Whenever you notice your mind drifting toward distracting thoughts, immediately refocus on the recording.

Feedback for Exercise 8.1

If you had difficulty dealing with the distractions, continue to practice this exercise until you feel comfortable with your reaction or lack of reaction to the interruptions. The more you practice with distractions, the less you will be affected by them in an actual performance situation. If you were unable to smoothly resume your topic after a distraction, you might find having an outline helpful (see page 142).

4. Increase the Organization of Your Information

The more organized your information is, the better you will be able to remember it. Identifying the organizational structure of your presentation as soon as possible helps you transfer the information from your working memory to your long-term memory.

If you've already prepared your speech, go over the main points of your talk and identify its organizational structure. You may need to read it a few times before you recognize the inherent order. If you can't identify it, start by identifying the purpose of your talk. When you identify the reasons you are giving a talk, relate each part of your presentation to that purpose. This way, your organizational structure will likely emerge. Once you've clarified the structure, make sure to establish a clear relationship between each point you want to make and the purpose of the talk. This will improve your ability to recall it.

In many cases, there is organization in the material you want to remember, but you may not be aware of it. Here is a simple example. Look at the following number: 2346698. If you were asked to memorize it, how would you go about it? When I presented this task to my university students, most of them reorganized it. Some grouped it as follows: 234-6698, as if it were a telephone number. Others grouped it in three chunks: 234-66-98, because each grouping has a specific type of meaning. The first three numbers (234) are sequential, the next two (66) are the same, and the last three (98) are the grades they were hoping for on their midterm exams. Now, take a look at the numbers again, and see what happens when you look at every other number:

Every other number represents the addition of *two* or *three*. If you happened to recognize the organization here, it would not only help you to remember the order of the numbers, but you could also remember a number a mile long using the pattern that was established here.

Identifying the organization inherent in your presentation should be done while the information is still in your working memory. Examine any material you have to remember and present. If you can detect a meaningful pattern, you will remember it better.

Whether or not you've already prepared your speech, the best course of action to improve your ability to recall the information is to create an outline, which you can have on hand during the presentation. See "Creating and Using an Outline" on page 142 for some helpful information.

5. Use Mnemonics (Memory Aids)

Sometimes what you see is what you get, and you simply won't be able

Creating and Using an Outline

A surefire way to improve your memory using your presentation's organizational structure is to make an outline. You can use the outline as a guide to keep you on track while practicing—and perhaps even during your presentation. When working with an outline, consider these few practical suggestions to make it more useful:

- **Create an outline that reflects the conceptual organization of your topic.** Standard outlines generally include a series of major topics followed by subordinate topics, reflecting a hierarchy of ideas. Being familiar with this hierarchy can help you keep the structure of the material fresh in your mind.

- **Make the outline easy to read.** It's best to type your outline and use a font that's large enough for you to read from a comfortable distance. Since you want to be looking at the audience, you should be able to read your outline with a quick glance down. A larger font also makes it possible to read in a dimly lit room if necessary.

- **Color code your information.** Color code key items in your outline so you can recognize them more readily. Color-coding can also help you instantly differentiate between various types of information in your outline. For example, you can use a red font to indicate which items are concepts, blue for explanations, green for stories, and purple for supporting data and examples. This will decrease the reaction time necessary to identify each item and keep you on track. If you don't have a color printer, you can use highlighter pens.

- **Use keywords and phrases.** Your outline should contain keywords and phrases that you set perhaps in a **bold font**. These terms and phrases can represent stories and anecdotes you want to tell or main points in the presentation. For example, one of my outlines includes the topic "Use Outlines" and my key phrase is **"Safety Net Story."** This bold item prompts me to tell the story about a confident speaker who never used outlines—he didn't need a "safety net." But when the executive vice president showed up unannounced during one of his presentations, the "confident" speaker completely lost his focus and had nothing to turn to.

- **Practice using your outline.** When you rehearse for your presentation, use your outline. Be sure to glance away from the outline from time to time to see if you can find your place quickly. If not, you'll want to increase its readability. If you get distracted easily, you may find it useful to keep your finger on the current topic. The more you practice, the more familiar your outline will become and the less likely you will need it during your presentation.

- **Determine your outline's effectiveness.** The best way to determine how effective your outline is to record yourself giving your presentation as you did in previous exercises. When you watch or listen to the recording, try to identify moments when you hesitated or lost your place. You may want to revise that portion of the outline. Then, once you're comfortable with the outline, increase the level of distractions, dim the lights, and indulge in some serious self-monitoring. Your outline should help you get back on track. If not, you'll want to revise your outline for increased effectiveness.

to identify any organizational structure in what you have to say to your audience. If this is the case, consider using mnemonic (*neh-mon-ic*) techniques—memory devices or tricks. Here's a common example: when children are learning the names of the notes on the treble clef lines (EGBDF) in music class, they are often taught the following mnemonic: *Every Good Boy Does Fine.* Notice that the first letter of each word in the sentence represents one of the notes, in order. In fact, the real value of a mnemonic is being able to memorize a list of words in a specific order. Here's another common example: Most of us know the names of the planets in our solar system but are hard pressed to name them all and in order. Take a look at the following list: *Mercury, Venus, Earth, Mars, Jupiter, Saturn, Uranus, Neptune,* and *Pluto.* How likely are you to remember the order of planets by reading the list just once? With mnemonics, it's easy: *My Very Elegant Mother Just Sat Upon Nine Porcupines.* Whenever you have to remember any sort of list, particularly in order, create a mnemonic to remember it.

Pluto is on the chopping block, and the planet mnemonic is in jeopardy! Let's keep our fingers crossed that we can keep it. A good mnemonic is hard to find.

It will probably be a rare occurrence when you'll need to recite a list in front of an audience, but if you find yourself in such a situation, mnemonics can help. If you would like to read more about this, consider reading *The Memory Book* by Harry Lorayne and Jerry Lucas.

6. When All Else Fails—Write It Out

If you are convinced you might really panic up there on the platform and totally freeze up as a result, write out the complete text of your speech as if you were going to say it. That is, write it as a speech to be listened to in a conversational manner, not as a formal paper meant to be read by someone. Once you've done that, write your outline in the margin of the paper so that each section corresponds to an outlined item. Make sure it is easy to read and follow. Then practice reading the entire speech aloud. When you've done that several times, practice the speech by looking only at the outline. Take this a step further and start at various places in your speech by skipping ahead or backtracking to various parts of the outline.

Using your outline and having the complete text of your speech available to you if you need it will give you the peace of mind that if you do begin to have a problem, you can start reading your speech at any point. To make this seem more natural, try to come up with a few transition lines to explain to your audience why you've begun to read. For example, you can say, "This next section is so important that I want to make sure you get it exactly as I planned it, so I'm going to read it to you." Joe B. followed this advice and here's how it went:

The Case of Joe B.

Joe B. was promoted to the position of senior vice president of a large loan company. As part of his new duties, he was called upon to give the dinner speech at a large company retreat. Although he was used to speaking in meetings, he had never had to face an audience this large. He was expected to be clever and entertaining as well as informative and was worried he would choke under pressure. Just thinking about the speech gave Joe anxiety attacks.

Joe and I decided he needed a serious backup plan. He agreed to write out the entire text of his speech and to practice reading it aloud. He also rehearsed the stories and jokes he was afraid he wouldn't be able to deliver. Finally, he practiced giving the speech from the outline in the margin of his written-out text.

After the actual speech, Joe was delightfully surprised that it came off so smoothly and that he didn't have to resort to reading the text. Having the speech written out made him feel secure—like a baby with a security blanket. Joe was very proud that he didn't have to read a word of his presentation.

I've advised many people to write out their speeches and practice in the manner described above. *Not one of them has ever had to resort to reading his or her speech.* Just knowing they had the speech and could read it if they had to was the safety net they needed to feel comfortable. It was the answer to their worst-case scenario. They knew that whatever happened, they would still be able to get through their presentation by reading it if worse came to worst.

WHAT YOU HAVE LEARNED AND WHERE YOU ARE GOING

When it comes to public speaking, the most commonly expressed fear is the fear of going totally blank and forgetting everything. While it's very unlikely you will forget *everything* you planned to say, forgetting some parts is not unheard of. As you now know, the best way to remember anything is to increase its organization. Information that is well organized is easier to store and ultimately retrieve. In addition to organizing your information, you can take other important steps to improve your memory. As discussed in this chapter, one of these steps is practicing. In fact, the next chapter focuses on this very important topic. Obviously the more you practice—and practice properly—the better you will be able to remember nearly everything you want to say to your audience.

9

PRACTICING FOR OPTIMAL PERFORMANCE

The BIG Idea

After you have thoroughly learned your material, practice under performance conditions. Try to simulate every detail—the minor ones as well as the main ones.

There is an old saying, "For every psychologist there is an equal and opposite psychologist." By reputation, psychologists agree on very few "universally true" facts. One of the few that all of them agree on is that practice helps performance, learning, and memory. But it has to be *good* practice. A classical guitar teacher once gave me some very valuable advice when he noticed I was playing too fast. "If you practice slowly," he said, "the speed will come, but if you continue to practice too fast, your playing will always be sloppy." As I thought about his statement, I realized he was talking about way more than the guitar. Whatever the task, practicing must be done correctly to make it pay off. Poor practice builds bad habits that must often be unlearned, and the correct skills must then be relearned. This becomes much more difficult than learning something correctly the first time. This chapter discusses the basic principles of good practicing. Practice them well, and you will see real results.

PRACTICE PRACTICE PRACTICE CORRECTLY

Poor practice builds bad habits. Whatever the task, practicing must be done correctly to make it pay off.

PRACTICE FREQUENTLY

It's been said that repetition is the mother of retention. When you are preparing to give a speech or presentation, it's important to practice frequently. You'll soon discover that the more often you've explained a concept or told a story, the easier it becomes to deliver. A good example of this is joke telling. Most people find that they stumble through a joke the first time they tell it. But after they've told that particular joke a few times, their ability to tell it improves significantly.

Once you've practiced your speech a few times, you'll notice that you just get used to certain phrases, examples, and ideas. Whole phrases will leap from your mouth easily, and you can add nuances when appropriate.

People often think that if they practice too much—or overpractice—it will lead to a flat presentation that lacks spontaneity. They are mistaken. Overpracticing is liberating. It frees you of the worry of having to remember what you will be saying next. It also frees you up to take advantage of anything that occurs in present time. If you are secure in what you are going to say and you think of a great ad lib, you can insert it. If a plane flies by, or you drop your notes, or you end up on the wrong PowerPoint slide, you can easily make a joke out of it or find a graceful way out because more of your mind is free from trying to remember your talk. Overpracticing is a huge confidence builder. The audience's presence and the excitement of the moment should keep your talk from becoming stale.

PRACTICE WITH A VIDEO OR AUDIO RECORDER

Recording yourself giving a practice speech puts realistic pressure on you and provides helpful feedback.

In Exercise 1.1 in Chapter 1, you were instructed to record yourself giving a practice speech. Doing this has several advantages. First, it simulates a presentation because you cannot stop and restart your speech; you must continue as if you were on the speaker's platform. Then, watching or listening to the practice presentation can provide you with useful feedback, such as helping you identify the parts of your speech you're comfortable with and parts you are not so comfortable with. You can also identify sections of your talk that seem informative or entertaining and which parts seem slow. Having this information gives you the opportunity to adjust your presentation as necessary. You can use a video recorder as your laboratory, trying out different types of delivery, attitude, and even attire.

PRACTICE IN FRONT OF FRIENDS, FAMILY, OR COLLEAGUES

After you've recorded yourself a few times, try out your presentation in front of a small audience. The more that audience matches your actual audience, the better it is. But any audience is helpful in simulating the experience of giving the talk. The optimal practice session is to have a small group of colleagues listen to your talk and give you feedback. There is an old phrase, "Feedback is the breakfast of champions." Take notes on their feedback. If you disagree with anything they say, keep it to yourself and reflect on it. Even if they misinterpreted what you said or didn't really understand it, they may be representative of other audience members who will respond in the same way. It's good information for you to know. You can then decide if it is something you choose to deal with or ignore.

PRACTICE AS YOU WILL PERFORM

When you are practicing, try to simulate every aspect of your performance to eliminate surprises. Surprises are great distracters and will surely disrupt your presentation. Find out as much as you can about the conditions under which you will be performing, so you can simulate the actual conditions as closely as possible. For example, find out how many people you will be speaking in front of, if you will be using a microphone, what mode of dress is expected, and anything else that will affect your performance. If you don't plan to make jokes during your performance, don't make jokes during practice. If you plan to use notes during your talk, practice with the notes. If you will be using an overhead, use the overhead during your practice session.

Merely reading your notes to yourself is not practicing. It's just not enough. You must read your notes aloud! If you will be speaking to more than ten to fifteen people without a microphone, practice your talk using a loud speaking voice. A loud speaking voice feels different from a low speaking voice, and you should familiarize yourself with it. Say a few words aloud as if you were speaking to a handful of people, and then say the same thing as if you were speaking to a person in the back of a room fifty feet away. Notice how different it feels to you. Practice it the way you will be saying it.

If you will be speaking into a microphone, practice doing that. Find out if the mic will be attached to a podium that you must stand behind or if you will be holding it and can walk around. It makes a big difference in terms of how it feels.

Also, be sure to find out how the room will be lit. If it is in a regularly lit room, you should not have problems. But if you will be on a stage or platform with bright lights shining in your eyes, and you are not used to those lights, you will find it very disorienting. When you are used to watching the reactions of people as you speak and all of a sudden you can't see a soul out there, it can make you very uncomfortable. If the lights will be dim, make sure you can still read your outline. Make your outline larger and darker so you can read it under any light. Don't let yourself be surprised.

Don't be surprised by how loud your voice sounds when you use a microphone. Familiarize yourself with it beforehand.

I once worked with an opera singer who went for an audition and didn't check out the room first. She assumed it would be held in a large theater, with her on stage and the director sitting in the audience in the middle of the theater. She believed she was expected to project her voice throughout the room as opera singers always do. She walked into a small practice room with an upright piano and the director was about eight feet away. She panicked because opera singers rarely sing in such intimate settings. The surprise spoiled her audition.

Also, practice in the clothing you will be wearing. I was working with a manager who had to give his first formal talk at a company convention. He was the keynote speaker at a black-tie dinner. He was not accustomed to wearing a heavily starched shirt and bowtie, and was enormously distracted by his attire. Many musicians complain about the same thing. They practice in blue jeans and t-shirts and get unnerved wearing tuxedos and not being able to move as they normally do.

Sometimes it won't be possible to simulate all the performance conditions. In that case, you may want to use imagery. For more on this, see "That's Using Your Head" below.

PRACTICE DEALING WITH HOSTILE QUESTIONS AND HECKLERS

The audience's attitude can make a huge difference in how you perform. Do you know if your audience will be friendly, neutral, or hostile? With a neutral audience, you'll want to have a plan in place to get them to know you. With a friendly audience, you'll have to make sure that the familiarity doesn't interfere with your role as presenter. But what about a hostile audience? How do you plan for that to avoid being unprepared

That's Using Your Head

There may be occasions when you have the *time* to practice, but not the *place* to practice. Fortunately, we've all been bestowed with the gift of imagery, which we can use anytime, anywhere. Successful athletes and musicians will attest to the fact that practicing through imagery can be very powerful.

When you've got the time, imagine giving your presentation, being sure to recreate every detail of the performance conditions in your mind. This is a great way to spend your time on an airplane or while standing in line at the grocery store. Although using imagery in this way can be almost as effective as actually practicing, nothing beats actual rehearsals.

and taken by surprise? Fortunately, there are ways to deal with a hostile audience to minimize their antagonistic behavior.

The first thing you must do is research the points of contention and be prepared to address questions *before* they are asked. In other words, don't present only your point of view and then wait to be challenged during a question-and-answer period. Cover those areas of contention *during* your talk. It's essential that you be the first one to bring up those points to show that you are aware of and respect the audience's point of view. More important, however, is that this gives you the power to control how the hostile point of view is presented. Take advantage of this by presenting it in its mildest form to make any opposition easier to deal with. By presenting these viewpoints in their mildest form, you can point out the flaws in the argument with less effort.

Develop a reflex to compliment the asker of a hostile question. For example, you can use a generic compliment such as, "That's a very interesting question." This will keep the issue from becoming personal as well as help diffuse the issue. If the hostile question concerns an area you've already covered, simply repeat what you said earlier. If the person asking the question wants to take it further than that, politely invite him or her to speak with you after the presentation. If the question isn't something you already addressed, paraphrase the question in a milder form and answer it that way.

If there are rude audience members who actually heckle or harass you, remember that you are not on stage at a comedy club. Counter-attacking them directly and harshly makes it more likely the audience will identify with the intrusive audience member. So, above all else, be sure to maintain your dignity no matter how rude and obnoxious the audience members are being. If their position has any validity, acknowledge it and address it. If they persist in trying to humiliate you or push a matter, ask them to kindly speak with you after the presentation. This should put an end to the matter. If it doesn't, perhaps that person needs to be asked to leave the auditorium or meeting room. When someone becomes that overbearing and rude, other members of the audience or staff will surely come to your aid.

Don't be caught off guard by hecklers in your audience. Plan ways to dodge the "tomatoes" during your practice sessions.

The best way to prepare for handling difficult questions is by simulating the situation. Ask a few colleagues or friends to listen to your presentation. Have them ask you a series of difficult questions when you're finished. When you get better at responding, tell them to turn it up a notch and increase the stress level by asking more difficult questions and by making critical comments. Practicing under fire will help you prepare for a difficult audience.

PRACTICE INCIDENTALS

Do not confine your practicing to the substantive part of your presentation. Practice every aspect of it. Practice walking up to the podium to give your talk, thanking the person who introduced you, and then accepting the microphone. This will help keep you calm as you are about to begin your talk, which is the time people are most nervous. Practice taking your notes out and arranging them on the lectern and adjusting the microphone. Look out at the audience before you begin to speak. Figure out how you will get them to finish their conversations and quiet down so you can begin. People rarely pay attention to these details and end up looking a bit awkward because they failed to practice them. Don't make that mistake.

PRACTICING PHYSICAL SKILLS

While this book is mostly about speaking in public, sports and music performances can also cause a performer a great deal of anxiety and stage

Exercise 9.1. Practice Presentations

In this exercise, you will practice your presentation *exactly* as you plan to give it. Be sure that you have practiced beforehand as if you were about to give the actual presentation, spending more time on any particularly difficult or confusing parts. Then, make every effort to simulate all the physical aspects of the actual situation. For example, locate a room that's approximately the same size as the one you will be speaking in. If you will be using a microphone, use one during the practice session. Wear the clothing you plan to wear for the presentation. And so on. To further help you simulate the actual presentation conditions, do the following:

1. Videotape your presentation.

2. Ask friends or colleagues to sit in the audience during the taping. They should ask you questions when appropriate and even challenge you on points they may disagree with.

3. Ask friends or colleagues to watch the video and provide critical feedback.

Feedback for Exercise 9.1

The key to this exercise is to make your practice presentation seem as close to the real thing as possible. Listen very closely to the feedback you get from your practice audience. Gather your own feedback as well by watching the video closely. Be very attentive to details as you watch the tape. Listen for places in your presentation when you seemed to slow down and "grope" for the next idea or sentence. This is a good way to diagnose any area that needs more practice.

fright. In these cases, regular practice is also essential. However, when it comes to practicing physical skills, there are additional complications.

Physical skills have both a mental and physical aspect. When you first learn a physical skill, you usually must guide your body by thinking about each aspect of the skill as it is performed. For example, if you take tennis lessons, you know that there's a lot to think about and remember. Your instructor will keep reminding you to bend your knees, watch the ball, keep your elbows in, follow through, and about twenty other things.

Once you have thought your way through the skill time and time again, your muscles will begin to remember the skills by themselves. This is called "muscle memory." You no longer have to think about how to make your body move. Once you get to this stage, it becomes difficult to break down and isolate each aspect of the skill as you learned it. If you try to alter your muscle memory, you will begin to understand how powerful muscle memory is. If you are a regular tennis or golf player who needs improvement, you know how difficult it is to relearn or correct what felt to you like a "comfortable" swing or stroke.

The problem with performing physical skills under pressure is that most people practice by relying on their muscle memory. But when under pressure, they often find they can't rely on it. This is because the physical aspects of anxiety, specifically tense muscles, interfere with your muscle memory. The feedback your nerves send from your muscles feels different from the feedback you received when you were calm, and your movements no longer come automatically. So, you generally turn to the mental aspect of how to do it, which throws off the natural feel you achieved by relying on muscle memory during practice. Under these conditions, many people may actually forget how to perform a physical skill—and panic.

This was something I discovered as kid during a basketball game. I was at the free-throw line as the game was ending, and my two free throws would determine who would win the game. I was so tense that I couldn't remember how to shoot a free throw, although I'd shot several hundreds of them in the past. It suddenly seemed like a totally new act to me. I missed both shots. The next day, in the schoolyard, I started analyzing how I was shooting the ball—my knees were bent slightly, my left foot was back, and my right foot was slightly forward. I noticed how I shifted my weight and that I was staring at the front of the rim. I analyzed the entire shot, and rehearsed the steps in my head as I practiced taking the shot. I vowed that if I was ever in the same situation, I would

"Practice does not make perfect, perfect practice makes perfect."

—Vince Lombardi

be able to "talk" my way through the shot if it didn't "feel" right. This paid off handsomely.

So, take a lesson from me and practice a skill you must perform under stressful situations by relying on muscle memory but also by thinking about each movement as you execute it. In other words, spend some time thinking about the skill as you do it as well as just doing it. The next time you find yourself tensing up during a performance, you will be familiar enough with the thought process of performing the skill so that you can fall back on it. As you did with your practice presentations, simulate the conditions of the anxiety-provoking performance to practice "talking your way through" the skill. Alternatively, you can use imagery to approximate these conditions.

WHAT YOU HAVE LEARNED AND WHERE YOU ARE GOING

The manner in which you practice ends up being as important as how much you practice. As you learned in this chapter, simply reading your notes to yourself is not good practice. You must practice aloud and practice under conditions that are a close approximation of the actual performance conditions.

In the next part of the book, you'll learn specific ways to improve your presentation skills. We'll start by taking a look at the various tools you have available to you.

PART THREE

BROADENING YOUR PRESENTATION SKILLS

10

The BIG Idea

Organize your presentation for maximum effectiveness. State a clear intention for your talk, establish your credentials, and make use of your presentation skills.

USING THE PUBLIC SPEAKER'S TOOLBOX

I n the tradition of film-making, this chapter breaks down your presentation into three sequential stages—preproduction, production, and postproduction. Preproduction includes everything that goes into the preparation of your speech or presentation. Production involves making the actual presentation or giving the speech. Postproduction refers to factors that should be considered after the talk has been given. Of the three areas, preproduction, or preparation, takes the most time. This is where you have to research your topic and your audience's background as well as determine the organizational structure of your presentation. Once you have completed the preparation, then you may begin the actual practice for the production, or giving the speech. The postproduction part will have you evaluating your presentation to determine which parts were effective and which need more work. This chapter also includes a discussion of an important tool and how to use it properly—presentation software.

Lights,
Camera,
ACTION!

THE PREPRODUCTION STAGE—
PREPARING YOUR PRESENTATION

When you are scheduled to give a speech or presentation, you will need to do a great deal of preparation to increase the likelihood of success. This includes various types of research, writing and editing, preparing the speech, and determining ways to gauge its success. The following sections discuss the general steps of the preproduction process.

Identify Your Audience

Because identifying your audience is so essential to a successful talk, this should be your first consideration. I once had the pleasure of interviewing John Scully, former CEO of Pepsi and Apple Computers. When I asked him why he was such an effective public speaker, he said it was because he always told the audience what they wanted to know. With a degree in marketing, he knew the importance of researching his audience before preparing a talk.

Every decision regarding the preparation of your speech should be based on who will be in the audience. There are several key questions you should consider: *Why is the audience here? What are their expectations? What is their point of view?* Misreading the audience can have a disastrous result. If they are there to be entertained, you don't want to give them dire predictions for the future. If they want specific answers to vital questions, you don't want to be general—or even worse, entertaining.

Every decision regarding the preparation of your speech should be based on who will be in the audience. Why is the audience here? What are their expectations? What is their point of view?

The composition of your audience can help you determine your purpose; the main content of your presentation; and the type of examples, stories, anecdotes, and jokes you select. Knowing who will be in the audience even helps you determine the kind of language you will use, what you should wear, and the type of body language you should aim for. For example, there's a big difference between how politicians conduct themselves while talking to supporters at a political rally and how they behave during a televised debate with an audience made up of both sides and undecided voters.

Make sure you know what the audience came to hear. If you don't know what that is, do some research. Talk to people who will be there or who are representative of the audience you will have. Read trade magazines. Talk to other speakers who have addressed similar audiences. Make sure you know what the audience dislikes as well as what they like. If they have a bias toward lower taxes, golf, or Pro-Life, you should know that rather than stumbling upon it.

Choose a Topic

In many cases, your topic will already have been chosen for you. Most people who engage in public speaking are generally asked to give a speech, usually because of their *experience* and *expertise* in a certain field. Should you find that you are ever called upon to speak in public and are given the opportunity to select your own topic, the two key words in the previous sentence should guide you in making a wise choice: Select a topic in which you have *expertise* and *experience*. It is always easier to give a talk when you know more than the audience does.

Be sure to choose a topic your intended audience will find both interesting and useful. You must make sure the topic you select can be covered adequately in the time allotted to you. Moreover, you'll want to make sure that you have the necessary resources to present your topic. In some cases, you may need multimedia equipment and appropriate graphics; in other cases, you may need certain props or materials to illustrate your points.

Determine a Purpose

In Economics 101, you learned about supply and demand. In Geology 101, you learned about the three types of rocks—metamorphic, sedimentary, and igneous. And, in Public Speaking 101, you learned that there are three types of speeches: informative, entertaining, and persuasive. Your geology and economics professors were on the up and up, but your public speaking professor wasn't honest with you. There is only one type of talk—persuasive. You may think that you are giving an informative talk, but what you are really doing is persuading your audience that you are well informed and entertaining or at least interesting.

When you are preparing to give a talk, it is important to begin by identifying what you want to persuade the audience to do. Be as specific as possible, and try to make the purpose observable and, better yet, something you can measure. For example, if you are holding a breakfast meeting to persuade potential clients to give your company business, gauge your success by keeping track of how many business cards you are offered, how many business cards you hand out, or how many luncheons you are invited to.

Always remember that your overall goal is to achieve your purpose. Make every element in your talk relate to that purpose. American novelist, playwright, and screenwriter, William Goldman—known in part for famous works such as *Butch Cassidy and the Sundance Kid*, *Marathon Man*, and *The Princess Bride*—uses the phrase, "Never include anything unless it is related to the spine of the story." Likewise, never sacrifice information for the sake of entertainment. However, if there is a choice between two pieces of information, choose the one that's more entertaining.

You probably think that the purpose of a talk should be apparent to the speaker, but this isn't always the case. It takes some thought. Take the Case of Mary U., for example:

What Do You Want?
When you are preparing to give a talk, it is important to begin by identifying what you want to persuade the audience to do. Always remember that your overall goal is to achieve your purpose.

The Case of Mary U.

Mary U. was a wedding planner who attended one of my stage-fright workshops. She was preparing a one-day seminar on wedding planning for recently engaged couples. When I asked her to state her purpose for giving the seminar, she quickly replied, "To educate people on how to successfully plan a wedding." A skeptical participant in the workshop pointed out that she'd be making herself obsolete by sharing her secrets and skills. The group got a good laugh out of this until they noticed Mary's red face.

Mary further explained the problem: She had far too much information to present in a single day, and when she'd held the seminar in the past, many of the couples left feeling overwhelmed. When Mary thought about it, she realized that her purpose was very different from the one she had stated. "Now that I really think about it," she said, "I guess my purpose is to 'scare' them with all that could go wrong so they realize they'll be safer in the long run if they hire my services."

Once Mary figured out what her true purpose was, she was able to prepare a much more effective presentation. Every point she made was tied in to her purpose. This brought cohesiveness to her seminar and helped reduce her fear. Her purpose *was* achievable.

Determine How You Will Establish Your Credibility, Integrity, and Expertise

Audiences will always show you more respect once you have established your credibility. One of your main areas of preparation should be to figure out how you will let the audience know enough about you to earn their respect. There are two components of credibility you must demonstrate: your integrity and your expertise.

You can establish your integrity through stories and anecdotes, endorsements from others whose integrity has been established, or through your previous behavior that is now a matter of record. Audiences want to be assured that you are concerned about them and that there are no conflicts of interest. If you ask your audience to take some action, they have to be sure that they too will benefit from it—rather than help you achieve your personal goals at their expense.

As for your expertise, there are several ways you can demonstrate it. The most straightforward is to list your degrees, credentials, awards, and past and current positions. This can be followed up with stories and anecdotes of your achievements. Endorsements that will have meaning to your audience are also useful for demonstrating expertise. Also, you can request that the person who introduces you include relevant mention of your expertise.

If you decide to incorporate this type of information into your speech, you can do it directly or indirectly. For example, I can say that I received my doctorate at the University of Southern California. Or I can say, "When I was in the doctoral program at USC, I met a psychologist who . . . " The second example is a bit more discreet and sounds less like bragging. You can also pass bypass the whole issue by passing out a handout that includes a biographical sketch.

Seek Out Examples That Are Specific and Clarify Your Points

Providing your audience with examples they can relate to is key to an effective presentation. Good examples illustrate, explain, and broaden your concepts, giving them life and color. Whenever possible, use stories and anecdotes to enhance your examples Also, if you are attempting to explain a difficult concept, find two types of examples: 1) what it is, and 2) what it isn't. The defining characteristics of a concept can usually be clarified by giving examples that illustrate the factors that make something a member of that concept or not. For example, if you were trying to explain to your audience what a web browser is, you would mention and discuss the functions of Internet Explorer and Netscape. You could clarify this by explaining that search engines such as Yahoo and Google are not browsers but work within a browser.

Good speakers paint pictures with words. Always try to use examples that are lifelike and easy to imagine. The more the audience can make an empathic connection with your examples, the better they will receive your talk. In other words, don't say *pet* when you can say *dog*, and don't say *dog* when you can say *poodle,* and don't say *poodle* when you can say a *black standard poodle with a puppy cut.* Turn your examples into images your audience can envision, so that they can see what you are seeing.

Identify Important Information by Brainstorming

Before you develop an outline or prepare your speech, hold a brainstorming session so you don't miss any important points. Brainstorming is a technique for generating and developing ideas. To make this technique work for you, focus on *quantity*, not *quality.* The more ideas you can generate, the better.

If you are brainstorming alone, free associate on a pad or into a voice recorder—that is, come up with an idea or point and record any related words, phrases, or ideas that come to you without censoring or judging them. Generate as many ideas for your talk as possible. If you have a

Good speakers paint pictures with words. Try to use examples that are lifelike and easy to imagine.

Note to Self . . .

Whenever you get an idea for something clever to include in your presentation, make sure you can record that idea immediately. It would be wonderful if all the good ideas came when you sat down to organize your talk with pad and pencil. Unfortunately, the good ideas are just as likely to come in a restaurant, on the freeway, or while standing in line at the bank. If you don't already have one, you might want to invest in a digital voice recorder or micro-cassette recorder. Small enough to slip into your pocket or purse, it will always be handy for those "light-bulb" moments.

group of friends or colleagues willing to help you, you can come up with even more ideas.

Don't immediately discount anything as being too wild or risky, since such ideas can lead to creative connections you wouldn't have thought of otherwise. Even bad ideas have a place in your brainstorming sessions—they're always good for a laugh later.

When you are satisfied that you have a lot to choose from, begin to evaluate the ideas. It is easier to eliminate bad ideas than it is to come up with ideas once you get stuck. When you are evaluating the quality of your ideas, ask yourself these questions:

• Does the information help me achieve the purpose of my talk?

• Will the audience find it relevant?

• Will the audience find it entertaining?

• Is this the best way I can present the information?

• Is there a way to make it clearer?

• Have I found an example or story to clarify my point?

Focus Your Outline on a Few Important Points Rather Than on Several

Whether you create an outline to help you prepare your speech or you create an outline from the speech you've already prepared, a major pitfall is trying to cover too much information. Unsuccessful speakers usually do this when developing their outlines from scratch. They may have an outline listing twenty to thirty "important" points they want to cover, but have only thirty minutes to make their presentations. On top of that, they fear they've left something out!

In thirty minutes, a speaker is lucky if he or she can make five or six good points that will be remembered. Trying to include too much information is a fatal mistake. That reminds me of a scene from a cheesy martial arts movie I'd seen as a kid: A young, eager student approaches a wise master and says, "Master, teach me everything you know." "Certainly," responds the master, "but first we drink tea." The student holds out a tiny cup, and the master begins to pour the steaming hot beverage. He continues to pour until the tea overflows onto the student's hand. The student drops the cup and pulls his scalded hand away. The master shakes his head and says, "The vessel is not big enough to hold everything you want to put into it." So, take a lesson from this, and know that your "thirty-minute vessel" will not hold twenty pieces of information.

Think back to a time when you went to hear a speaker you really liked who was giving a seminar or lecturing on a topic you found fascinating and, perhaps, even life altering. The next day, still glowing from such an inspiring talk, you tried to tell your friends everything you could remember about it, but you could only recall a few of the most important points. How long did it take for you to retell it? Five minutes or so? But the lecture itself was probably an hour long. What happened to the other fifty-five minutes of information? Like you, audiences typically walk away from such presentations remembering very little of what they've heard. Therefore, your job is to make it as easy for them to remember the most important points. If you cram your talk too full of information, they might not retain anything of importance.

A good strategy is to tell your audience just enough to get them interested if you are trying to solicit their business or attention. Aim to make them curious enough to want to learn more about you. This requires a very tight outline, with a couple of points you can cover in several different ways. In all cases, be sure each point relates directly to the overall purpose of your talk. Then, at the end of your talk, hand out

Four Score and Seven Years Ago . . . Considered one of the most famous speeches in hisotry, Lincoln's Gettysburg Address was fewer than 200 words and was delivered in well under five minutes!

Time's Up!

There is rarely a reason for your presentation to exceed the time you have been given. It is certainly always better to leave your audience wanting more. Most talks are given a time limit for a reason. Whether it is a class (which will interfere with students' next class if you run over) or a panel (in which case you will usurp the next speaker's time), or simply a dinner where the organizers only wanted a short bit of entertainment before dessert, do not take more than your allotted time.

any printed information or your website address so they can learn more about you and/or your topic (see page 167).

Identify the Beginning, Middle, and End of Your Speech

Every presentation or speech needs a beginning, or an introduction. This opening is the audience's initial exposure to you. It's the time when they are going to decide if they like you, if they should pay attention to you, and if they're going to find anything useful in your talk. Therefore, your opening should grab their attention. Avoid beginning your talk with information that has no real content or interest value. Instead, begin with an interesting story that segues into your topic. Or tell an amusing anecdote to let them know you plan to entertain them and they'd better pay close attention if they don't want to miss some wonderfully amusing nugget.

The following is a typical, but poor, introduction to a speech.

> Good afternoon, ladies and gentlemen. I'd like to thank your organization for having me here. I think you all perform a wonderful service for the community, and you deserve a lot more recognition than you get.

This introduction tells the audience several things about you: 1) you are not afraid to be traditional and conservative, 2) you are willing to pander to an audience, 3) you are not afraid to be boring, 4) you don't want to call a lot of attention to yourself, and 5) you want to give the audience a chance to finish their conversation topics and maybe start a new one. I hope it's clear that you don't want your introduction to take this route. For some good ideas on how to begin your speech, see "Let's Skip the Introductions!" on page 163.

Next, be careful that the body of your talk is the *middle*—not the *muddle*. Since the middle basically determines the length of your presentation, keep in mind the old saying, "Nice guys finish fast!" Don't drone on, and be sure to take steps to make your middle memorable! Research tells us that people usually remember the beginning and end of a talk best. So, to make your middle more memorable, select only essential information and clear examples. Including too many details will make your talk tedious. Personalize your stories, anecdotes, and jokes to give them more meaning. When I give a speech, I try to make it a series of connected talks with short middles to make the information more memorable—bite-sized pieces rather than whole mouthfuls. I usually do something dramatic every five to ten minutes—for example, I might tell a joke or use an example that's counterintuitive and shocking, or I may hold a demonstration in which I get the audience to participate. This keeps my presentations interesting.

As for the conclusion, this is your opportunity to "cinch the deal"—in other words, to accomplish your purpose for giving the speech. If you want your audience to take action, summarize why they should take such action and tell them how to go about it by presenting a clear path. If you are trying to change their minds about something and are attempting to get them to see your specific point of view, the conclusion is where you should make your strongest appeal. You must end your speech on a high note. Never end your talk like this: "Well, I guess that's it . . . any questions?"

When you write your conclusion, keep in mind that Patrick Henry's famous line "Give me liberty or give me death!" were simply the final words of a lengthy speech. And it's all most of us remember.

Let's Skip the Introductions!

When you are giving a speech, there's no need to be traditional: "Good afternoon, ladies and gentlemen. My name is Daniel Dullman, and I have a degree in marine biology. I am here this evening to inform you caring people of the worldwide decline in diversity among ocean predator fish."

Could you be any more boring?! Instead of making this fatal mistake, be creative with the introductory part of your presentation to get your audience interested right from the get-go.

Experiment with the ideas below. Try each one out for size to see which works best with your particular presentation. Take note of how they all jump right in and attempt to grab the audience's attention right away.

- **Begin your speech with a question.** Here's an example from one of my workshops on the downside of technology:

If technology saves you time, why are you spending more time than ever using technology? If faster Internet connections allow you to work faster, why are you spending more time on the Internet? Tonight we're going to examine the seductive quality of the new technologies and help you develop an immunity to their addictive power.

- **Tell an anecdote.** Here's an example from one of my workshops on public speaking:

One night, I had just begun to deliver my presentation to a group of seniors, when one elderly lady in the back raised her hand and said, "Honey, we already know all of this. Why are you wasting our time?" I replied, "Madam, clearly your time is very valuable, but if you give me just a little more of it, you'll see that what I have to say will actually save you time in the long run."

- **Tell the reason why you're qualified to speak.** Here's another example from one of my workshops on public speaking.

When it comes to public speaking, you can be sure I've made way more mistakes than you have. And that's why I'm here tonight—to teach you how to avoid my mistakes. And who's better qualified for that?

Notice that in all three of these examples, I just jumped right in. I didn't thank anyone or tell the audience how pleased I was to be there. Each intro came equipped with a hook that grabbed the audience's attention.

Don't Touch That Dial!

When you are planning the beginning of your speech, imagine that each member of your audience will be holding a remote control. We'll call this remote control their attention. You know from experience that when you've got your remote control in hand, you don't linger on a station waiting for it to entertain you. If it doesn't grab your attention right away, you click to the next channel. Well, that's how long your audience is going to give you too. So, be sure to grab your audience's attention as soon as you get up in front of them. Once your opening has gotten them to put their remote controls down, you can go on to tell them what your presentation is all about, including a basic outline of what's to come. The clearer the structure of your talk is to your audience, the more they will follow and remember it.

Write Out the Full Draft of Your Speech

In Chapter 8, I suggested that you write out your presentation and use it as a safety net if you truly believe you'll freeze up in front of the audience. Even if you don't have such a fear, you should still write out the full draft of your talk so that you can develop it through the editorial process. Write out a draft of your speech exactly as you intend to give it. Don't forget to use conversational language, which will make your presentation easy to deliver and understand. Double or triple space the draft. This way you can easily make revisions between the lines when working on paper.

Don't be too judgmental of your first draft. Very few great presentations are completed on the very first go-round. Once you've completed the first draft, walk away from it for a while, and reread it later and reflect on it. You will invariably see improvements you can make. And although I've mentioned this many times, once you have your final version in hand, don't forget to practice, practice, practice! Review Chapter 9 once again to make sure it's "good" practice.

Figure Out Ways to Get Your Audience Involved

According to an interesting bit of research, university students rate their professors most favorably when they are given the opportunity to interact during class. You'd think a professor who hands out good grades or has a great sense of humor would be the highest rated. But not so. The more students get to talk and participate, the higher they rate their professors. That's obviously because, by nature, people would rather interact than be lectured to. So, whenever possible, find ways to involve your audience in your presentation.

The most common way speakers do this is by inviting questions from the audience. But you can turn the tables and ask members of your audience questions. Both of these techniques are good, but they usually only involve one or two people. Here are a few more ways to increase interaction.

Group Responding

Rather than asking one person in the audience a question, ask the whole audience a question, one that's open-ended and requires some reflection and problem solving. Then, have your audience break up into small groups of two to four people. Request that they discuss the question among themselves for a few minutes. Then, ask a member of each group to present their best answer or solution. This way, you're involving the entire group. Everyone will listen closely because they'll want to compare their answers with the others. It is usually a good idea to have your own version of the response ready in case you are asked for it.

Help Audience Members Relate to the Information

I once consulted with an Internet company whose unsuccessful sales presentations included a lot of data. They'd bombard the audience with what they thought were meaningful statistics that would persuade the audience members to contract for their services. But this backfired. I recommended that instead of telling the audience how much the average company spends on collecting web-based data, for example, they ask the audience to come up with their own estimates of the costs—numbers that would be more meaningful to them. Then, when the speaker gave them the actual data, the audience realized how much they would save. Now that the audience was working with figures that were more personally relevant, they were easier to persuade. If you need to present statistics to a group, take a lesson from this, and get your audience involved in a guessing game of sorts. When they become personally involved, the numbers will have more meaning to them.

When sharing statistics as part of your presentation, figure out how to make the figures meaningful to your audience.

Ask Counterintuitive Questions to Surprise Your Audience

A counterintuitive question is a question whose answer is contrary to what common sense would suggest. Try to find information or examples that will surprise the audience, and before discussing it, ask a question about it that they will likely get wrong. A wrong answer will pique their curiosity and make them want to listen closely. For example, during a discussion of international copyright laws, I asked the audience to call out which products they thought had the most copyright infringement in China. They shouted out things like music and movies. There was a buzz around the room when I told them the correct answer—Prozac!

Design Exercises and Demonstrations

The more hands-on you can be with your audience, the better. Whenever possible, bring up members from the audience to participate in a demonstration. Your audience will pay closer attention to a demonstration that seems real than they will to one that seems staged. Moreover, the presentation will be more persuasive if audience members can personally sample a product or strategy versus watching the presenter doing the same thing.

During one of my presentations, I wanted to give an example of how the mind affects the body. I used an exercise I'd seen at a martial arts demonstration that's commonly used in Aikido. I instructed the audience members to pair up, and asked one member of each pair to touch their thumb to their index finger, forming a circle. Then I told them to hold that position and not allow their partners to separate their fingers. Of course, it was fairly easy to separate them. Next, I asked them to imagine that a strong, circular steel rod was running through their thumb and index finger. Everyone participating was stunned to see how much more difficult it was to separate the fingers. This was a strong demonstration of the power of imagery, made stronger by the audience's participation.

Solicit Comments from the Audience

If you are very knowledgeable about your topic, you can solicit comments from the audience and use their comments to launch into other related areas. Doing this guarantees your talk will be relevant to the members of your audience. In many cases, their comments and the discussion that results will have more of an effect on the audience than if you had simply made the comments yourself. Mary U., the wedding planner, used this technique with much success. Take a look:

The Case of Mary U. (Continued)

When Mary realized her purpose was to "frighten" her audience into using her services, which she considered honorable because she believed they really needed her help, she designed a new opening for her presentation. Instead of telling the audience all the things that could go wrong at a wedding, Mary had the audience tell her. With light-hearted humor, she asked them to shout out all of the things they'd ever seen go wrong at a wedding. As they shouted out one disaster after another, they became more and more competitive, trying to outdo each other. Although the participants were laughing at this point, the sheer volume of potential problems had succeeded in scaring them. Mary hadn't even begun the talk, but she had already achieved her purpose!

An interesting sidelight is that this technique also helped Mary calm down. Like most people, she'd be most nervous at the start of her presentation. But during those first few minutes—the scariest for most people—Mary had her audience do most of the talking and just chimed in when she wanted.

Prepare Useful Handouts and/or a Website Address

Since you'll rarely have the time to include all of the information you want in the time you are given, take advantage of the opportunity to hand out further information following your presentation. A well-designed handout is a good way to highlight your main points and present additional information. Be sure to pass out the handout *after* not *before* your speech. You don't want to compete with the written word. If you put reading material into your audience's hands, they will probably read it, which will take their attention away from you. However, if your audience is expected to take notes, there is an exception: it may be a good idea to provide them with an outline with blank space available for note-taking.

Websites are also a good way to provide your audience with additional information. An interactive and informative website that provides useful links can greatly benefit your ultimate purpose. If you are computer savvy, you might want to look into creating a website that suits your needs and that will further educate your audience. If you or your company already has a website, be sure to tell your audience. Keep in mind, however, that although the Internet is a great convenience, it does take effort to log on. Therefore, you might want to provide your audience with a handout in addition to your website address.

Create an Outstanding Slideshow

There are many factors involved in determining whether or not you will be using a slideshow. The time you have available to you, the data you want to present, what's expected of you, and what type of audience you are presenting to should all come into consideration when you are making such a decision. For some people, a slideshow can be a great benefit. This is especially true in the case of people who have dyslexia—

a neurologically related impairment of the ability to read and write—and, as a result, tend to rely more on images than on words. If you have dyslexia, see also "Public Speaking and Dyslexia" on page 174 for some helpful advice when it comes to making presentations.

Computer-based presentation programs such as Microsoft Power-Point allow you to integrate graphics, text, and other media into your presentation to make it more informative, entertaining, and captivating. Programs such as these essentially replaced the chalkboard or dry-erase board, overhead transparencies, and slide projectors (some of which are still in use, of course).

Be careful when using presentation software—it has the potential to either improve or reduce your effectiveness. I've often heard people groan when faced with a speaker who uses PowerPoint. Why? Because PowerPoint is so easy to use—everything is practically done for you—that slideshows often lack uniqueness and creativity. The program's features and stock clipart and backgrounds, which were designed by computer engineers for simplicity, *simply* make everyone's presentation look the same. So, if you want your presentation to come across as unique and interesting, avoid using the templates.

If you are using PowerPoint in particular, don't let the "AutoContent Wizard" take over. Choose the "Blank Presentation" option and make the presentation as unique as you are. Think outside the wizard! But, if you truly feel you cannot do without the wizard, watch out for two common errors: the wizard may call for a category of information that you don't need to include, but you think you must because the programmers felt it was relevant. The second error is omitting relevant information because the wizard doesn't ask you for it.

A main point to keep in mind when using a program such as Power-Point is to go heavier on the graphics than on the text. You want your audience to *listen* to your presentation, not *read* it. Likewise, don't end up reading the text on the screen to your audience. (They can read it in their heads *much* quicker than you can say it. They'll be waiting at the finish line bored and listless until you catch up, so don't do it.) Instead, use the text to highlight your main points and to keep your audience focused. Elaborate on the text you have placed on the screen rather than designing the text to elaborate on what you are saying.

Always remember that you—not the computer program—are the presenter. The slideshow is simply a tool to help you get your information across to the audience and persuade them to see things the way you do. It is just a tool, so make it fit your needs. Use it when you think it is appropriate. You do not need a slide for everything you say. You want

Always remember that you—not the computer program—are the presenter. The slideshow is simply a tool to help you get your information across to the audience.

your audience to pay attention to you, not the screen. If you don't have a compelling graphic or key words or phrases to make a point, you don't need a slide. And don't be afraid to "let it B." In PowerPoint, the "B" key makes the screen go blank. You do not want to compete with a screen, so keep it blank until you need it.

The following sections discuss some important things you'll want to keep in mind when designing your presentation.

Make the Text Large Enough to Read

If possible, visit the place where you will be giving your presentation to find out the dimensions of the room. If you can't visit the site in advance, call ahead and ask for the dimensions. The size of the room will help you determine how large to make the text in your slideshow. Here is the safest rule for projected text: for every 10 feet from the screen, add a half inch (36 points) to your font size. The following guidelines should help:

- If the room is 10 feet long use a 36-point font.

- If the room is 20 feet long use a 72-point font.

- If the room is 30 feet long use a 108-point font.

- If the room is 40 feet long use a 144-point font.

- If the room is 50 feet long use a 180-point font.

There are few mistakes that rival a font that's too small for your audience to see. Following these guidelines guarantees that everyone in the room will be able to read your slides from anywhere in the room.

Use Enough Contrast Between the Text and Background

Your audience will not be able to read the text on the screen if it is too similar in color to the background. For example, the audience will have to strain their eyes to read a light blue font on a white background. So, be sure to use a text color that contrasts with your background color—for example, dark blue on white or black on yellow. There should be enough contrast between the text and background so that even the smallest text is easy to read.

> There should be enough contrast between the text and background so that even the smallest text is easy to read.

Limit the Amount of Text on Your Frames

A general, conservative rule is that type that is projected on a screen should follow the six-by-six rule. That means no more than six lines on a screen and no more than six words per line. The purpose of text on the screen is to focus the audience's attention on your main points. It is not supposed to present a large amount of information. Ideas should be summarized in brief phrases.

When college students are reading their textbooks, they are used to seeing pages with graphics and text divided by heads and subheads. Occasionally, they turn the page and find only text. You can tell when this happens because they slump over and instinctively look at their watches. This is what your audience will do when you bring up a slide with too much text. If you have a lot of text to present, put it in your handout (see page 167). Always remember that *you* should be the one providing the words, not the screen. That's why they call you the speaker.

Choose Your Fonts Carefully

It's best to use a simple sans-serif font for your slideshow presentation. A *serif* is a short, fine line stemming from the main strokes of a letter to make a font more decorative. Arial is an example of a sans serif font (*sans* is the French word for "without"), and **Times** is an example of a serif font.

Avoid difficult-to-read fancy fonts in your presentation.

Be aware that many fonts are unreadable when they are projected on a screen. A fancy, exotic font may look cool to you but may be difficult for your audience to read. Consider Old English, for instance: 𝕮𝖆𝖓 𝖄𝖔𝖚 𝕽𝖊𝖆𝖉 𝕿𝖍𝖎𝖘 𝕰𝖆𝖘𝖎𝖑𝖞? You certainly don't want your audience struggling to read what you've placed on the screen.

Also, be sure to avoid using too many different fonts, even if you've avoided the fancy ones. There's a secret code among professional presenters: *too many fonts equals amateur.*

Don't Forget the Graphics but Be Discriminating

Plain text does not make the best use of your presentation software. Text is for speaking and graphics are for seeing. Well-chosen graphics can help you communicate your message. In fact, I've met some excellent speakers who used absolutely no text in their presentations, just graph-

Is the Room Too Bright?

Even the most fabulous slideshow will flop if your audience can't see it. Be sure you can cover windows and turn off lights in a room where you will be playing your slideshow. If you don't have control over the lighting in a very bright room, it's best not to use that room to make your presentation. In a bright room, the slides will be too washed out to see and the glare will greatly compound any problems, such as blurry graphics and small text. So, if you're planning a slideshow, find out where you'll be presenting it to make sure the lighting is within your control.

ics. When used properly, graphics can help your audience grasp information and increase their retention. (By the way, bad graphics are way worse than no graphics at all. If you know that a slide is an eyesore, don't show it!)

When used solely for decoration, graphics will interfere with communication. They should either communicate the content of your presentation or be eliminated. By all means, avoid repetitious animations such as animated gifs—they are extremely distracting.

Limit the Colors You Use

Too many colors used for text and objects can result in the "rainbow effect" where the brain tries to make sense of all the colors and goes offline. In other words, too many colors will distract your audience. Limit the font color to a maximum of two colors per slide, being sure they contrast with your background. The purpose of colors is to cue the audience in to what's important. Any more than a couple of colors per frame will obscure your message. As for color selection, use whatever suits your taste but do avoid complementary colors such as red and green, which would make it difficult for people with colorblindness to see. Likewise, make sure you maximize the contrast. For example, don't put black letters on a dark blue background unless you want your presentation to end up "black-and-blue."

Choose Your Special Effects Wisely

Transition effects are usually used to move from one frame to another during a slideshow. However, whirling, twirling text and other special effects can distract or disorient the viewers. Although your presentation software may provide a multitude of options, it's best to limit yourself to one, unless you feel strongly that the effect serves a specific purpose. For example, transition effects can be useful to help the audience prepare themselves for the next frame. For example, you may employ one main effect, and then use a different one when the next frame is a graphic. In this way, transition effects can signal the type of information that's coming up next.

Whirling, twirling text and other special effects can distract or disorient the viewers.

Once again, try to use transitions functionally. It's not uncommon for a few audience members to gasp when they see a dazzling triple spin transition. It's like watching an Olympic gymnast stick a landing. However, you must ask yourself if the triple spin adds quality to your presentation. Nine out of ten times, the answer will be no. Moreover, most of the people who let out a gasp are probably doing so because the effect made them dizzy.

Keep Frame Design Simple

Too many items in one frame—especially if some of them are moving—can make it difficult to focus on any one particular thing, such as text. If there's something important enough for it to be included in your slideshow, your audience shouldn't have to play "seek and find" to figure out what it is. Make it easy for your audience to find it by using a simple, clear design that's free of distractions.

Use Sounds Sparingly

Unnecessary sounds interfere with communication when they are used solely for effect. Sounds should be used to help communicate the content of your slideshow and for no other reason. Even soft music can be distracting to your audience. And by all means, be wary of cheesy sound effects. Canned laughter and other strange sound clips can be more annoying than amusing.

Make Use of Controversy

If you want your slideshow to help generate a discussion, put something controversial, but related to your presentation, on one of the frames. I don't mean something vulgar, but rather an issue you know the people in your audience will feel strongly about. If the slide itself doesn't generate conversation, be prepared to ask questions about it to elicit a response from the audience. For instance, you can ask what the item represents, what would be a good caption for it, or even why they think you are showing it.

Know Your Slideshow and Your Options

Remember not to use your slideshow as a teleprompter. Instead, know your material inside and out. Know exactly where each slide is in your presentation and how to get to it. This will keep you from having to look at the screen or computer to figure out where you are.

Also, make sure you are familiar with all of the keystroke functions associated with your software. There may be times during your presentation when a question or comment will prompt you to jump forward in your slideshow to make a point or clarify something. In PowerPoint, for instance, you have two options for doing this: you can either create a button to make these jumps or you can simply enter the frame number and hit ENTER. With options like these, you don't have to stumble back or ahead, you just go straight there—it looks more professional.

CENSORED

If you want your slideshow to help generate a discussion, put something controversial, but related to your presentation, on one of the frames.

Check Your Compatibility!

Beware: not all computers are compatible, and not all presentation software responds the same way. If you have prepared a slideshow to go with your presentation, it's a very good idea to make sure all the equipment and software you will be using is compatible. Moreover, any built-in graphics, sounds, or fonts in your slideshow may not be available when played on someone else's computer. Be sure to check for compatibility at least a few days before the presentation so that you can work out any problems if necessary.

If you plan to run the slideshow from your own laptop, great, but don't let that lull you into a false sense of security. You'll still need to have the appropriate cables and adapters to hook up to the projector. Also, you'll want to check the resolution and luminosity of the projector so that your presentation will look the way you expect it to.

Employ the "PowerCounterPoint" Principle

PowerCounterPoint is the powerful synthesis of two concepts: *Counterpoint* and *PowerPoint*. Counterpoint is a musical concept that refers to music that has two or more melodies played at the same time. While they are separate melodies that may each be good, together they may create music that is more interesting and more beautiful than the sum of its parts. At any moment in time you can listen to either melody, or look at the harmony between the notes being played at the same time. If you enjoy listening to Johan Sebastian Bach, you have heard some of the most effective and beautiful use of counterpoint. When you are thinking about counterpoint, understand that you and your PowerPoint slides are playing *at the same time*. You can interfere with each other, cancel each other out, or propel each other to greater heights than either can soar to alone.

The key to PowerCounterPoint is that you must always be aware of the relationship between what you are doing and what's on the screen. The screen should never work against you by distracting your audience with text or graphics. When you have something interesting on the screen, you must direct the audience away from you and toward the screen. You can do this with your body by turning away from the audience and gesturing toward the screen with your hand. This way, you are controlling their attention, and you can get it back by turning your back away from the screen and facing the audience when you want their attention back. You also have the choice of leaving the image on the screen for reference or blanking out the screen so that you are the total focus of their attention.

Dyslexia and Public Speaking

When I was learning how to digitally edit video from a well-known expert, I became privy to an interesting bit of his history. He explained that he has dyslexia. As a young boy, he dreaded going to school, and he painfully recalled how each day was just another day of torture. He was alternately labeled by his teachers as stupid, bright, under-achieving, and emotionally disturbed. Then, one day, a representative from a nearby camera factory visited his school to show off a newly developed inexpensive plastic camera. Each student in the fifth-grade class was asked to try it out. My instructor explained that the moment he took his first picture, his life had changed. From that point on, he used photographs to express himself in school; he relied heavily upon photos with captions in his reports and papers. A few years later, he was introduced to motion graphics and never looked back. I was moved by this story.

Only in the last few decades has the field of education come to understand dyslexia and the problems associated with it. Previously, children with dyslexia were ridiculed and made to feel ashamed. It is now well known, however, that dyslexia is totally unrelated to intelligence. It is more a matter of how information is processed by the brain. People with dyslexia tend to do most of their thinking in images and have difficulty processing two-dimensional and symbolic objects, such as letters and numerals. This difference in brain structure is present at birth and the condition is hereditary. Current estimates suggest that between 5 and 15 percent of the U.S. population is dyslexic. Interestingly, dyslexia is rarely seen in countries where pictorial writing is used, such as China. In languages where symbolic sequential alphabets are used, however, such as English, dyslexia is relatively common.

Having dyslexia doesn't mean a person can't succeed professionally. In fact, you would be quite sur-prised by the number of successful entertainers, inventors, scientists, athletes, writers, artists, and business/political leaders with dyslexia. I could name dozens upon dozens, but since my space is somewhat limited, I'll just list an even two dozen so you can get the point: Agatha Christie, Albert Einstein, Babe Ruth, Bruce Jenner, Charles Schwab, George Burns, Hans Christian Andersen, Henry Ford, John F. Kennedy, John Lennon, Leonardo da Vinci, Magic Johnson, Nelson Rockefeller, Pablo Picasso, Robin Williams, Steven Hawkings, Steven Spielberg, Ted Turner, Terry Bradshaw, Thomas Edison, Tom Cruise, Walt Disney, Whoopi Goldberg, Will Smith, and Wolfgang Mozart.

Clearly, dyslexia is hardly a limitation. In fact, it can provide a person with the drive and incentive to overcome this difficulty and achieve great things.

When it comes to public speaking, people with dyslexia may face two different types of problems—in addition to the anxiety-related fears shared by many public speakers. The first may be related to self-esteem issues stemming from years of academic difficulties. Since most people with dyslexia are able to come up with creative strategies to overcome academic problems and are able to use their gifts to achieve success, the fear of public speaking for them has more to do with the second problem: not being able to use notes or an outline during a presentation. If this is you—and you don't want to memorize everything you are going to say—the following information should help.

Preparing Notes for Your Presentation

Before you prepare any notes, review what you want to say and organize it into sections that make sense you. You can organize your speech by identifying key points, specific stories/anecdotes that illustrate your points, and/or recommendations you have for the audience. Learn each section well and practice saying each section aloud until you feel comfortable with it. Each section will then be one part, or chunk, of your notes. By learning the material as a series of chunks, the individual parts will be easier to identify with whatever cues you choose to use, whether they are words, pictures, or colors.

To make your notes easier to read, limit the number of words you use. Avoid whole sentences and phrases; instead, stick to a few *key* words that can cue you in on what you want to say. Write those few words in large, bold letters to help you recognize them more easily. This will also help if the lighting is dim or if lights are shining in your eyes. You might also want to write the key words in different colors to help you identify the items more readily. If you've developed a transcription code over the years, make use of it in your notes. The goal is to be able to recognize each item as quickly and easily as possible. You also might find it helpful to use graphics instead of text. If you can sketch pictures, logos, and/or line drawings to key you in to each part of your talk, do it. If you can't draw, feel free to use graphics from magazines, photos, or the Internet.

What's most important, obviously, is that with a quick glance down at your notes, you are able to immediately figure out where you are in your presentation and what comes next. Before you move on to the next step (practicing with your notes), make sure you can quickly and accurately identify each entry by glancing down at them. If you cannot, you'll need to change the entry until you find one you can quickly recognize.

Practicing With Your Notes

Preparing your notes is a great first step, but you must practice using them. You've learned each section of your talk as a separate entity and provided a key word or graphic in your notes to cue you in on what's coming up. Next, you will integrate those two crucial steps into your practice.

First, practice giving your speech by looking at your notes, and then present the section that goes along with each specific key entry. Practice this until you can do it smoothly. Overlearning and overpracticing are your allies. Remember that the actual talk generally causes more anxiety than your practice session and there may be a drop off in your performance. You can compensate for this with extra preparation. Also, since people with dyslexia are very good with images, if you haven't already, you'll want to read the section "Create an Outstanding Slideshow" on page 167. Using a slideshow with mostly graphics can be a great advantage for people with dyslexia.

Finally, practice without referring to your notes. Every time you forget or stumble, you have diagnosed a weak area. Go back and practice more on that area. Each time you falter, practice using your notes with the graphic cues you have inserted. Once you know you can pick up anywhere if there is a problem, your confidence level will rise. This alone will lower your anxiety level and improve your performance.

PRODUCTION STAGE—
MAKING YOUR PRESENTATION OR SPEECH

As you may have guessed, the production stage is the part where you will actually be giving your presentation or speech. This is what you've been preparing for. Although you will want to focus all of your attention on your topic, there are certain tools you can employ just before and during your presentation. Let's take a look.

Do Your Relaxation and Breathing Exercises

While you are waiting to be called up to the podium or before entering the room in which you will be presenting, spend a few minutes doing your breathing and relaxation exercises (see Chapter 6). Not only will this relieve some of your anxiety, but it will also help you to be present and more alert. Also, when you do begin your presentation, speak slowly and deliberately, and take a breath between each sentence. If you've done the exercises in Chapter 6, this should come naturally. Remember, an important benefit of taking deep breaths during your speech is that your voice will have more strength and power.

Make Effective Use of Your Voice

Writers often use various ways to convey the emotion of their words. For example, some words will appear in boldface for greater emphasis, some in italics for distinction, and some in all caps to represent a strong feeling. Ellipses (three dots to indicate a pause) and various other types of punctuation all play a role in getting the writer's intention across. Still, this isn't much of a tool palette. As a speaker, you have many tools at your disposal. Be sure to put them all to good use. Here are a few tools to incorporate into your practice and later into your presentation.

Volume, pitch, and speed are important tools in your public speaker's toolbox. Listen to talk radio and pay close attention to how the hosts use these tools.

- **Volume.** Loudness is a sign of heightened emotion and forcefulness. It also conveys excitement. Softness indicates intimacy and privacy. It is a message not intended for everybody. You can increase the volume of an important point, or soften it to draw everyone in close to you.

- **Pitch.** When you raise your pitch, you signal excitement. A high-pitched voice is another way to show heightened emotion. A drop in pitch signals seriousness or a warning. Too many speakers lull their audiences to sleep with a monotone voice. They drone on in the same pitch and may awkwardly raise or drop a note at the end of sentence. Avoid this by varying the pitch of your voice during practice.

- **Speed.** Increasing the speed of your words also increases the excitement. Decreasing your speed shows that you are serious and careful about what you are saying.

Have you ever listened to talk radio? The announcers have only their voices to convey their emotions. Listen to how they use and vary the volume, pitch, and speed of their voices. Once again, recording and listening to your practice sessions can help you practice using these tools. Employ them at key points during your speech to make your presentation more dynamic, but be sure to not alter your normal speech patterns. If you were to listen to a recording of a discussion you've had with a friend or family member, you'd hear yourself using all of these features naturally. Under pressure, however, people tend to retreat to conservative speech. It's essential to allow your personality and feelings to come out during a speech by using these features the same way you would when having a relaxed conversation.

Appear to Be Enjoying Yourself

No one is telling you that you must be having a good time while you are giving a speech or presentation. But, to be effective, you must *look* like you are having a good time. The audience will never detect how nervous you are if you appear to be in control.

Don't Apologize!

By no means should you ever tell the audience that you're nervous, not an expert, or inexperienced. A common way people deal with stage fright is to try to lower the audience's expectations with an apology. For instance, *I'm not really an expert in this area; You'll have to excuse me, but I'm a bit nervous tonight;* or *I'm sort of new at this, but . . .*

An audience who pities you cannot respect you. When you tell them you're nervous, you are directing their attention away from your talk and toward a search for any signs of anxiety you might be showing.

This strategy does *not* work. It's foolish to think that if you admit you are nervous and then you don't do very badly, the audience will rate you better because they had low expectations for you. They may even have a little sympathy for you during the talk. The sad news is that an audience who pities you cannot respect you. When you tell the audience you are nervous, you are directing their attention away from your talk and toward a search for any signs of anxiety you might be showing. You might as well be saying, "Please examine my hands to see if they are trembling," or "Take notice if I'm sweating," or "Listen for my voice to crack." It will be okay if they discover on their own that you're nervous, but certainly don't point it out for them.

If you tell the audience you aren't an expert in the area you're covering, you'll simply annoy them. They didn't come to listen to a nonexpert. They will be looking for evidence to show that you don't have the competence to address them. Imagine your dentist talking to you just before he begins your root canal. "I'm not real good at this type of procedure so just bear with me. Oh, and I tend to get a little nervous when I start drilling, but don't worry."

Don't Talk About Things That Make You Uncomfortable

Audiences are very good at detecting when you are uncomfortable about a topic, joke, or example. If you are in doubt about whether to include it, follow this simple piece of advice, DON'T! This goes double if the material may possibly be in bad taste. Sometimes you'll be able to make this decision in the preproduction stage, but sometimes you may have to make a judgment on the fly depending on your audience. The careers of Al Campanis (a major league baseball executive), Jimmy "The Greek" Snyder (a football commentator), and Earl Butz (a U.S. government official) would have been much brighter if they had heeded this advice. All three lost their prestigious jobs because of politically incorrect comments or racial jokes.

Make Eye Contact

Reach Out and Look at Someone

Making eye contact with members of your audience makes them feel personally involved.

When you make eye contact with audience members, it makes you appear more comfortable to them. It also gives you some feedback, because it allows you to briefly take note of how the audience is responding to your talk. In one-on-one interactions, both no eye contact and total eye contact are considered strange behaviors. People in a one-on-one conversation feel most comfortable with eye contact about 50 percent of the time. So, aim for that. When you are speaking to a larger group, try to make eye contact with as many different people as you can. You can use no eye contact to indicate thoughtfulness. If you are thinking of a response to a question and look up or down, it appears that you are giving the question a great deal of thought before answering.

From here on in, you're on your own. Good luck to you. If you've taken all the preproduction steps in this chapter, your production should go smoothly. If you've participated in all of the exercises presented so far in this book, all the better. Once you've completed your presentation, you'll want to gauge your success. That brings us to postproduction.

THE POSTPRODUCTION STAGE— AFTER THE SPEECH OR PRESENTATION

There is an old saying, "Smart people make mistakes; dumb people repeat them." The purpose of the postproduction phase is to assess your presentation so that you can learn from your mistakes and even improve on the good parts. To do this correctly, you will need three types of data:

1) your memory of how the talk went; 2) the feedback you received from people whose opinions you value; and 3) a video or audio recording. If a video of your presentation is not available to you, an audio recording is the second best thing. With the size of recorders these days, you can easily slip one into your pocket and hit record just before you begin your presentation. This type of feedback is extremely valuable in assessing how you did.

When you've had a chance to examine the data, try to determine what improvements you can make for next time. If there is a formal structure for feedback in place, such as written evaluation forms, be sure to review them carefully. If no formal feedback is available, approach participants if possible, colleagues perhaps, and ask what they thought of your speech or presentation. If someone invited you to give a speech, ask that person if you provided what was needed. In most cases, you'll have the opportunity to speak with the people who were in your audience. If they offer feedback, great. If not, join conversations and solicit any information you can get. When you were determining the purpose of your speech (see page 157), you were asked to identify any specific results of achieving it. Now is the time to evaluate those results.

WHAT YOU HAVE LEARNED AND WHERE YOU ARE GOING

This chapter likened giving a talk to making a movie. During preproduction, you write the script and rehearse it. Then, you're on the set, shooting your film. Later, you see how it did at the box office. If you took the preproduction stage very seriously, it should be a blockbuster!

The next chapter will help you create a lasting impression on your audience, specifically the impression you *want* to make.

11

The BIG Idea

Certain strategies can help you be more effective with your audience. Analyzing your audience provides a great deal of information that can improve their impression of you and your presentation.

CREATING THE RIGHT IMPRESSION

A troubled man is walking along a deserted beach. He stops and shouts up to the heavens, "God, I've been a devout believer all my life! Reveal yourself to me and grant me a wish!"

"You are right, my son!" booms a voice from the heavens. "You deserve a reward. What would you like?"

The man shouts back, "I live in California, but I love Hawaii. Build me a bridge so I can drive there whenever I want."

The voice booms back, "That's a little more than I had in mind. Choose something else."

"Okay, Lord," shouts the man. "I have to give a speech next week. Tell me what the audience really wants."

And the Lord replies, "Do you want two lanes or four?"

Clever, yes, but these days, that's considered an outdated joke. In recent years, psychologists have been examining the question of what audiences want, and believe it or not, we have some answers. In fact, we know quite a bit about how an audience evaluates a speaker, how a speaker can gauge if he or she is succeeding, which of a speaker's characteristics influence an audience, as well as the strategies a speaker can use to create a favorable impression.

In this chapter, you'll learn when and how to create the impressions you want to make on your audience. Next, you'll learn some management strategies that will enable you to present yourself in the best light possible. The last section presents strategies for handling difficult issues. Let's begin with a general discussion of impression management so you can get a feel for what it's all about.

> "Sometimes one creates a dynamic impression by saying something and sometimes one creates as significant an impression by remaining silent."
>
> —Dalai Lama

IMPRESSION MANAGEMENT

The term "impression management," coined by social psychologists, is just what it sounds like. It refers to the strategies you can use to present yourself so that your audience can form the impressions *you* want. Does this sound a bit manipulative and maybe even dishonest? Actually, it is what virtually all of us do constantly. It would be strange if people stopped paying attention to the impressions they make upon others. Imagine how odd it would be if you were in an audience when someone walked up to the podium to address the local chamber of commerce and had no regard for what they thought. Picture a speaker in tattered jeans and a dirty sweatshirt belching into the microphone before beginning the speech. This person would be viewed as highly inappropriate, even bizarre. It's hard to imagine such a scene really happening because we all care, to some degree, about what others think of us.

How much should we care about the impression we make? Look at the graph in Figure 11.1. It illustrates that if you don't care enough or if you care too much, the audience will *not* think you are effective. You will be most effective if your level of concern is right in the middle. Our starting point then is to examine how concerned you are with making a good impression.

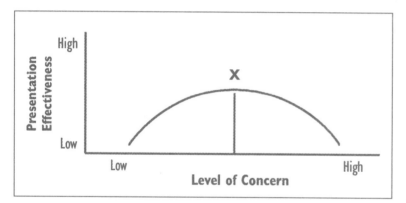

Figure 11.1.
The Relationship of
Level of Concern
to Effectiveness

If you are not concerned enough about how you are perceived by your audience, there's a good chance your audience won't get what it wants and/or expects from you. There are many types of mistakes you can make if you care too little to prepare correctly—you may dress too casually or too formally, tell inappropriate jokes or stories, come off sounding too familiar or too aloof, and so on.

If you care too little, you probably won't put enough effort into your preparation and will likely give an unenthusiastic, poorly structured presentation. This can result in a lifeless performance that lacks energy. For example, imagine an overworked executive who is coerced into giving a talk to a small group of people. Believing this talk won't affect his future in any way, he puts out very little effort in preparing his presentation. Not surprisingly, he'd likely be judged as a poor speaker because he cared so little about it.

On the other hand, if you are too concerned about the impression you make, you are also putting the success of your presentation at risk. If you care so much that you painstakingly take care to avoid making any mistakes at all, your presentation will often end up being too conservative, both in *what* and *how* you present. You might be so afraid to take any chances that you'll wind up being boring and predictable—just to be on the safe side.

Moreover, if you care too much, you may start to overanalyze the impression you're making during your presentation. As you know, this is called self-monitoring—one of the main causes of stage fright. This distraction will take your attention away from your presentation, resulting in a poor performance. If it seems to the audience that you're trying too hard to make a good impression, they may perceive you as insecure or even insincere. This is not the impression you want to make.

Clearly, both caring too much and caring too little can hinder the effectiveness of your presentation. Fortunately, there is an optimal point in the middle that, if you can reach it, will enable you to perform at your peak. The key word here is "moderation." Now that you care "just enough," the next question becomes, "How should you use these skills?"

USING YOUR IMPRESSION-MANAGEMENT SKILLS

The real question is not *when* you should use impression management, but *how much* you should use it. As I said before, everybody tries to make a good impression to some extent, and this requires impression management. Here's an old joke, "How can you tell if a lawyer is lying . . . when you see his lips moving." If we use the technique "joke switching," which is covered in Chapter 12, we could come up with this joke: *How can you tell when a person is impression managing? . . . Whenever someone else is around.* It's a joke, but it's quite accurate. As soon as a person becomes aware that he or she is being observed (and likely being judged or evaluated), impression management kicks in. The degree of impression management varies depending on several factors. Here are a few of the more common ones: Who is in the audience, whether or not you will see the audience members again, and how confident you are. Let's take a closer look.

- **Who's who in the audience.** The people who make up the audience play a large role in how much you want to make a good impression, and this will determine the amount of effort you put into impression management. There is a great deal of research showing that people are more likely to employ this strategy when their superiors are in the audience

Don't Try Too Hard!
If you try too hard to impress others, you might wind up sounding ignorant or looking awkward.

than when the audience is made up only of their subordinates. If there are people in the audience who can influence your future, you will be impression managing on all eight cylinders.

- **Future interaction.** Are you ever going to see these people again? The more you will have future interaction with the people in the audience, the more likely you are to try to manage their impression of you. There's usually little motivation to shape impressions if you think you'll never see the people in the audience again. Interestingly, if you know the people in the audience *very* well, the motivation also declines. In that case, you feel that you've already made your impression on them, and it won't change with a single presentation.

- **Your confidence level.** How confident you feel about yourself and what you are about to present also plays a role in the degree of impression management. The less confident you are—in other words, the lower your self-esteem is—the more you will try to manage the audience's impression of you. The difference between how you *want* to be seen and how you *think* your audience sees you relates to your self-esteem. The larger the gap, the more likely you will try to curry favor with the audience. If you take this to the extreme, your audience will not think kindly of your efforts to win them over with flattery, favors, or promises.

In all of the above cases, you'll want to make sure that you are properly employing your impression-management strategies so you don't come across in a negative light. You don't want your efforts to backfire! Moderation is always key.

HOW A SPEAKER'S TRAITS INFLUENCE THE AUDIENCE

Good impression management is a delicate balance between a speaker and his or her audience. Each adds to the mix, and the more you understand about the speaker, the audience, and how they interact, the better you can use impression management to your advantage. There are many factors that influence an audience's evaluation of a speaker above and beyond the content of his or her speech. For instance, the *tone* of one's speech can have a positive or negative effect on the audience. Also, non-verbal communication—in other words, body language—plays a larger role than you might think. In addition, physical characteristics can influence how a message is perceived. The following sections discuss a few of the traits that have been shown to influence an audience's opinion of a speaker.

The Speaker's Tone

Research shows that audiences react better to a speaker who expresses positive emotions than one who expresses negative ones. Keep in mind that these findings relate to the tone of the talk, not to the content. Audiences prefer uplifting messages over depressing ones—unless of course the negativity is aimed at a target the audience dislikes.

If I were to announce that the stock market has just gone up, I could be focusing either on the good times ahead or on the disasters that might occur if people rushed in foolishly. My tone—not the news I'm giving them—will shape the audience's reaction. In other words, it's not *what* you tell them, but *how* you tell them that determines their impression of you.

Audiences like to be uplifted. They want to feel optimistic about the future or want to feel like they're on an important mission to make things better. So, be sure to state your information in the most upbeat way possible—unless your goal is to convince your audience that things are even worse than they seem.

Here is a good way to remember this point:

> "I'd be a pessimist, but it probably wouldn't work out."
>
> —*Author Unknown*

A mother takes her identical twins to a child psychologist. "My boys are identical in every way," she explains to the psychologist. "But this one is much too pessimistic, and this one is much too optimistic. Can you help them?"

The psychologist reassures her that he can. He places the pessimistic boy in a room containing every conceivable toy and tells him to play with them to his heart's content for the next three hours. With a smug look at the mother, the psychologist says, "Let's see him not have fun in there."

Then, he places the optimistic child in a room full of horse manure, and says to the mother, "Let's see how happy he is after three hours in there."

Three hours later, he goes into the first room and finds the pessimistic twin sitting sadly in the corner. Not one toy has been touched. "Why didn't you play with any of these fantastic toys?" the psychologist asks.

"These toys are so great," says the boy. "If I played with them, I'd just feel worse when I had to leave them. I thought it was better to not get involved."

The psychologist shrugs his shoulders and says, "Well, at least I'm sure we've straightened out his brother."

But when he opens the door to the optimistic twin's room, he sees the boy laughing and whistling. The psychologist asks what there is to be happy about in a room full of horse manure. The boy replies, "With all this horse manure around, there's got to be a pony in here somewhere!"

Make Them Feel Good!
Audiences want to feel optimistic about the future or want to feel like they're on an important mission to make things better.

Audiences like ponies. Even if your ultimate message is one of "doom and gloom," present it in such a way that your audience comes away feeling hopeful and positive.

The Speaker's Body Language

I once read that you should never keep your hands in your pockets when you're giving a speech. Much like all of the other advice on the effective use of body language, this is foolish. If you are comfortable with your hands in your pockets, keep them there—especially if taking them out will distract you. If you like to pace when you talk, go ahead and pace—as long as you aren't stuck behind a podium with a stationary microphone. If you normally make gestures with your hands, go ahead and gesture. If you don't feel comfortable gesturing, don't worry about it. Unnatural gestures are ineffective and sometimes laughable. In short, the only rule you need to follow regarding body language is to be as natural and as comfortable as you can be.

If you are really unsure of what to do and it makes you worry, videotape yourself talking. Notice what you like and don't like. Then, work on adding thing you can do to feel better about your presentation while maintaining your comfort level. There are very few things you can do

The Intricacies of Smiling

Smiling is generally an expression of positive emotions. When you smile, it shows your audience that you're comfortable and feeling good. While this is true in most cases, what fun would it be if I didn't point out a few wrinkles to complicate matters?

Some research suggests that insecure people smile more often than secure people. Even without this research, we know that people often smile politely in awkward situations to ease tension. Some people smile out of nervousness, and some people smile to hide their true feelings. Smiles can be interpreted suspiciously when someone is asking for favors or trying too hard to get someone to like them.

It's important to know that most people have pretty good intuition and can distinguish between a false smile and a genuine one. Therefore, you have to do more than simply "turn that frown upside down" to make a favorable impression on your audience.

One way to effectively enhance the sincerity of your smiles—especially in situations that don't warrant it—is to use imagery. Actors use this technique all the time to make emotional scenes more convincing. Bring to mind things that genuinely make you happy, and your smile will be genuine. If you are going to use imagery like this, make sure you plan it out well in advance and practice it a lot so that it won't take your attention away from your presentation.

that are worse than adding movement, or stopping movement, that doesn't feel natural to you. It looks bad and will distract you, causing other problems. Even if you notice something like a repetitive physical habit such as tugging on your earlobe, it may cause more trouble changing it than leaving it there and remaining comfortable. Use the video to give you the answer.

There is one bad nonverbal mistake you can make. If you get physically nervous when you talk, especially if your hands shake, do not hold a piece of paper no matter what it contains. Your hand-shaking will be amplified by the paper so that even people in the last row of the room will not miss it. Except for this one unbreakable rule, just be comfortable.

The Speaker's Physical Attributes

As unfortunate as it is, there's a great deal of research supporting the fact that physically attractive people are evaluated as more dominant, intelligent, socially adept, and well adjusted than unattractive or ordinary-looking people. They also tend to be more persuasive.

We've all been given the looks we were given, and short of making an appointment with a plastic surgeon, there's not much we can do about it. We can, however, make the most of what we have with proper grooming and by taking care of our bodies. Keep in mind, also, that what is physically attractive to one group or audience may not be so for another, so don't worry too much about it. What you should concern yourself with is how to dress for the occasion—in other words, how your audience expects you to dress for the occasion. If you give them what they expect, they will be pleased—no matter how attractive or unattractive you think you might be.

If You're a Bit Bizarre . . . Flaunt It
Many professional speakers and comedians make use of their out-of-the-ordinary body language, which sets them apart from others. It's better to be a bit playful than to be stifled, so don't go out of your way to tone down your natural body language, even if it's a bit bizarre.

The Speaker's Leadership Qualities

Whenever you speak or give a presentation, you are being placed in a leadership role. In order to be accepted by the audience, they must consider you a leader. In his book *Self-Presentation: Impression Management and Interpersonal Behavior*, psychologist Mark Leary identifies several characteristics an audience looks for in what they consider a good leader. The most basic of these characteristics is competence—the audience wants to be convinced you are good at what you do as well as skilled at making your presentation. Unfortunately, trying to get your competence across to the audience presents an interesting problem. It's called the self-presenter's paradox. If you don't promote yourself, the audience may never discover your competence. On the other hand, people think that if you are competent, you shouldn't need to self-promote. The best solution here is to get this across in the stories you tell the audience. Place the emphasis on what you did, not who you are. Audiences don't look favorably upon boastful people, so be careful. They prefer modesty. (See "The Art of Modesty" on page 189.)

Likeableness is another important factor. Everyone wants to *like* their leaders. You run the risk of not being liked if you make your audience feel uninformed or unintelligent in the manner you present your material. You want your message to be new and useful, but you don't want to make the audience feel like idiots for not understanding what you're talking about. Audiences like speakers who make them feel good about themselves. If you make yourself important at the audience's expense, you run the risk of not being liked, even if your information helps them. With that said, however, if being liked interferes with being seen as competent, choose competence. This is especially true if you are in a position of authority.

Other qualities audiences find favorable include morality, level-headedness, and decisiveness. The way to communicate these traits to your audience is through stories and anecdotes. Pay close attention to the role in which you portray yourself in your stories. Avoid anything that sounds like bragging. Be sure not to mention your characteristics directly. Allow them to emerge so the audience can infer them from your stories. In other words, don't say, "I'm a very moral person." Instead, relate a story where someone's immoral behavior upset you and made you rush in and take charge.

The Speaker's Willingness to Give

Audiences appreciate it when you make an effort on their behalf and are pleased when they can give something back to you. This is known as the principle of reciprocity. They key to putting this principle to work for you is to give less than you expect back. Giving or offering too much can seem like bribery. And, the more you give, the more desperate you appear. So, as ironic as it seems, the less you give, the more you get back in results.

As a speaker, you can often ingratiate yourself to your audience by showing that you have made an effort that exceeded their expectations. For example, many years ago, I was hired to give a technology workshop. Learning that I'd be giving this "workshop" to *three hundred* participants was the first of many unpleasant surprises. To me, workshops are

> "An ounce of image is worth a pound of performances."
> —*Author Unknown*

The Art of Modesty

As a speaker, you will be more effective if your audience has a highly favorable opinion of you. This opinion can come from one of two sources: 1) your good reputation precedes you, or 2) you create the impression of modesty during your presentation by what you say and do.

In general, if a speaker is already highly regarded by his or her audience, a modest self-presentation has proven to be more effective than a strong one. This way, the speaker is not perceived as bragging, and since the audience's opinion of the speaker is already high, there really is no need to brag. However, care is required here: A successful person who displays too much modesty can come across as *smug*.

On the other hand, if the audience does not have a preexisting high opinion of you and you are too modest in your self-presentation, your modesty can be taken at face value, which can end up devaluing your accomplishments and abilities. In addition, your modesty could be taken as a sign of insecurity. In the event the audience doesn't know about your accomplishments, you must find a way to inform them. You can do this by having someone else introduce you or by working the information in obliquely. For example, instead of saying, "I am a Harvard graduate," you can say, "When I first walked on Harvard's campus as a freshman, I was stunned to see that all the buildings looked alike." The first form seems to say, "Look at me . . . see what I've done," while the second comes closer to saying, "I went to Harvard, but I don't brag about it."

Like many of the factors discussed in this book, modesty must be used in moderation for it to be effective. Furthermore, it must be used in the right instances. Audiences generally like a speaker to be modest in areas of obvious strength. To be immodest in an area of strength makes a speaker come off as a braggart, which can turn off an audience. It is possible to "boast modestly," depending on how much attention you are calling to yourself.

Here are some principles of modesty presentation from psychologist Mark Leary: Once people know you and what you have already achieved, your modesty will pay off. For modesty to be effective, the audience must already know your accomplishments. If the audience doesn't know that you have already achieved something, they may believe the diminished version of your modest story. Moreover, slight modesty is viewed more favorably than extreme modesty. Too much modesty is like asking for praise. It looks like you want the audience to say, "Oh, come on, you're way better than that." Avoid looking like you are asking for a compliment. People just don't respond well when you have achieved something significant, and then downplay it too much. In the end, it is better to acknowledge your triumphs modestly than downplay or brag about them.

hands-on presentations in which people participate rather than just watch and listen passively. That was not going to happen with three hundred people! To make matters worse, a few days before the *six-hour* workshop, I discovered that the conditions would be dreadful. I'd be the only one with access to a computer. And, if that wasn't bad enough, the workshop would be taking place in a long, narrow room. To make matters much worse, the projector equipment of the time was inadequate and at least half the participants would be unable to see the screen clearly, if at all. I realized I was going to have to give my audience something to make up for all of these problems.

Using the principle of reciprocity, I created samples of every programming concept I was presenting. Then I hired one of my graduate students to copy the files onto three hundred floppy disks so that I could give each one of them a copy to take home and work through. That way, even if they couldn't see a thing, they still had a copy to play with at their leisure.

When I began the workshop, I announced what I had done and started distributing the disks. I got a very pleasant surprise—the audience applauded my efforts. What could have been an awful day turned into a success because of the audience's appreciation of my efforts.

The Speaker's Expressions of Character and Virtue

"The secret of success is sincerity. Once you can fake that you've got it made."
—Jean Giraudoux

Although audiences appreciate dedication and morality in a speaker, they don't appreciate those virtues when the speaker flaunts them. Once again, like so many of the factors discussed here, moderation is the key word. While we may admire a person who lives a healthy lifestyle, we do not enjoy when he or she critiques us while we're eating a burger and fries for lunch. Audiences simply do not like sermons. They like people who make them feel good about themselves. If you place yourself on a higher moral plane than your audience, even if you deserve to be there, they will not like you for it. You are reminding them that they should be better people. That's a message for which you do not want to be the messenger.

REVEALING YOUR CHARACTER THROUGH THE STORIES YOU TELL

When you try to manage the audience's impression of you, you'll probably want to come across as some or all of the following—honest, dependable, friendly, loyal, reliable, responsible, self-confident, understanding, trusting, and unselfish. In most cases, you won't want to appear withdrawn, commonplace, slow, too formal, slipshod, hurried, quick, mild, awkward, or superstitious. How do I know this? A team of psychologists asked people to rate the importance of 300 character traits in terms of their importance in describing what a person is really like. The ten most likable and unlikable traits are shown in Table 11.1 on page 191.

Most successful public speakers are good at creating the impression that they have at least most of the top-ten likeable traits. You should too.

TABLE 11.1. THE TOP-TEN LIKABLE AND UNLIKABLE TRAITS			
Most Likeable Traits		**Least Likeable Traits**	
1. Honest	6. Responsible	1. Retiring	6. Slipshod
2. Dependable	7. Self-confident	2. Superstitious	7. Hurried
3. Friendly	8. Understanding	3. Commonplace	8. Quick
4. Loyal	9. Trusting	4. Slow	9. Mild
5. Reliable	10. Unselfish	5. Formal	10. Awkward

Once again, you'll present these positive characteristics to your audience through the stories you tell. Here is an example of a story that illustrates the speaker's sense of morality.

> When I was fourteen years old, my uncle Albert was in an industrial accident. He lost the use of both legs. The insurance company and their team of lawyers gave him a settlement of $28,000—hardly enough to make up for his loss. Uncle Albert spent the rest of his life in misery and near poverty, despite much financial help from friends and family. He died a broken man. There wasn't much I could do at the time—but I knew that by someday becoming an attorney, I could help people like my uncle Albert who were unfairly treated by their insurance companies.

This story doesn't say, "Look at me—I am devoted to a cause! I am sympathetic! I make things right!" However, as a listener of this story, you can pick up those traits in the speaker, especially if there is true feeling behind the words. Examples like this are much more convincing than direct statements. Sharing personal anecdotes allows the audience to construct a picture of who the speaker is. In Exercise 11.1 on page 192, you will be identifying stories from your past that you can share in an effort to illustrate your traits to the audience.

ASSESSING HOW YOU COME ACROSS TO THE AUDIENCE

Even if you do everything "right," the impression you are trying to make won't always match the actual impression you are making. For example, if you try to impress an audience with your sophistication, you may be successful or you might end up coming across as affected or haughty.

EXERCISE 11.1. Creating a Self-Exposition Story

In this exercise, you will be coming up with a true story about yourself that describes a trait you want to convey to the audience. You can perform this exercise for many different traits.

1. Identify the trait you want to impress upon your audience and record it below:

_____

2. Find an example of something that really happened to you or something you did in which this particular trait was exemplified. Record a brief synopsis of what happened below:

_____

_____

_____

_____

_____

3. Relate the conflict in the story to the trait you want the audience to know about, and write out the complete story below.

_____

_____

_____

_____

_____

_____

_____

_____

_____

Feedback for Exercise 11.1

Read your story to determine if you think it will hold the audience's attention. There's no point in telling the story if your audience won't find it interesting. Also, make sure your story clearly illustrates the trait you want your audience to identify. Be sure your story is straightforward and honest and can't be misconstrued as bragging about your great qualities. Once you feel comfortable with the story, share it with others and ask for their feedback.

Unfortunately, people aren't particular good at assessing themselves when it comes to impression management. They are, however, better at assessing the entire audience's impression than they are at assessing the impression they've made on individual audience members.

The *way* an audience processes your presentation has as much importance as *what* you are presenting. If they like you, they will process what you say differently from how they would if they don't like you. Audiences, as a whole, may be skeptical or accepting, optimistic or pessimistic, and so on. Their overall attitude can determine how likely they are to accept what you say as well as the impression you make on them.

Be careful about how you evaluate your effects on the audience, however. For example, one or two critically vocal people may make you feel like no one in the audience is enjoying your talk although the rest of the audience may be very approving of the job you're doing. Likewise, be wary of selecting out, and focusing on, only negative data, when there is positive data to consider as well. Below is a case taken from my own sordid past. I was guilty of falling into the trap of only looking at the negative data.

The Case of Peter D.

When I was a graduate student, I did not like to present papers in seminar classes. I would get very nervous before and during presentations. I had more than a few doubts about how I would like teaching at a university. I was very nervous walking into my first university class as a professor. Yet, within a few minutes of starting my first class, I knew that I was *home*. In that first semester I taught a class with sixty students. Every day I walked in and felt like I was talking to sixty of my best friends. They laughed at every joke, marveled at every revelation, and thought everything I said was fascinating. I couldn't wait to see my student evaluations at the end of the school term. When I got the evaluations, I eagerly ripped open the envelope and was devastated by the results. I ignored evaluations from the fifty students who loved the class. I dwelt on the evaluations that were lukewarm, and obsessed about the three students who seemed to think I was the devil. This small group of students disliked everything I said and did. When I pulled myself out of the bowels of depression, I realized that I had rediscovered the "normal curve."

I gained a few insights from this experience: There will always be a few people in a group who oppose the views of the main group. They actually define themselves by their oppositional behavior. I was foolish to think I could please everybody. Although you can generally tell how an entire audience is reacting, you cannot assess how specific people in the audience respond to you. Although it took a few years for me to learn the final lesson, I finally discovered that if I don't irritate at least a few people, then my presentations are lifeless, boring, and way too safe. The key is not to irritate more than those few people.

IMPRESSION MANAGEMENT AND THE CHARACTERISTICS OF THE AUDIENCE

There's a good deal of research showing that if you share characteristics with your audience—in other words, the more like them you are—the more they will like you. This is because you have traits, skills, or talents the audience understands and values—or at least you come across as if you do. If that's the case, good for you! The more you believe your traits or abilities are valued by your audience, the more relaxed and confident you will be when making your presentation. (For an example of this, see the inset "Perceived Similarities" on page 195.) Keep in mind, however, that you can't just assume your audience will accept you, and you can't just assume that every audience you appear in front of will relate to who you are and what you're about.

In order to successfully manage the impression you make on the audience, you'll need to become aware of important audience characteristics that can affect how they see and evaluate you as a speaker. Having this information will help guide you in the preparation of your presentation and shape the way you deliver it. Among other things, this information will determine how you will dress; the examples, stories, and jokes you tell; and how formal or informal you should be in your presentation. It will also determine what information to include in your introduction and any advanced promotional materials presented prior to your talk.

Let's take a look at some of the most important audience characteristics in the following sections.

The Audience's Goals and Objectives

Why did the audience come to hear you? If the audience heard about the topic and chose to be there because of it, you have an ideal situation. If they were coerced to attend by their bosses, spouses, or state law, you have a much tougher audience to deal with. The most important thing for you to know is what they expect or hope to come away with. One of the best ingratiating strategies devised is to give the audience what it wants. You'd be surprised how often this does *not* happen. In most cases, the speaker never identified what the audience wanted. In other cases, the speaker couldn't deliver it, or for some foolish reason, the speaker wouldn't deliver it.

There are several decisions you must make once you know the audience's goals and objectives. The first and most important decision you need to make is whether you want to meet their objectives now or show

Perceived Similarities

There is a great deal of research showing that the more similar a person is to us, the higher we would rate his or her performance. You can take advantage of this by adapting yourself to your audience. While you don't want to come across as phony, you can usually successfully alter your tone, language, behavior, and dress to match the audience's. As long as you can pull this off, your audience will likely receive you with more warmth than they would if you seemed different from them in some important way.

Here's an example: When I was a graduate student, I studied sociolinguistics at a government research lab. What fascinated me most was the process of code switching—when a person changes his or her dialect to blend in with others, in this case, to blend in with the audience. Since I was specifically researching Black English, also called "Ebonics" (a nonstandard variety of English, or a dialect, spoken by some African Americans), I attended every presentation made by a certain prominent, local black politician. When he addressed audiences made up of well-educated professionals, he sounded like he had graduated from an Ivy League university. But when he spoke to groups who were less well off and less educated, his speech incorporated more slang expressions, as well as grammatical and pronunciation features associated with Black English. Moreover, he also changed his manner of dress depending on the group. In both cases, this politician worked hard to seem more like the people in his audiences. He won the election.

them that you have the skills to give them what they want and get hired on to fully meet their goals for a fee. You must determine if you can meet their goals within the time limit of your talk. If you have a short time and can only talk about topics superficially, you must decide how to handle the situation. Do you want to prepare additional materials and handouts to meet their goals? Do you want to send them to your website? Think carefully how you can give your audience what it's looking for.

The Audience's Background

Unless you are giving a very general talk, it is essential to know the background of your audience. For instance, if you are talking about technology, does your audience have the necessary background to understand the information you want to present? If they have a great deal of technical expertise, is your information too basic? You can lose an audience both by talking above them and by talking below them.

If your audience does not have a great deal of technical background and your presentation deals with technical issues, there are some interesting research results that should guide your preparation. There is one main mistake experts make when talking to nonexpert audiences.

Experts are good at selecting the right introductory topics, but as they are making their presentations, they assume that the audience understands the *relationships between the concepts*. They don't seem to understand that the audience doesn't have the same mental organization for understanding the complex relationships between each idea that they have. It is easy to put the audience to sleep or make them feel dumb. To avoid these outcomes, if you present technical information to nontechnical people, limit the scope of the talk to fewer concepts so that you can explain how they relate to each other. Then, give them a path to find out more. Indicate both what they need and how to make sure they can understand it.

The Audience's Beliefs, Opinions, and Prejudices

"Your audience gives you everything you need. They tell you. There is no director who can direct you like an audience."

—*Fanny Brice*

If you believe that playing hopscotch is a good way to test for landmines, go into a talk without knowing much about the positions your audience holds on controversial issues. Once you know their views, you want to be clear on your own goals. Are you there to change their viewpoints or use their strong feelings to get them to perform some kind of action such as signing petitions, persuading friends to come to meetings, donating money, and so on. Chapter 10 discussed the importance of defining a clear intention for your talk and then organizing the talk around that intention. Here is your opportunity to do so. If your audience does not like the viewpoint you hold, that doesn't mean they don't like you personally. It's still important to treat them with dignity and respect. It is also helpful to employ self-effacing humor to help break down their resistance toward you (see Chapter 12).

The Audience's Demeanor—Hostile or Friendly?

It is important to know the mindset of your audience. There are certain venues where the audience is predisposed to being friendly and accepting. An awards banquet is an example of a setting where the audience is going to be warm and friendly. They will laugh, at least politely, at every joke told. They will applaud at every opportunity. There are also audiences that are predisposed to being somewhere between skeptical and hostile.

One of my younger colleagues once asked me why university faculty always seemed so negative. All doctoral-level graduate students, whether they are studying French history or physics, go through a similar training ritual. They all attend university symposiums where famous scholars visit and talk about their current research and theories. If a graduate student wants to look intelligent in front of his colleagues and professors, he tries to find flaws in the presentation. Every time a scholar formulates a new theory, it is done by finding problems with the older theory he or she is trying to replace. We all learn that the way to appear intelligent is by showing that we are smarter and trying to find flaws in everyone else's presentation. I would call that a hostile room. This environment exists in many places besides universities. It is common in boardrooms, military meetings, and family discussions—particularly if there are teenagers involved. You need a very different set of strategies for presenting to hostile audiences. Chapter 9 presents some skills you should practice for dealing with hostile audiences.

The Audience's Preconceived Notions

Does the audience have any preconceived notions about you, your occupation, your age, your gender, your lifestyle, your organization affiliations, or your beliefs? In other words, are they likely to stereotype you? For example, if a speaker begins a talk by announcing that she's an accountant, I let out an involuntary yawn. I just assume I'll be bored. If I hear that the speaker is from a religious organization, I think I will be in for a conservative and moralistic talk. Fortunately, I'm wrong quite often. But you must be aware of the stereotypes that are out there about every demographic category you fit into. While you're preparing for your presentation or speech, you should try to determine how you can either use the stereotype to your advantage or convince the audience that you don't fit it. Preparing for this in advance gives you the element of surprise.

The Size of the Audience

Earlier in the book, we discussed how the size of your audience can have an effect on your anxiety level. Now, let's look at how the size of the audience can affect the individuals who make up that audience.

Members of a small audience are more likely to pay attention to what you have to say or risk being thought of as rude by other audience members. They are also more likely to become involved in discussions. However, audience members in a large audience have a sense of anonymity. They feel that they can safely daydream, be distracted, or even talk during your presentation without being noticed. To engage a larger audience, you need to employ different strategies than you would with a smaller audience. First of all, members of a large audience expect to be entertained by you. Plan to do that by setting up dramatic events or

Members of a small audience are more likely to pay attention to what you have to say. They are also more likely to become involved in discussions.

some type of surprise during the presentation. You also need to get your audience involved in your presentation somehow to make it more personally relevant to them. The more an audience interacts during a presentation, the higher they are likely to rate your performance.

The Age of the Audience

Sometimes you will face an audience whose members span many generations. Other times, however, they will all be roughly the same age. It is essential to find out the age range of your audience. This will help you to determine the nature of the examples you use. You'll want to fashion your presentation around what that particular audience would find interesting and relevant.

The Audience's Culture

Be an Audience Culture Vulture

As a speaker, it is essential to discover as much about the culture and the rules that govern your audience as you can. Quiz a few members of that particular group by asking, "Would XYZ be an appropriate topic to discuss with your group?"

Every group you make a presentation to has its own culture. Corporations have cultures, clubs have cultures, schools have cultures, and so on. Every situation in which you speak has a series of rules and codes. Sometimes, these rules and codes are quite clear, but sometimes they are implicit, unwritten rules. Cultural rules and norms are always well known to everyone within the group, but not necessarily to someone, a speaker, coming into the situation for the very first time. A member of a group may not be able to explain the culture of the group, but he or she will always know when a cultural rule has been violated. As a speaker, it is essential to discover as much about the culture and the rules that govern your audience as you can.

If you don't know the culture of the organization you are speaking to, you can limit your effectiveness and even create serious problems for yourself. If you went to speak to an all-male rugby club, it might be very appropriate to tell an off-color joke. It might even be appropriate to tell a joke that makes fun of women. Imagine how this same behavior would be looked at during a PTA, university, or church group meeting. It is essential to know the culture or climate of the group or organization to which you will make a presentation so you can plan your content and examples to fit in with their culture.

The norms for any situation are tricky because sometimes they dictate what *to do* and sometimes what *not to do*. At the beginning of a speech, the norm in a formal setting may be to acknowledge certain key officials or dignitaries. In some situations, you may open with an introduction, a joke, an announcement, but not with an insult. On the other hand, at a roast or a retirement dinner, opening with an insult may be a requirement. If you are not well acquainted with the norms of the group you will be speaking to, talk to a member of that group or someone who has had experience with them.

SELF-PRESENTATION STRATEGIES FOR DIFFICULT ISSUES

It's easier to be likable and friendly when you are presenting information that ranges from neutral to nice. However, if you are presenting controversial information or disclosing unpleasant facts about yourself, you might need to employ some strategies to get your audience to view you in a more positive light. The following sections provide some helpful information.

Role Distancing

In most cases, you want to show your audience what kind of person you are, but in other cases, you may want to show the audience the kind of person you are *not*. "Role distancing" is what psychologists refer to when someone is attempting to show that they are not part of a group, do not accept a position with which they have been linked, or do not possess a trait they have been associated with. Quite often, we see politicians disavowing associations with groups that have bad or extreme reputations. For example, several years ago, certain members of congress were accused of having ties with ultra right-wing, white-supremacy groups because they were guest speakers at their meetings. It caused quite a scandal, and the congressmen denied the ties quickly, vehemently, and often. If you are going to engage in role distancing, as a rule, it is better to speak against a more abstract position or philosophy than to make a direct, personal denial. For example, if you were somehow linked to having rejected the idea of affirmative action, don't deny that you spoke against it. Instead, talk about its merits and what you like about it. This makes it clear to those who listen that you wouldn't have said anything against affirmative action because your position is clearly for it.

Disclosing Negative Information

Evidence suggests that disclosing negative information early on in a presentation is evaluated more favorably than delaying it. Delaying the disclosure tends to get the presenter evaluated as shady or dishonest.

The sooner you deliver it, the more time you will have to recover and win over the audience. More important, by disclosing it sooner, the audience will not think you were trying to deceive or manipulate them.

Apologies and Admissions

If you have done something wrong, apologizing is an effective technique for gaining favor from your audience. There is a good deal of research showing that people who apologize are viewed more favorably than those who do not. Apologies are also most effective when done quickly. The more responsibility you accept for the wrong-doing, the more favorably you will likely be viewed. Half-hearted and insincere apologies are harmful not helpful, so be genuine.

Self-Handicapping

Always guard yourself against the need to self-handicap by preparing well in advance and practicing frequently!

While not recommended, a technique for dealing with public-speaking anxiety is to give yourself a "handicap"—some believable excuse for a poor performance. This strategy will *never* help you give a *better* talk; rather, it can be used to cushion your fall when your speech or presentation fails miserably. For example, if you gave a bad talk, you can explain it away to others by saying you were on mind-numbing medication for your cold. Other excuses include not having had the time to adequately prepare, a poor night's sleep the night before, or a personal problem. In other words, self-handicapping helps you explain away failure. It works as a safety net.

I worked with a very successful executive who did not enjoy speaking in public. He used an interesting form of self-handicapping. He kept himself under a tremendously busy schedule. His calendar was always full, and he volunteered to take on much more than he could ever handle. He made sure that everyone knew how full his schedule was. When he had to give a speech, people were just glad he showed up. They never expected him to be very prepared. He was too busy for that. He trained people to develop low expectations of him and to be grateful that they got anything at all. Being harried all the time was a very effective strategy for him.

Self-handicapping is not offered here as a strategy for you to use. You should always guard yourself against it by preparing and practicing. But, if worse were to come to worst, you could fall back on it. Just make sure you only fall back on it once. It probably won't work a second time on the same audience.

Admitting Weakness

Often, if a speaker appears weak and admits to it, the audience will be sympathetic. However, don't aim for this by any means. This is simply another way to deflect from a very poor performance. This can help you avoid some audience criticism, but it won't help you achieve your goals and can actually hinder them. This is not a good strategy except under the most *extreme* circumstances. I once worked with a well-known classical cellist who said, "I enjoy performing when I am sick, especially when my symptoms are obvious to everyone, like when I have a bad cold." I asked if being sick diminished his ability to perform, and he said it didn't. He believed the illness worked to bring down the expectation level of the audience and the orchestra he was playing with. He also believed that they now thought he was a real "trooper," not wanting to let the orchestra down. It freed him up to play better because he felt so loose. This might work for the cellist, but I don't recommend trying this at home—or on the speaker's platform.

Using Poor Presentation Conditions to Your Advantage

It's good to know that if conditions are poor in the presentation room, a speaker will get a lot more latitude from the audience. If there is a lot of ambient noise, a failing PA system, or a poor projection device, a poor performance is more likely to be overlooked. More interestingly, there is research to show that speakers performing under poor conditions have decreased anxiety because they can attribute their problems to the distracting environment. If you find yourself in a situation where the presentation conditions are less than ideal, do the best you can and let your audience know that you are trying to compensate for the problems.

WHAT YOU HAVE LEARNED AND WHERE YOU ARE GOING

It helps to know what an audience looks for and how they judge speakers. Take the information in this chapter very seriously. You don't want to become obsessed with what the audience is looking for, but you don't want to ignore it either. Always remember the key word "moderation."

The next chapter takes impression management a bit further—if you want your audience to be impressed with your good sense of humor.

12

USING HUMOR IN PUBLIC SPEAKING

Sigmund Freud said that to get a laugh, a joke needs to create a certain amount of tension. If there's too little, you'll barely get a chuckle. Here's an example of a joke with very little tension: *Ducks go under water to liquidate their bills.* At best, a joke like that will get a groan, and the last thing you want is for your audience to groan! On the other hand, if there's too much tension in a joke, you risk offending your audience, which is something else you certainly don't want to do. (For a painful example of this, see "How I Offended My Audience: Part One" on page 204.)

This chapter will help you understand what humor is all about and how best to use it in your speech or presentation. You'll learn how to select the best jokes for your needs, as well as how to avoid offending your audience—and, if you accidentally do, how you can save face.

HUMOR IS A DOUBLE-EDGED SWORD

It's a great feeling when you know what to say to make your audience laugh. But you must remember that what makes one audience laugh may offend another audience. You must also remember that some of what you and your friends find humorous may not be appropriate for your colleagues or supervisors. If you use fail to use humor appropriately, you can lose your audience—and if you are inappropriate enough, you may even lose your job. When I'm trying to decide if a particular joke is appropriate for an audience, I turn to this old joke for some guidance:

> A little boy picks up a crumbled shirt and shouts to his mother, who is in the next room, "Mom, is this shirt dirty?!" Even though she can't see him or the shirt, she shouts back, "Yes!"

Be Colorful . . . Not Off Color

Most cooks will tell you there's no such thing as a little bit of garlic. Likewise, there's no such thing as a little bit of smut.

Bad joke . . . good moral. The boy's mom knew that if her son was asking if his shirt was dirty, it must be dirty. So, likewise, if I'm asking myself if a joke is inappropriate, it must be inappropriate. If you are even remotely in doubt about the appropriateness of a joke, don't use it. (By the way, not only shouldn't you ever tell jokes in bad taste, but you shouldn't even laugh at such jokes. It's like guilt by association. You will be judged as guilty as the person who told it.)

By this point, you should have a healthy dose of paranoia about using humor in your presentation. But you're probably wondering, *if humor is so potentially lethal to a speaker, why should I even consider using it?*

How I Offended My Audience: Part One

Freud's words—*a joke needs to create a certain amount of tension*—were racing through my head one day as I faced 350 straight-faced people in a lecture hall. What was I lecturing to them about? *How to use humor successfully.* And I was failing miserably! I was supposed to be an expert on the subject, but I wasn't getting *any* laughs. So what went wrong?

Here's a little background: A month earlier, I was hired by the administrator of a conservative religious university to give a talk on the topic of instructional humor—a skill speakers use to get their points across with humor. The administrator cautioned me that my audience would be older, conservative, and religious. I worked very hard to censor my speech, and two weeks later, I delivered a very well-received talk. In fact, it went so well, the administrator asked me to give it again two weeks later. I was very pleased with myself.

A day or two before the lecture was scheduled, I revised the material a bit by adding some new information so it wouldn't seem repetitious to the people in the audience who'd already heard it.

Because my first talk was so well received, I walked out to the podium with confidence. However, within a half hour, it was clear I was dying. That's when Freud's words came to me, and I realized what the problem was. I was being *too* conservative. I wasn't giving them *enough* tension. I was using "liquidate their bills" humor, but they wanted something more intense. At the time I was talking about how an effective form of humor comes from children who misunderstand adult situations. At that point, I decided to add more tension. I did a quick mental calculation and reasoned that they already knew and accepted me, I was a university professor talking to a group of students at a university, and the joke that I was about to tell was only mildly off color but should provide the tension I was missing. I told it. I won't make the mistake of retelling it here.

Imagine the sound of 350 people gasping for air at the same time. I had offended the entire audience. As it turns out, the new audience members were much more conservative than the previous ones had been, and clearly my off-color joke was too much even for the audience members who already knew me from the previous lecture. I made the mistake of creating too much tension. As I finished my talk, which lasted another hour, consisting of complete silence and hostility from the audience, the administrator walked by and handed me a check without even making eye contact.

There is a lesson here. Later in this chapter, I'll tell you what I could have done to remedy that horrible situation.

Here's your answer: If you use humor well, it is a powerful antidote to stage fright. It can give you a great deal of confidence on the speaker's platform. If you know you have material your audience will love, you'll look forward to speaking rather than dreading it. Humor can help you captivate your audience, make you memorable, and maybe even have you evaluated as brilliant and creative. Humor can make important information more enjoyable and can also help clarify difficult concepts. Moreover, if necessary, it can help you diffuse difficult or awkward situations. The following section contains a rundown of the research on the effects of humor, so you can begin to understand its potential.

SOME RESEARCH ON THE USE OF HUMOR

There is quite a bit of research on the effects of humor. The findings are generally favorable. In the discussions to follow, you'll see how humor affects the audience's perception of a speaker, how it can affect one's recall of information, and how it can make a person seem more accessible to others.

> "Once you get people laughing, they're listening and you can tell them almost anything."
> —Herber Gardner

How a Person Who Uses Humor Is Perceived

A few of my colleagues and I recently completed a study in which several hundred people were asked to rate their managers' use of humor, both in terms of how well it was used and how often they used it. What we found is that managers who used humor effectively were perceived by their employees as more intelligent, competent, and creative than managers who didn't.

Our findings concur with similar studies on the effects of humor—it seems most of us just tend to perceive funny people as being a cut above the rest of us. What this suggests is that your audience will see you as more creative, competent, and intelligent if you successfully use humor in your presentations. So, go ahead and make 'em laugh.

How Humor Relates to Learning and Retention

Several colleagues, graduate students, and I performed a series of studies on the relationship of humor to learning and retention. In one of the experiments, two groups of college students received a packet of information that they were instructed to study. The first group received information that included jokes related to the material. The second group received the information without the jokes. Although the jokes did not help the students recall the information, the students who received the humor-filled packet reported that they had enjoyed the task, while the other students did not.

This study notwithstanding, there is a good deal of research showing that university students tend to remember jokes and funny examples much more than they would dry lecture material. But overall, from what researchers have put together, there's nothing magic about humor that makes information more memorable. It does, however, tend to make audiences more attentive, thereby making it more likely that what's being presented will be remembered.

Humor Reduces Anxiety

Humor has been proven time and time again to reduce anxiety. One of the best research examples I know is one in which a university professor created two versions of his midterm exam—one with humorous questions and one with serious questions. His intention was to test out the effects of humor on test anxiety. Although test anxiety can come with a myriad of mental and physical symptoms, the main concern is its effect on one's ability to think clearly and recall the necessary information. As it turned out, the students who received the exam with the funny questions performed much better than the students who took the humorless test. Clearly, the humor had reduced the students' test anxiety.

When you are anxious, humor can come to your aid as well. There is a relatively new phenomenon called "Laughter Yoga" that was started by Dr. Madan Kataria, a physician from Mumbai, India. Laughter Yoga is now practiced throughout the world. Practitioners learn a series of yoga breathing exercises combined with simulated laughter, which often turns into real laughter when practiced in a group. The result is a marked decrease in stress levels. While this is a great way to reduce tension, nothing beats the laughter that erupts when someone says or does something funny.

Self-Effacing Humor Increases Accessibility

If You Have a Self, Efface It!
Woody Allen has made a career out of self-effacing humor with sayings like "Most of the time I don't have much fun. The rest of the time, I don't have any fun at all."

Self-effacing humor—humor in which you make yourself a target—shows that you don't take yourself too seriously. Demonstrating a willingness to laugh at yourself can make you seem more approachable. In fact, my colleagues and I performed a study which found that managers who use self-effacing humor are perceived by the members of their staff as being much more open-minded and approachable than managers who use hostile humor. The study also suggested that a manager's use of self-effacing humor can reduce a worker's fear that a question he or she may ask will be responded to aggressively. Moreover, it can reduce a worker's fear of reporting a mistake. People generally withhold such information from managers who use hostile or aggressive humor out of fear of being humiliated.

Like managers whose employees are not afraid to approach them, speakers who make use of self-effacing humor during a presentation are nonthreatening to their audiences. Not only does the use of self-effacing humor show that a speaker is confident with him- or herself, but it also makes it more likely that audience members will be willing to ask questions and get involved with the presentation—in other words, it gives them more confidence too. This is because they will have no fear of being attacked by the speaker for asking a "dumb" question or for being deficient in some manner. Another benefit of the use of self-effacing humor is that it gives one's audience a feeling of superiority. An intimidating speaker who flaunts his or her talents and intelligence can make the audience members feel worse about themselves. While you want to demonstrate your competence, self-effacing humor helps you show your humility, an admired quality.

> "All higher humor begins with ceasing to take oneself seriously."
> —Herman Hesse

When using self-effacing humor, there's an important rule to keep in mind: be careful to make fun of yourself only in your strong areas. Self-effacing humor in areas of weakness will only amplify your weaknesses or make you seem unsure of yourself.

RECOGNIZING HOSTILE HUMOR

How many people does it take to tell a joke? According to Freud, it takes at least three people: the joker, the jokee (the "butt of the joke"), and a third party, one who acts like a judge. If the judge laughs, the joke is considered successful. If the judge doesn't laugh and declares the joke in bad taste, then the joke is seen for what it is, a direct attack.

Think back to a time when you were the butt of a joke and everybody was laughing but you. You were probably too keenly aware of the hostility behind the joke and how bad it made you feel to find it funny. This is what hostile humor does—it makes people feel bad about themselves. Jokes about sex can also be seen as a form of hostility. For example, a vulgar joke told in mixed company can be perceived as an unwanted sexual advance. This kind of joke can be invasive and injurious and could be taken as sexual harassment in a professional setting. Avoid these jokes.

The following are some examples of relatively innocent hostile jokes. Examine each one and try to identify the target of the hostility.

Q. Why did Mrs. Desberg name her son Peter?

A. Because she couldn't spell "blech"!

_____

Wife to her husband: Your fortune says you are handsome, debonair, and wealthy . . . look, it has your weight wrong too!

_____

Two women approach a golf pro at a city golf course. The pro turns to the first one and asks, "Do you want to learn to play golf?"
"Oh no," she says, "it's my friend here who wants to learn to play . . . I learned yesterday!"

_____

Q. What's the definition of tragedy?

A. A busload of lawyers going over a cliff—and two of the seats are empty.

_____

A consultant is someone who borrows your watch to tell you what time it is . . . and then walks away with the watch.

I hope you could see the hostility in all of these jokes. In each case, there is a clear "jokee"—me, the husband, the golf pro, lawyers, and consultants. Certain professional groups, like lawyers and talent agents, are regularly attacked through hostile humor—a "civil" form of attack. How a joke like this is perceived by the butt of the joke depends on just how hostile the joke is and if the joke was really told in jest.

But I Was Just Kidding

If you ever decide that a situation calls for hostile humor, make sure your joke focuses only on a person's or group's obvious and recognized strengths. Only then will it be clearly taken as a joke.

If you ever decide that a situation calls for hostile humor, make sure your joke focuses only on a person's or group's obvious and recognized strengths. Only then will it be clearly taken as a joke. Numerous people have gotten themselves into trouble by telling hostile jokes, so remember this basic rule: If you don't say it, they can't repeat it, and you won't get into trouble!

If you do not wish to use hostile humor, be very careful to determine whether a joke you intend to tell is a personal attack. The butt of the joke will surely recognize a hurtful joke even if you do not. Also, be sure that the joke is appropriate for you to tell personally; otherwise, it could also be considered a hostile attack. Take the Case of George M., for example.

The Case of George M.

George M. was giving a talk at a psychological convention when he used an old joke by Dorothy Parker, the famous Algonquin Round Table wit. Dorothy Parker had been asked to use the word "horticulture" in a sentence, and she said, "You can lead a horticulture . . . but you can't make her think." When George delivered this joke, the women in the audience booed him and gave him a hostile reception during the rest of his talk. It may have worked for Dorothy, but for George, it was construed as a hostile, sexist joke.

SELECTING JOKES FOR YOUR TALK

I keep a large database of jokes on my computer. When I need a joke for an upcoming presentation, I can search through it by multiple references, You can begin a joke file simply by printing out jokes you like and keeping them in a binder. If you really get into it, you can also create a database. While I prefer to use spontaneous humor, it's good to have some jokes stored up that can help you get an important point across to your audience. The following few sections will help you identify the types of jokes to be on the lookout for and how to make them suit your purpose.

Be on the Lookout for Opportunities to "Joke Switch"

While taking a walk across the "State University" campus (not the university's real name), I met up with the university's baseball coach. We walked side by side for a bit, and I told him the following joke:

A rich Texan called each of his sons into his study one by one. To the first, he said, "Son, I've got all this money, and I'd like to buy you something really nice. What would you like?"

The first son said, "Father, I've always wanted to learn to fly. Can you get me a little single-engine Cessna airplane?"

The Texan went out and bought his son a Boeing 747 jumbo jet.

When asked the same question, his second son said, "Father, I've always wanted to learn to sail. Can you get me a single-mast Sabot?"

The Texan went out and bought his son the Queen Elizabeth III.

When the third son was asked the same question, he said, "Dad, I just came back from Disneyland in Southern California. I'd just love a little Mickey Mouse outfit."

So, the Texan went out and bought his son the "State University" baseball team.

At this, the coach laughed really hard. Nearly breathless, he asked, "Where did you ever hear a joke about the State University baseball team?"

The coach didn't understand the concept of *joke switching*—altering a joke to custom fit a situation. This joke could just as easily have been about the Republican Party, the American Medical Association, or your local cable company. It could be used to make fun of any organization you want to poke fun at. A joke that can be custom fit to your situation makes it a very powerful joke. Be on the alert for jokes like this.

Some shorter jokes can also be altered to fit your needs. Here's an example:

> A man visiting a cemetery notices a tombstone that reads, HERE LIES A LAWYER AND AN HONEST MAN. He goes up to the caretaker and asks, "Say, since when have you been burying people two at a time?"

You've probably heard a huge number of lawyer jokes in your lifetime. Because lawyers generally have a reputation for being dishonest, this joke works well for them. But it could just as easily been a joke about another profession that highlights a negative characteristic associated with that profession. For example, *Here lies a psychologist and a well-adjusted man . . .* or *Here lies a doctor and a humble man . . .* or *Here lies a teacher and a rich man.* In fact, the U.S. Department of Labor's *Dictionary of Occupational Title,* Vols. 1–2, lists thousands of occupations. With this one joke, you can fit it to any one of them. Now that's power! Be careful when using occupational jokes, however, because sometimes the joke may make reference to something that works only for a specific profession—for example:

> A doctor was so egotistical that every time he took a woman's pulse, he had to subtract ten beats for his personality.

Although this joke works for doctors both because they are often thought of being egotistical and because taking someone's pulse is a common part of their practice, it wouldn't work for a carpenter or accountant. The key to joke switching is to match the traits and characteristics of various professions or groups.

Be on the Lookout for Jokes That Help Make Your Point

Be on the lookout for jokes that make your point. You can use the joke as your lead in to the topic you want to talk about. After the joke, you can transition into your message. Here's an example.

An American rowing team was scheduled to race against a Japanese team. Both teams practiced diligently to reach their peak performance levels.

They raced, and the Japanese team won by a mile.

The American team was humiliated by the loss.

The American Corporate Management Group decided they must discover the reason for this humiliation. They hired a consulting firm to investigate the problem and recommend a solution.

Here's what the consultants found: The Japanese team had eight people rowing and one person steering. The American team had one person rowing and eight people steering.

After six months of diligent investigation, the consulting firm concluded that there were too many people steering and not enough rowing on the American team.

The following year, the American team was sure they would win the race. Their team had been completely restructured: they now had four steering managers, three area steering managers, and a new performance review system for the rower to provide work incentive. That year, the Japanese team won by *two miles*!

Humiliated, the American Corporate Management Group laid off the rower for poor performance and gave the steering managers a bonus for identifying the problem.

From here it's easy to launch into topics such as the problem with corporate America. Jokes that make a point often clarify issues for people. Here's one of my favorite jokes. I have used it very frequently in my work as a psychologist.

A man is driving out in the country when he gets a flat tire. He stops his car, opens his trunk, takes out his spare, and then notices he doesn't have a jack in the trunk.

He remembers passing a farm a mile or two down the road so decides to walk there to borrow the farmer's jack.

As he's walking, he starts to think, *What if the farmer doesn't have a jack . . . then I'm stranded out here . . . or what happens if he has one, but won't lend it to me. I've heard that farmers often don't like city folks . . . or what happens if he decides to take advantage of me and won't lend me the jack, but tries to rent it to me? He might charge me $100 just to borrow his jack. $100 for a jack is ridiculous.*

Just then he finds himself at the farmer's door. He knocks and the farmer says, "Hi, may I help you?"

The man says, "Why don't you take your jack and choke on it!"

Remember the discussion about finding alternative explanations in Chapter 3? This is a great example of how the process works. Once I have told this joke, it opens up the whole topic of inner dialogues and how much we can start to believe them when they have no basis in reality. By introducing it as a joke, it makes the concept easier to take in. I also use this joke to talk about motivation, optimism, and pessimism.

Find Jokes That Can Help Ease Negative Emotions and Reduce Anxiety

Using humor to reduce anxiety is one of the best ways you can employ humor in your presentation. All of us have sat in a tense movie and seen the effects of comic relief. Humor gives us a way out of painful emotions. Years ago, I went to hear an R & B singer who was blind. He had to be guided out onto the stage. Before the audience could feel sorry for him because of his disability, he grabbed the microphone and said, "How are you all doing tonight? I'm outa' sight!" While the audience was laughing at this, he quickly added, "The reason I'm feeling so good is that I just got a great new lawyer. This guy has so much clout, he just got me a driver's license!" The audience saw how well adjusted this singer was, and they were able to sit back and enjoy the show. Likewise, in an instructional humor workshop I was giving, one of the participants was paraplegic. He had difficulty using humor in his presentations because people would always feel sorry for him. He learned to begin all his talks with the statement: "It's always a pleasure to address a *pre-handicapped* audience." Not only would this get the audience to laugh and lighten up, it would also get them thinking.

Don't Try This at Home!
George Carlin says, "...it's the duty of the comedian to find out where the line is drawn and cross it." This might work for him and other successful comedians, but always keep in mind that you are a public speaker, not a comic.

Avoid Jokes That Are Discriminatory or Dirty

We have spent a lot of time on this one already, but if repetition is the mother of retention, then this is a mother of a rule. Remember it. In case you need more convincing, here's a good story: Years ago, I was teaching a university course on the use of instructional humor in public speaking. One day I brought in a hilarious, but controversial, George Carlin recording. I had planned to play Carlin's "Class Clown" bit to illustrate the point of the lesson. But after I made my point, I made the mistake of mentioning that Carlin's monologue called "Seven Words You Can Never Say on Television" was also on the tape. "Let's hear it!" shouted one student in the back of the room, and before I knew it, the entire class was chanting, "Let's hear it!"

The next day's news headline ran through my mind: PROFESSOR FIRED FOR SUBJECTING STUDENTS TO OBSCENITIES. "Oh, no!" I said quickly. "I can't play *that*." But this just made the chanting louder. I'm sorry to say I folded under the pressure.

"Class dismissed," I said. "I'm going to stay here and listen to Carlin's seven words. If you *choose* to stay, I can't forcibly make you leave. But, I warn you, this material is *very* offensive." No one moved, and we listened to the entire monologue. When it was over, the class left and I headed back to my office. I wasn't in my office five minutes when I heard a loud knock on the door. My heart started pounding and my face grew hot.

"Who . . . who is it?" I called out.

It was the dean.

As the door creaked open, the headline flashed through my mind again. *Why, oh why, had I given in to the pressure?!*

"Peter," he began. I gulped. "I'm having a small party at my house Saturday evening, and I'd like you to come."

I let out the breath I'd been holding. I went to the party and had a great time, but I learned a huge lesson that day: never do or say anything you don't want to be held accountable for.

LEARNING TO DELIVER YOUR JOKES SUCCESSFULLY

There are many people who believe they can't tell a joke. Some people claim they can't even remember them. Although I've heard comedians say that comedy is a skill that can't be taught and you either have it or you don't, joke telling is a skill that can be practiced. What's left up to chance is whether or not your joke will get a laugh at any particular time. Even comedians believe that there's no way to predict if an audience will find a joke humorous. But the more skill you have, the greater your chances are of getting a laugh. In this section, you'll learn some essential techniques and tips for delivering jokes to maximize the probability of getting a laugh.

Desberg's Law

Every joke is funny . . . if you find the right audience.

Learn a Joke Before Telling It

There are few things more frustrating than listening to someone tell a joke or story and then stop in the middle, groping for details because he forgot some part of it. Often the joke will be over, make no sense, and then a flicker of recognition will come over his face as he says, "Oh yeah, I forgot to mention that he was a . . . " and you receive the part of the joke that would have given the punch line some sense. Be sure to memorize a joke before you tell it, and practice it a few times even before you try it out on someone you know.

If you have trouble remembering jokes, here's how to approach it. First, read the joke below and try to memorize it. Next, cover up the joke and answer the questions that follow to see how well you remembered it.

> One day, three contractors were touring the White House. One was from Chicago, another from Kentucky, and the third from Florida.
>
> At the end of the tour, the official guide asked them what they did for a living. When they each replied that they were contractors, the guide said, "Hey, we need one of the rear fences redone. Why don't you guys look at it and give me a bid." So they went to the back fence.
>
> First up was the Florida contractor. He took out his tape measure and pencil, did some measuring and said, "Well I figure the job will run about $900—$400 for materials, $400 for my crew, and $100 profit for me."
>
> Next was the Kentucky contractor. He also took out his tape measure and pencil, did some quick figuring and said, "Looks like I can do this job for $700—$300 for materials, $300 for my crew, and $100 profit for me."
>
> Then the guide asks the Chicago contractor how much. Without so much as moving the contractor says, "$2,700."
>
> The guide, incredulous, looks at him and says, "You didn't even measure like the other guys! How did you come up with such a high figure?"
>
> "Easy," says the contractor, "That's $1,000 for me, $1,000 for you, and we hire the guy from Kentucky."

"A sense of humor is part of the art of leadership, of getting along with people, of getting things done."

—Dwight D. Eisenhower

Now, cover up the joke and write down the answers to the following questions, and then check your answers: 1) Where were the three contractors from? 2) Where were they visiting? and 3) What part needed repairing?

Here are the answers—it doesn't matter, it doesn't matter, and it doesn't matter. Although this joke takes place in Washington, D.C., you could make the joke happen in Colorado or New York. The part that needed repairing could be any part you want. People waste too much energy trying to remember the joke *just as they heard it*. The most important part of the joke, the one that you *must* remember is the punch line. In this case it was, *"That's $1,000 for me, $1,000 for you, and we hire the guy from Kentucky."* To make it work, identify the elements in the buildup or setup that are necessary. You need the following elements: 1) a place or occupation where you want to show corruption, and 2) amounts that will add up to the final amount. You can select any that you want; just make sure they add up and are substantial enough to be funny.

You can customize everything else to fit the area you want to make fun of. This puts a tiny burden on your memory. The mistake people make is hearing a big laugh and assuming that they must tell the joke exactly the same way. This joke could deal with the high-tech industry, medicine and HMOs, plumbers, or any other industry.

Use the Rule of Three

Basic jokes are structured by the *rule of three*. The rule of three helps you set up a joke structure. In the first part, you establish a pattern. In the second part, you confirm the pattern. In the third part, you violate the pattern with a surprise. Here is an example:

> While commuting into the city, three men were discussing which man's wife loved him most.
>
> The first man said, "My wife says I'm a wonderful dancer, and she wants to go dancing with me every weekend."
>
> The second man said, "My wife says I'm very sensitive, and loves to cuddle with me on the couch and watch movies every night."
>
> "Well," began third man, "my wife loves me so much that she wants me all to herself! Whenever I have an unexpected day off from work and someone comes knocking on the door, she shouts, 'Go away, my husband's home!'"

Almost all jokes are based on being able to see something two ways. In this joke, you are being led through a pattern in which each man seems to be trying to outdo the other. Then, you are surprised and entertained by the third man's gullibility; he totally misunderstands why his wife is shooing away "visitors." In shorter jokes, parts one and two are generally understood and all that's needed is a subject about which we have a preconceived notion, the situation, and the punch line.

Always End the Joke With the Climactic Word

If you tell the punch line before the joke is finished, you'll be "stepping on your own laughs." The punch line should always finish up the joke for the desired effect. Here's an example:

> One day, a man's beloved dog passes away, and he wants to have it buried. So he takes the dog to a Protestant minister to ask if he can bury the dog on the church grounds.
>
> "Blasphemer!" shouts the minister. "You can do no such thing!"
>
> Next, the man goes to see a rabbi to ask if he can bury the dog on the

grounds of the synagogue. Like the minister, the rabbi is terribly offended and asks him to leave at once.

Now, a bit discouraged, the man goes to see a Catholic priest to ask if he can bury his dog on church grounds. Again, the clergyman is greatly offended and shouts, "A dog has no place in heaven!"

The dejected man lets out a deep sigh and turns to leave. Shaking his head, he says, "I wonder if any house of worship will honor my request—and accept the $10,000 donation I was going to make for a proper burial."

"Wait!" shouts the priest, as he rushes toward the man. "Why didn't you tell me the dog was Catholic?"

The key word here is "Catholic," and that is the final word of the joke. Do you think it would make a difference if the punch line was, "The dog is Catholic? Why didn't you tell me?" The same message is getting across, but the person listening to the joke would hear the word "Catholic" and begin to laugh. Then, he or she would notice that there was more and stop laughing to listen, but the joke is already over and so is the laugh. That's what comedians call "stepping on your laughs." It is to be avoided if at all possible. Always edit your punch line to make sure the climactic word comes at the end of the joke. Perhaps a better way to say this is, edit your punch line to make sure that the final word is the one that is *climactic*.

Change Jokes Into Stories

Surprise is a big advantage in using humor. If you start off a joke with an introduction like, "That reminds me of the old joke about . . . " or "Did you hear the one about . . . ," you minimize the surprise. Instead of saying, "A guy walks into a restaurant . . . " you can begin with, "The other day, *I* walked into a restaurant . . . " Turn your joke into a story about you or someone in the audience. It helps get the audience into your joke because they can actually picture someone they know taking part in the story. This will heighten the surprise when the punch line comes.

Don't Laugh at Your Own Jokes

Laughing at your own jokes is an obnoxious habit that seems to offend most audiences.

Laughing at your own jokes is an obnoxious habit that seems to offend most audiences. You might as well say, "Hey, I'm really funny, don't you think so too?" Unless you are in character and have a particular reason for laughing at your joke, avoid doing it. It's a form of bragging. This is not a good way to endear yourself to an audience.

Don't Repeat the Punch Line for a Joke That Works

Some people think that if a joke happened to get a laugh, they can repeat the punch line and get more laughs. They will not. They miss the point that it was the surprise of the punch line, not the punch line, that got the laugh.

Don't Explain Jokes That Don't Work

If you want to get an audience to really dislike you, begin by telling them a joke that is not very funny. Then, when the audience does not laugh, assume that they did not get the joke, and explain it to them. Now, you have not just bored them, you have also insulted them. I have seen audiences turn on professional comedians who did not follow this rule. It was ugly.

Try to Tell Jokes or Stories That Get Laughs on the Way to the Punch Line

Jokes that get laughs on the way to the punch line increase the number of laughs you will get because you do not need a new setup for each punch line. It is very economical. Here is an example:

> John was terrified by the thought of public speaking. After years of nagging, his wife finally convinced him to take a public speaking course. On the first night of class, the instructor explains that he'll be assigning everyone a topic to research and report on the following week. John's topic is sailing. He throws himself into the subject and can't think about anything else. Using his wife as a sounding board, he practices his speech—over and over and over again, until she was sorry she'd ever recommended the course.
>
> The following week, John arrives in class, prepared to give his talk on sailing. He's the first to go. He stands up in front of the class and clears his throat. That's when his instructor says, "Class, I have a surprise for you. Today's lesson is on how to be spontaneous. The topics I assigned you were a ruse. John, your actual topic is sex."
>
> All of John's newfound confidence flies out the window as he begins to haltingly recount the tales of his love life. But he picks up speed and really gets into the topic and wows the other class members with his description of how sex and love have blended beautifully throughout the many years of his marriage. The group was spellbound. John's talk was a success.
>
> The next day, one of John's classmates runs into John's wife at the market.

"You would have been so proud of John's speech. His recount of his firsthand experiences had the class in awe!"

"Really?!" asked John's wife. "But he only did it once.... And he threw up twice while doing it."

Turn Your Head to Indicate the Speaker in a Dialogue Joke

When you tell a joke in which two people are speaking, turn your head from side to side to indicate who is speaking. This will relieve you of the burden of saying, ". . . and then the second guy says to the first guy . . . "It is difficult to follow such jokes, but easy if you use the head turn. Here is a joke with all of the "who saids." First read the joke as it appears below.

Two pregnant women are in the delivery room.

The first one says, "I'm so nervous. Have you ever had a baby before?"

The second woman replies, "Yeah, this is my fourth."

The first woman says, "Really? What does it feel like?"

The second woman says, "Well, take your index finger and put it between your lip and gums, then massage in a slow, gentle circle."

The first woman says, "Ooh, that feels good."

The second woman says, "Okay, now pull your lip over your head."

Now, read the same joke without all of the "who saids." When you turn your head to indicate the speaker, give each woman a different attitude—for example, make the first woman sound really nervous and the second one sound a bit bored. Notice how much better the joke flows when you do this.

Turning your head to indicate the speaker is a very effective way to keep the listener clear on the flow of a joke or story. Practice doing this in front of a mirror or video recorder until it feels natural.

Learn to Recover When a Joke Doesn't Work

Jokes don't always work, so it is essential to learn how to save the situation. If a joke bombs, the audience will generally sense your discomfort and will feel sorry for you. If people feel sorry for you, it becomes difficult for them to laugh at what you say next, and it also makes it difficult for you to be persuasive. *When* a joke fails (not *if*), you must use a *saver*.

A saver is anything you can say or do to distract the audience and keep them from noticing that the joke failed. Once the audience begins to feel sorry for you, it's hard to get them back.

Whenever I speak in front of a group, I always carry a few small pieces of paper in my pocket. If I tell a joke that fails, I immediately make a show of taking one of those pieces of paper out of my pocket, crumpling it up, and throwing it as far as I can. Sometimes, if it was a really bad reaction, I'll say something with it like, "Never use a joke told to you by a [and then I insert a group that the audience dislikes]." Another strategy I use is to come out with a horrible, groaning pun. If I'm a speaker at a luncheon and a joke doesn't work, I'll say, "I don't really enjoy luncheon speaking, I'm just in it for the bread." The audience will then react with a groan or even "boo," but they have now been distracted. They realize I'm in control of the situation and they don't have to feel sorry for me.

Remember my humiliating story at the beginning of this chapter? I told you I would let you know how I *could* have handled it. See "How I Offended My Audience: Part Two" below.

So now that you know a bit about what goes into joke telling, you're ready to learn a joke and deliver it. This is what you'll be doing in Exercise 12.1 on page 220.

How I Offended My Audience: Part Two

When I realized how much damage I had done by telling my off-color joke to the conservative audience, time seemed to slow down. In those excruciating moments, the following saver came to me:

When I give this talk, I usually warn people against telling jokes that are in bad taste. The audience dutifully takes notes . . . which they will probably never look at again. But this is just too important to be dismissed. I wanted to make sure you didn't just hear this point, but also that you FELT it. I wanted you to experience, first hand, how it feels to be on the receiving end of inappropriate material so that you would NEVER make this mistake. Even though this was only an example of what not to do, notice

how uncomfortable it made you feel. And this was coming from a professor. Imagine if you made this mistake OUT THERE. Hopefully, after this intense demonstration, that will never happen to you.

That's what I *should* have said. What I actually said sounded more like, "OK, uh, mmm . . . let's go on." I was stunned, and although I could have said that little speech above, I was worried I might make it worse. Now I'm experienced enough to know that it would have worked really well. Sometimes hindsight isn't that comforting. I still shudder when I think of that incident. *Always* be ready with a saver or two of your own if you are using humor in your presentation.

EXERCISE 12.1. Learning and Delivering a Joke

Identify a relatively long joke that you personally think is funny. (You can use one from this chapter if you'd like.) For maximum effect, edit the joke to fit a particular situation that has some connection to an upcoming presentation you will be giving or just has some relevance to you. Write the joke in the space provided below. Tell the joke to ten people within the next few days. Take note of your comfort level each time you tell it.

_____

_____

_____

_____

_____

_____

_____

_____

_____

_____

_____

_____

_____

_____

Feedback for Exercise 12.1

You'll notice that the first time or two you tell your joke, you get stuck on a word or phrase. As you continue to tell it, whole sections of the joke will begin to emerge smoothly from your lips. Once you've told your joke seven or eight times, you'll probably notice that you've reached a plateau. The delivery of that joke is going to be as good as it gets. That's a good thing.

Take note of the responses you get when telling the joke. Even if you've learned to tell it as well as you can, you'll probably notice that some people laugh at it and some people don't. Don't be discouraged by the people who don't laugh at it. Not everyone has the same sense of humor. But, if you do find a joke that *everyone* laughs at *all* of the time, mail me a copy!

HUMOR AND ACCEPTANCE

Humor can be a wonderful way to gain acceptance from your audience. It is particularly effective in an environment where it is not expected. When you go to a comedy club to hear comedians, the audience frequently has a tough attitude of "make me laugh!" In most cases, however, an audience is very grateful for a chance to laugh. At the university, I find that students laugh appreciatively because their expectation level for being entertained in a classroom is so low. My student evaluations are very highly correlated with the amount of humor I use. In most business situations, humor is even more appreciated.

I look forward to the opportunity to do any form of professional public speaking. After years of experience, I am comfortable doing it and believe that I have something important to say, but that is not why I look forward to it. I believe that I am going to enjoy the experience. I make sure that I will be including material that will please my audience, and while I'm at the podium, I look forward to the next entertaining moment. Using humor is at the pinnacle of such moments. I try to use humor to get my points across and make those points memorable. I also know that my audience will enjoy those times and that is the lure that keeps bringing me back.

My gift to you is a few sample jokes to start your joke file. Use them well:

Move On

If a joke fails to get a laugh, don't fret. It probably just wasn't the right joke for your audience. If the same joke consistently fails, however, it's time to trash it and move on to the next one.

A new manager at a failing company began his meeting by saying, "There are going to be a few changes around here, and I'd like some input from you. Those who oppose these changes may signify their opposition by saying, 'I quit.' "

The better the news, the higher ranking the official who announces it.

Retreat into analogies and discuss them until everyone has forgotten the original problem.

To spot the expert, pick the one who predicts the job will take the longest and cost the most.

People would rather live with a problem they cannot solve than a solution they don't understand.

A true friend will not laugh at your joke until she retells it!

WHAT YOU HAVE LEARNED
AND WHERE YOU ARE GOING

When you are able put humor to good use in your presentation, it can lift what might have been an ordinary speech to new heights. However, when used inappropriately, it can have devastating consequences. Always be wary of the targets of your humor. Learn to identify or create appropriate jokes and stories and practice telling them so you can deliver them successfully in formal settings.

The next chapter applies the principles you've learned so far to a specific setting, the interview. There are several different types of interviews and ways to prepare for them to increase the likelihood of your success.

13

The BIG Idea

The keys to interviewing successfully for a new position are research, preparation, and practice. Take all three very seriously.

INTERVIEWING SUCCESSFULLY

When you go on an interview, you will be the center of attention, and no one is hiding the fact that you're being evaluated. Moreover, the consequences of the interview will most likely be very important to you. These three factors play a big role in stage fright under any circumstances. But in the case of the interview, such factors seem magnified. During the interview, the interviewer or interview panel will be taking notes as you speak. You'll have no idea who else they've interviewed or how you are stacking up. Simply stated, interviews are pressure cookers—CPR training should be mandatory for anyone who takes an interview!

With so much pressure, how can you be expected to walk calmly into such a situation? Well, it should be calming to know that it's a level playing field out there—everyone has to go through the same ordeal when they interview for a position. However, after reading this chapter, you'll have an advantage over them. Why? Because you will be more than prepared for your interview.

In this chapter, you'll learn about the various types of interviews and how to prepare for each. You'll also discover that there's a common set of interview questions and strategies for answering them. Knowing what you're in for will eliminate a good deal of uncertainty and reduce the most common surprises. You'll learn how to create the right frame of mind by doing the appropriate research, by preparing and practicing, and by applying your relaxation techniques. Improving your interview skills can help you reap the rewards of career advancement and professional success.

"For job seekers, the interview represents a time to shine. Thorough preparation . . . is the key to avoiding potential pitfalls."

—Max Messmer

TYPES OF INTERVIEWS

There are many different types of interviews and each has its own characteristics, requiring different types of preparation. In some cases, you may be told what type of interview structure to expect, but other times, it may come as a surprise to you. For example, you may be expecting to be interviewed by one person and arrive at the interview only to discover that there's an interview panel.

If you aren't sure what to expect at an interview, make every effort to find out. If an employment agency or recruiting firm is sending you out on an interview, they will be able to tell you what type of situation you'll find yourself in. If you are interviewing at a company and know someone who works there, ask that person how their interviews are generally structured.

To help prepare you in advance, the following sections discuss the most common types of interviews.

Direct Interviews

In direct interviews, the interviewer follows a list of questions or an outline. Sometimes, he or she will use a formal checklist to score or record the candidate's responses. This rigid structure allows all of the candidates to be evaluated by the same criteria, making it possible to fairly and accurately compare them. This also makes it less likely a candidate can sue for discrimination. This type of interview procedure highlights fairness and gives all candidates the same opportunities.

The downside of a direct interview is that there's less of a chance the interviewers will get to know you personally. So, when you have the opportunity to answer an open-ended question such as "What have you been doing up until now?" or "What are your goals?" or "What can you tell us about yourself?" seize the moment! Express yourself as best as you can and allow your personality to shine through. Because direct interviews are often used when there is a lengthy list of candidates, your major goal is to stand out positively in the interviewer's memory during his or her review of the candidates.

Insert Personality Here
Think about which parts of your personality make you stand out, and figure out how to work them into the interview setting.

Screening Interviews

If an organization is very large, an initial level of interviewing is typically performed by the human resources department to determine an applicant's qualifications. Their job is to filter out candidates who don't have the necessary experience. These are trained interviewers who try to determine, among other things, if a candidate's resume is valid. Moreover, they will have a list of the job specifications and will systematically determine if a candidate meets each of the requirements. Since their main goal is to screen out unqualified applicants, they don't pay much attention to your personal anecdotes and stories. If you're simply not qualified for a position, there's very little chance you'll be able to win them over with your great personality.

There are two keys to performing well on a screening interview. First, present the facts the interviewer is soliciting in the clearest, most direct manner possible. Do not volunteer anything or you risk saying something that inadvertently takes you out of the running. Answer questions directly and be sure to cover every point. Allow the interviewer to lead the interview. In other words, don't attempt to shape or control the interview. Second, maintain a pleasant, nonconfrontational, noncontroversial attitude. Screeners cannot hire you; they can only reject you. If you present yourself colorlessly but competently, you have a good chance of moving on to the next round. However, if you seem like a qualified oddball, you will certainly be rejected.

Screeners cannot hire you; they can only reject you. If you present yourself colorlessly but competently, you have a good chance of moving on to the next round. However, if you seem like a qualified oddball, you will certainly be rejected.

Unstructured Interviews

In an unstructured interview, which is usually less formal than a direct interview, questions tend to be broad and general to get candidates to reveal as much information about themselves as possible. Because this type of interview usually follows a screening interview, it generally indicates that the company already considers you qualified for the position. Their goal now is to investigate your compatibility with the company— that is, how well you might fit in with their organization. In this case, you will usually be interviewed by the manager or managers you will be working under. The format of the unstructured interview can range from very supportive to stressful, but the goal remains the same, to determine if you fit the spirit of the organization.

If you're at this stage, it's no longer necessary to emphasize your qualifications. Your goal should be to establish compatibility. Be professional, while allowing the best parts of your personality to emerge.

Stress Interviews

As the term suggests, the purpose of stress interviews is to see how well you handle stress. This type of interview uses a combination of

"I Don't Know"
Don't be afraid to admit
you don't know the
answer to a question.
Trying to fake it will
likely make you sound
ignorant or dishonest.

challenges, silence, and brusqueness to purposely place the candidate under stress to see how he or she will handle the situation. You may be given examples of case studies, scenarios, or vignettes and asked to explain how you would deal with each situation. The key to performing well in this type of format is to not reveal any signs of stress to the interviewer, no matter how much of it you may be feeling. Fortunately, the stress interview is usually combined with other types of interviews, such as unstructured ones, which will give you the opportunity to relax at least for a few moments while answering questions that reveal your personality.

If a company uses a stress format, it is a good indication that the position you are interviewing for will be very stressful. For example, Susan B. interviewed with a major transportation company and was stunned by the pressure they placed on her during the interview. She ended up getting the job, but was sorry to discover that many of the key administrators had stress-related personal problems and health issues.

Group Interviews

In a group interview, there will be several people interviewing for the position and one or more interviewers. If a company has limited time and resources and there are many candidates, the group format may be used as a cost-effective timesaver. However, the primary goal is to allow the candidates' characteristics and personalities to surface in the group setting. Generally, a leader or two will emerge, shy or unassertive people will stand out, and team players will make themselves known. In some cases, the company will be seeking out the leaders. In other cases, they'll be looking for team players. This is why it's very important to do background research to find out what the company is looking for in an employee. One of your major goals is to be remembered favorably in this setting. Although this should be a goal at any interview, it is particularly important in a group setting.

Board Interviews

In board interviews, which tend to be very formal, one candidate meets with a group of interviewers. As you know, it's important to try to establish a rapport with the interviewer, but this is difficult to do when facing a group of people with different personalities. A good way to determine what's important to each member is to pay very close attention to the questions he or she asks. Since people tend to ask questions about the areas that interest or concern them most, focus on the question and attempt to establish a rapport with that particular person during your response.

Selection Interviews

When you've reached the stage of a selection interview, your qualifications have been acknowledged and you are being interviewed to determine how easy you will be to work with. Your goal is to demonstrate your style and compatibility with your potential manager and coworkers.

A basic rule for a selection interview is to be a polite version of yourself. Don't pretend to be something you aren't. By this time, the company has probably contacted your references and perhaps even former coworkers and managers to get a feel for who you are. They'll want to ensure that you match the profile they have of you (which got you this far in the interview process). Moreover, by presenting your true self, you'll be better able to determine if you'll be happy working with these people.

Some stress may be introduced during the selection interview to determine your compatibility. If you wish to disagree with something you are told, do so in a courteous manner after acknowledging the validity of the other's viewpoint.

COMMON INTERVIEW MISTAKES

There are some common mistakes people make during interviews that guarantee failure. Knowing what they are will help you avoid making them. And knowing that you are avoiding them will help reduce your anxiety level. Let's take a look.

Not Dressing for the Occasion

When you go on an interview, you want to put your best foot forward, and your potential employer is expecting you to do just that. How you present yourself initially tells them just how much you want the job as well as how courteous and respectful you are. Wearing wrinkled, sloppy clothing with scuffed shoes will spell disaster for your chances of landing the job. Likewise, wearing jeans and a t-shirt when a suit is called for is just as bad. Moreover, outlandish clothing and gaudy colors as well as strong cologne or perfume can be a real turnoff. (It's probably better not to use cologne or perfume since some people are highly sensitive to the smell.)

> "Never wear a baseball cap to an interview unless applying for the job of umpire."
>
> —Dan Zevin

Your first step should be to make sure your clothing is clean and pressed and that your shoes are in good condition. When researching the company, make an effort to find out what their dress code is. Many companies pride themselves on their casual style. If that's the case, you'd be better off not showing up in a pin-stripe suit with patent-leather shoes—especially if the CEO is wearing jeans. On the other hand, if the dress code is very formal, it's probably a bad idea to wear a sport jacket or a casual dress rather than the dark suit they're expecting. So, be sure to do your research to avoid this fatal mistake.

Arriving Late

"If, in New York, you arrive late for an appointment, say 'I took a taxi.' "

—*Andre Maurois*

Arriving late for an interview makes for a very bad first impression. Even if you are normally punctual and your tardiness was a fluke thing, the interviewer will assume that timeliness is not one of your strong points. He or she will probably wonder if you'll be able to make it to work on time in the mornings.

To avoid this mistake, confirm the time and place of the interview well in advance. Get directions. If you are unfamiliar with the route, make a test run a few days before. Have an alternate route planned out if there's traffic.

If you do get stuck in traffic, if there's an accident on the road, if the train breaks down, or anything else unforeseen happens that will keep you from arriving on time, call from your cell phone and explain the circumstances.

In any event, plan to arrive well before the scheduled time. You can use that time to look over your notes, to freshen up, or to do your relaxation exercises. If you've taken all these steps and you're still late, apologize profusely and offer a plausible explanation. But better yet, don't be late!

Interrupting the Interviewer

During an interview, one's communication skills come under a magnifying glass. When a candidate interrupts the interviewer, he or she is broadcasting this message: *I'm not a good listener and what I have to say is more important than what you're saying.* This is a very poor way to make a good first impression. Be courteous and listen carefully to what the interviewer is saying. Respond only when he or she pauses to wait for your response. Remember Fran Lebowitz's great quote "The opposite of talking isn't listening . . . it's waiting."

Using the Interviewer's First Name or Asking Overly Personal Questions

Using the interviewer's first name when you haven't been specifically invited to use it is a sign of disrespect. Asking personal questions that center on things such as religion, marital status, politics, controversial topics, or anything of the sort also shows a sign of disrespect and inappropriate familiarity. This is like standing too close to someone you are talking to—it makes them uncomfortable. In some cases, you may not realize a question is overly personal or invasive until you've asked it. So, to avoid this mistake, stick to questions that concern the company and the position you are interviewing for.

Being Inattentive to the Interviewer

Not listening to what the interviewer is saying makes it seem as if you are easily distracted, and if you're not listening, you probably are. You must not permit your mind to wander. First, be sure to get and remember the interviewer's name. Pay careful attention to everything the interviewer says, and allow it to settle in for a moment as you formulate a response. Be specific when answering questions to show that you were listening.

Hard-to-Believe But True Interview Tales

As you well know, the idea of interviewing for a job can be very anxiety provoking. So, let's take a moment out for a couple of stress-relieving laughs. When interviewers from large corporations were asked to describe their most unusual interview experiences, they came up with some extraordinary responses. Here are a few of them:

- A balding interviewee asked to be excused from the interview for a moment. When he returned, he was wearing a toupee.

- An interviewee phoned her therapist during the interview to ask for advice on how to answer certain questions.

- A woman wore a headset to an interview and assured the interviewer that the music she was listening to wouldn't interfere with her ability to hear to the questions being asked.

- An interviewer was challenged to an arm wrestle by an interviewee.

- One applicant said he would like to demonstrate his loyalty to the company by getting a tattoo of the corporate logo.

- One interviewee insisted on standing during the entire interview.

- An applicant arrived for an interview with a large dog in tow.

There's no chance you'll make mistakes like these. The simple fact that you're reading this book shows you care a great deal more about "doing the right thing" than these characters did.

This will give the interviewer the impression that you are sharp, which is one of the key things you'll be judged on during an interview.

Telling Inappropriate Jokes

Using sarcastic, hostile, obscene, or otherwise inappropriate humor will kill the interview and any chance you had of securing the position. Many people use humor to alleviate tension, and when used appropriately, it's a wonderful tool. (See Chapter 12 for more on humor.)

HOW TO CONDUCT YOURSELF DURING THE INTERVIEW

Now that we've covered the most common mistakes interviewees can make, it's time to focus on the correct things to do during an interview. Interviewers have certain expectations and a sense of the appropriate range of acceptable behavior. Knowing where they are coming from will help you interview more successfully. Fortunately, there are some easy-to-remember "rules" for proper interview conduct. A few of the more important ones are discussed below.

Be sure you know the person's name with whom you will be interviewing. Find out his or her full name when you set up the interview or ask the receptionist when you arrive for your appointment. Repeat the name a few times so you don't forget it.

Remember the Interviewer's Name

The first few minutes of an interview are usually the most stressful. This also coincides with the introductions. This stress will make it less likely you'll remember the interviewer's name if you don't already know it. So, be sure you know the person's name with whom you'll be interviewing *before* the interview. Find out his or her full name when you set up the interview or ask the receptionist when you arrive for your appointment. Repeat the name a few times so you don't forget it.

If you cannot learn the name in advance, use it as soon as you hear it. For example, you hear, "Hello, I'm John Sanders." And you say, "Hello, Mr. Sanders. It's nice to meet you."

Remember not to use the interviewer's first name unless he or she specifically invites you to use it.

Make Eye Contact During the Interview

While you don't want to make the person interviewing you uncomfortable by staring into his or her eyes during the entire interview, you must make an appropriate amount of eye contact. Constant eye contact violates the norm and would probably make a person uncomfortable in nearly any situation. No eye contact also violates the norm and will result in a bad impression. In a study of interviewee behavior, the majority of candidates made eye contact with the interviewer 50 percent of the time or less. It was common for the interviewees to make eye contact when questions were being asked and to look away as they began answering them. This is a good "rule" to follow.

The best thing to do is to behave as if you would when conversing with a friend—in other words, doing what feels natural and comfortable. Be sure to practice an appropriate amount of eye contact during your mock interviews (see page 240).

Highlight Your Strengths

By far the most important thing you can do during interviews is to identify your strengths. Use any chance during the interview to present yourself confidently without sounding as if you are bragging. Focus your attention and energy during the interview on making sure these points are brought to light. If you focus on the positive aspects of your presentation during the interview, you'll be less likely to make yourself anxious about difficult-to-answer questions or the things that could go wrong.

Avoid Personal Statements or Credos

Anything that falls outside the appropriate range of acceptable behavior during an interview will likely be defined as problem behavior. If you go out of your way to be different in some outlandish way—in other words, if you try to make a personal statement by deviating too far from the norm—you will greatly spoil your chances of being accepted. Take Alan B. for instance. He wore blue jeans to an interview for a position at a large legal corporation. He wanted his appearance to make this statement: *It's a person's performance that should count, not his appearance.* When he later contacted the interviewer to find out why he was rejected, the interviewer told him he suspected that Alan would always have some cause to champion, which could potentially harm the company's interest or just not help it.

Look Comfortable

Relax your body as much as possible during the interview so you appear comfortable. Holding yourself in uncomfortable positions will make you seem stiff and awkward. However, don't slouch, lean away from the interviewer, stretch your legs out, cross your arms over your chest, or do similar things you might do in a social setting. Find a good balance between professional body language and comfort. Also, take a few seconds for a thoughtful pause before answering a difficult question. During these few moments, take a deep breath or two, and respond to the question on the exhale. Having enough breath available to you during your response will make your voice clear and will show commitment in your response. If you run out of breath during your response, you may sound like you're mumbling. (See Chapter 6 for a discussion on deep breathing.)

Use Humor Wisely

While humor is generally a plus, be careful not to use it insensitively. If the interviewer asks you a serious question, respond in the same serious manner—in other words, don't answer with a joke or make light of the question. If you do, you'll be putting yourself in an unfavorable light.

Also, if you do wish to use humor, be sure to avoid put-down humor. Self-deprecating humor is more appropriate than making a third party your target. Even with self-deprecating humor, however, avoid it in excess. It could be taken as a sign of low self-esteem. Instead, use it sparingly to show that you don't take yourself too seriously in matters where you are obviously competent and secure. (See Chapter 12 for more on humor.)

Maintain Total Honestly but Keep the "Puffery Quotient" in Mind

> "One may sometimes tell a lie, but the grimace that accompanies it tells the truth."
> —Friedrich Nietzsche

Never lie about your qualifications or your past experiences. Dishonesty, once it's discovered, will surely disqualify you. There's an old Slavic saying: "Lies have very short legs." They cannot run very fast and tend to trip over themselves. While keeping this in mind, be aware that a little puffery or exaggeration is okay. For example, if you are asked if you would be willing to work more than forty hours a week, you can simply say "yes" even if you could only see yourself doing this on rare occasions.

Most interviewers expect you to slightly exaggerate your abilities and commitment because virtually everyone does. It is a rare occurrence when an interviewee lives up to all of his or her "promises" on an interview. As a result, an interviewer will most likely "deflate" things you say to compensate for this puffery. If you are totally accurate in all of your responses, chances are you will end up being evaluated a bit south of your true ability.

Use the Full Palette of Presentation Tools

In most cases, you will be only one of many candidates for a position. To set yourself apart from the other applicants, vary the tone of your voice during the interview. You can do this by varying pitch and volume. Far too many speakers only go up or down the equivalent of one musical note in their speech and, as a result, tend to sound robotic. A good speaker will go up or down a full octave to communicate a very important point. As mentioned earlier, listen to the way radio announcers use their voices. Don't worry about the content; just listen for the changes in pitch and volume. Refer to page 176 for more on this tool, and be sure to use it during your interview.

Be Sensitive to the Interviewer

While I was studying Wing Chun, a form of Kung Fu, we'd often practice an exercise called "sticky hands." The partners would press their wrists against each other and move their arms in a circular motion while trying to maintain equal pressure. Too much or too little pressure would allow one's opponent to gain the upper hand and strike a vital target. The only way to protect yourself in this exercise is to match your partner's force exactly. This is a great exercise for developing sensitivity to another person. An interview is the verbal equivalent of sticky hands. If the interviewer is acting light and relaxed, you should try to have the same relaxed attitude. If the interviewer is very formal, try to match that level of formality. If the questions coming at you are very specific, be specific in return.

Interestingly, many Asian businesspeople refer to Sun Tzu's book *The Art of War* as a major reference for conducting business. Being interviewed is hardly a war, but, as described in that book, the idea of being sensitive to the tone, manner, and style of your interviewer and responding in a like manner is essential.

Help the Interview Flow Smoothly

If the interviewer seems nervous or inexperienced, try to help him or her out by bringing up relevant topics. If the interviewer is very domineering, don't compete for dominance. Remember that the interviewer controls the questions, but you control the content through your answers. The interviewer asks questions because he or she is interested in the answers. Make sure you answer those questions directly. If you want to digress or expand on the question, ask permission to go outside of it.

Learn to Deal With Silence in the Interview

Some interviewers use silence as a stress tool. If you give a response that is greeted by silence, do not try to change your view or add to it. This will show a lack of conviction on your part. You have two choices here: Let the interviewer break the silence with a comment or question or ask a related question yourself.

Bring a Pen and Paper to the Interview

Make sure you have the tools for note-taking in case the interviewer asks you to take down some information. Don't embarrass yourself by having to ask for a pen and paper because you've come unprepared. Also, you might want to jot down a note or two before you begin answering a difficult question or a question that contains multiple parts. You can explain that you are doing this to properly organize your response. This shows that you are being thoughtful and methodical, and is another way to show that you will take the necessary steps to get the job done correctly. Then, when you leave the interview, write down any pertinent information you remember while it is still fresh in your mind. You can review it for future interviews with the company.

Have a pen and notepad handy for note-taking during the interview.

When going on interviews, keep all of the above in mind to increase your chances of having a successful interview. Be sure to present yourself in a way that fits the description of the position you are interviewing for and remain within the range of acceptable behaviors. To present yourself in the best possible light, be sure to thoroughly research the company and prepare your responses to interview questions ahead of time. This is the subject of the next section.

RESEARCH AND PREPARATION

In order to be able to effectively interview for a position, you must prepare for the interview well ahead of time. When you show the interviewer that you are prepared, your dedication and good work ethic will shine through. Start by researching the company. Next, prepare your material and familiarize yourself with it. Then, practice your answers by holding mock interviews. The discussions to follow will guide you on your way.

Researching the Company

Your knowledge of the company shows the interviewer just how interested you are in working there. You can demonstrate your knowledge by providing company-specific answers to the interviewer's questions. Being able to do this reveals your desire for the position as well as your intelligence level.

You can do a great deal of your research on the Internet by visiting the company's website. You can also visit your local library and search the indexes for recent newspaper and magazine articles about the company. (Be sure to focus on publications that serve your particular industry.) Moreover, you can ask your friends and/or colleagues in the field what they know about the company. At the very least, be sure to determine the following:

- What is the company's purpose? Do they produce goods or provide services, or both?

- Who are the company's major competitors, and how does this company distinguish itself from the competition? This information is essential if you are asked why you chose to interview at *this* company over others.

- What is the company's reputation is the marketplace? Keep in mind that this can be a sensitive issue. If there are any controversies raging in the marketplace, there's a chance you may be asked for your opinion. It won't bode well for you if you are unfamiliar with the issues. However, if you can offer an informed opinion, you'll come across as sharp and well informed.

- What is the state of the industry? Is the company growing or downsizing? You may be asked for specific suggestions on how you would handle various aspects of growth or decline.

- What are the major books, publications, and professional organizations associated with your field? Knowing the titles and the issues illustrates your serious involvement in your profession. Being ignorant in this area suggests that you have a superficial interest in your field. You may be asked if you are a member in any of these organizations or a subscriber to any of the publications.

- What are the current trends, alternative points of view, and competing theories in your profession? The interviewer may quiz you on this type of information to determine your dedication to your chosen field. Once again, being able to formulate knowledgeable answers to these questions shows your level of intelligence and the amount of time you put into preparing for the interview.

- What are the job specifications for the position you are interviewing for? Try to rank the precise qualities the interviewer is looking for in order of importance. That way you can tailor your responses to better fit the position.

Keep a folder of all the relevant information you gather. Take some time to study it and make notes. This will be extremely helpful as you begin to prepare for the interview.

Preparing for the Interview

Listening carefully to the interviewer's comments and questions is key. Stay focused on what he or she is saying, and ask questions if something is not clear.

There is an old expression in boxing, "Fights are won and lost in the gym." In other words, preparation is key. Once you arrive in the interviewer's office, it's too late to begin preparing answers to important questions. The interviewer will be controlling the interview by asking the specific questions he or she wants answered. Assume the interviewer has a specific purpose for asking the question, and try to answer it accordingly. A perceptive interviewer will note your ability to attend and respond specifically and thoroughly. This is the first indication you'll be giving your interviewer that you can follow directions and produce what is needed.

If some aspect of the question is unclear, ask for clarification. Doing this shows the interviewer that you are not likely to bluff your way through something. It also shows that you're not overly confident, a quality that could result in costly mistakes on the job. Asking for clarification also gives you additional time to frame your response to the question.

It is appropriate to take a few seconds before answering questions. Some interviewees worry that not responding immediately makes them look slow and uninformed, but on the contrary, it makes them look thoughtful and careful. Most interviewers will take this as a good sign.

Since many of the questions interviewers ask are universal, you can prepare your answers ahead of time and practice them. Be sure to formulate your answers so that you can highlight your strengths. Begin your preparation by preparing your answers to the seven most common interview questions, discussed below.

The Seven Most Common Interview Questions

Interviews are simply structured: the interviewer asks questions and you answer them. You can influence the content of the interview by emphasizing your strengths when responding. It helps to know ahead of time what might be asked of you. So, what is an interviewer likely to ask? Let's take a look.

1. Tell me about yourself. Although not phrased as a question, this statement is asking you to tell the interviewer what you consider important about yourself. This is usually the initial interview question. It may be the only opportunity you'll have to highlight what you want the interviewer to know about you. If you have an answer prepared, you'll be able to stick to the important points and avoid awkward interjections, such us "uh," "let's see," and "hmmm."

Generally, the interviewer is just as interested in how you will handle this open-ended question as in the content of your answer. Your style of responding here is very important. Above all, don't ramble. Select three or four highlights of your strengths and abilities and back up each point with an example or two from your past. The more your response can match the mission of the company the better. Some interviewers use this as a base from which they can ask follow-up questions.

2. Explain the conditions under which you left a former position as well as any difficult circumstances you encountered at that company. This can be a tricky question to answer. If you tell the interviewer that you left your job because you were unhappy at that place of employment, you may come off sounding like a hard-to-please person. On the other hand, if you say you liked your job but simply wanted more money or a "better position," you may come off sounding like a self-centered person who puts career ahead of company loyalty.

A good way to explain why you left a former position is to say you left in seek of career growth and additional responsibilities. You can talk about the educational aspects and new level of challenge associated with a new position. The key here is to find a way to reframe the issue in the most socially redemptive way possible. It simply sounds better to say you wanted an opportunity for professional growth rather than a bigger paycheck.

As far as difficult circumstances at a former company are concerned, tread lightly here. Don't go into too much detail. Telling negative stories about past job situations usually backfires. Only mention difficult situations if the interviewer presses very hard. While doing so, be sure to mention that you can only relate the circumstance from your perspective.

If you must discuss difficult circumstances in a former job because of the reference that company is likely to give, be sure to put yourself in the best light possible. If you had a personality clash with a former supervisor or some other difficulty, there are several steps you can take to ensure that his or her reference will not harm your chances of securing the position. See "Potentially Negative References?" on page 238 for some help with this issue.

Don't Quit Until You're In

Ironically, it's easier to get a job when you are already employed. It makes you seem more marketable. So, hold on to the job you have until you are offered a job you want.

Potentially Negative References?

It's virtually impossible to know what a former or current supervisor or manager will say when contacted by the interviewer or the human resources department. If you are concerned that a former boss's reference will cause problems for you, here are a few steps you can take:

- **Do a sample reference check.** Most employers are cautious when giving out references. If a bad reference is given without substantial documentation to back up the negative information, a former employer can be held liable in court. This is good to know. Still, if you're not sure what type of reference your former employer will supply, ask a friend or colleague to do a sample reference check for you. Have your ally contact your previous place of employment as a potential employer to determine what sort of information the company is giving out about you. Having this information beforehand allows you to formulate a response in line with the information the current interviewer will likely receive. If the reference is particularly negative, consider alternate references within the company.

- **Frame the reason for the problem honestly but in the best light for you.** Once you know what your former company is likely to tell a potential employer, make sure your response is compatible with the reference. Since you are the one present at the interview, you can relate the facts in a way that makes you look best. For example, if the person giving the reference is likely to say you were often late for work, you can explain to the interviewer that the traffic on your route was very heavy and you had requested an earlier/later shift but the company was unable to comply with your request. Make it a point to say that you often stayed late at the office or worked through part of your lunch to make up the time. Problems like tardiness are not easy for an interviewer to overlook, so if you can avoid giving that particular reference, do so. But, if you have no choice, be prepared to offer a plausible explanation.

- **Accept responsibility for past problems.** If, when checking your references, the interviewer is likely to find out that you had problems with supervisors or colleagues, you'll want to mention this. Without becoming defensive, briefly explain the role the other person played in the conflict. Also, be sure to accept some of the responsibility—for example, "I could have tried harder to . . ." Then point out how you would handle the situation differently based on what you learned from the situation. This shows the interviewer that you can admit you are fallible and that you learn from your mistakes.

- **Admit that you are uncomfortable with a particular question.** If you are asked a specific question about your former colleagues or boss that you feel you can't or don't want to answer, don't be evasive or cute about it. Specifically explain why you do not wish to answer it. For example, you can say, "I'm not comfortable discussing personality-related issues concerning my colleagues and/or boss, but on a professional level, I made every effort to work with them for the common good of the company."

The truth is, reference checks are a big part of hiring process. If there are problems with your references and you can't find alternate references, make sure you deal with them directly during the interview. Be sure to do this without coming across as a "problem employee." If you badmouth a former employer, you're the only one who will look bad.

3. Why do you want to work in this field or in this particular position? With this question, the interviewer's goal is to discover what motivates you and how motivated you are to work in the field or at the company. This question gives you an opportunity to present any anecdotes concerning what drew you to this area. It also gives you the chance to identify specific talents or skills you wish the interviewer to note. Moreover, you can use this opportunity to show how extensive your research was as well as how relevant your experience is.

4. Why do you want to work for this company specifically? When you answer this question, you have another opportunity to demonstrate your research and preparation. It is your chance to show that you have looked into this company and why you believe it is a good fit for you.

5. What are your career objectives? Your answer to this question reveals your level of aspiration. It can give the interviewer some insight into how long you would stay with the company if hired. It's a good idea to sound both ambitious and loyal to your potential employer, so you will need to prepare a well-balanced answer. If you've done your research, you should be familiar with the opportunities for growth in that company. Emphasize your desire to learn all you can from your new position and explain how that will help you grow and reach new heights within your profession. Mention a specific position you could see yourself filling in the future. Give the interviewer the impression that you see yourself going places, specifically within the company. Above all, avoid sounding like you have little or no ambition. If you do, you probably won't be considered a good "investment."

6. What are your unique qualifications? While this question gives you the opportunity to brag about yourself, it is important to frame your response in such a way that it doesn't sound like you're bragging. Try to sound self-confident without coming across as being too impressed with yourself. Rather than simply listing your qualifications, draw on your research concerning the specific job requirements. Then, discuss your abilities as they relate to the job requirements.

7. What are your strengths and weaknesses? This is a very common question. Identifying your strengths should be easy enough, and you have basically been doing this as much as possible during the interview. The difficult part is identifying your weaknesses.

It's a very bad idea to tell the interviewer that you don't have any weakness or that you can't think of any. This is a weakness in itself—that you don't have the awareness or self-knowledge necessary to identify your shortcomings.

Don't Compete With the Interviewer
If the person interviewing you asks about your aspirations, it's a very good idea to avoid mentioning you'd like his or her job someday—even if it's true.

You must find at least one "good" weakness to present. It shouldn't be too bad or extreme. Admitting to a serious weakness is a sure way to miss out on getting the job. For example, you'd never want to admit to being a substance abuser or that you have a tendency to pilfer supplies.

The basic rule here is to present a weakness with a plan for how you are dealing with it. It gives you the opportunity to show that you are always looking to improve. For example, you might mention that you are unfamiliar with all of the aspects of a computer program you are required to know, but then follow that up with a brief description of the actions you are taking to learn the program.

Of course there is no way to predict all of the questions you will be asked during an interview. The seven discussed above are among the most common. If you know someone who has been interviewed by the company, ask what questions they were asked and prepare for any that weren't covered above. Once you've prepared your answers, you'll need to practice your responses. You can do this by setting up mock interviews (see "Going on Mock Interviews" below). Still, no matter how prepared you are, there will be some lingering anxiety. So, let's focus on that aspect of the interview process in the following section.

MANAGING INTERVIEW-RELATED ANXIETY

As you know from earlier chapters, simply experiencing the symptoms of anxiety can increase your level of anxiety. You tell yourself that if you're that nervous, there must be a valid reason, and you get even more worked up. Believing these symptoms are obvious to others can further increase your anxiety. Then, thinking those symptoms will be taken as a

Going on Mock Interviews

The best way to practice is to simulate the interview situation as closely as possible. For starters, have a friend or family member ask you the common interview questions at the kitchen table. Respond as if you are on the actual interview.

After doing this several times, ask a colleague to give you a practice interview in his or her office. Dress the part to make the situation seem more realistic. After a few mock interviews of this sort, consider applying for some jobs you don't necessarily want just to get in some real interview experience. Also, consider going to an employment agency or a recruiter's office where you will be interviewed before being sent out to other companies. The more you practice, the more comfortable you will be during the actual interview.

sign of incompetence or a lack of confidence can make the anxiety even worse! But don't fret too much. The interviewer expects you to be nervous. It's how you handle it that counts. Take the Case of Stuart P., for example.

The Case of Stuart P.

Stuart P., a manager at a high-tech company, was ready to move up and was about to go on a round of interviews for the position of project manager. This position would require him to conduct weekly staff meetings. Since Stuart had a fear of public speaking, he came to me for help preparing for this aspect of the new position. But, as it turned out, Stuart was getting anxious about the interviews themselves.

We focused on Stuart's main symptom of anxiety—profuse sweating—because that's what caused him the most distress. Whenever Stuart was put on the spot or it was his turn to speak at meetings, he would sweat so much that moist rings would appear under his arms and his forehead would bead up with perspiration. In fact, he'd become so tense that just waiting for his turn to speak would make him sweat. To counter this, he'd wear extra layers of clothing to soak up the sweat, but this only made him warmer and caused him to sweat even more. He'd spend so much time willing himself not to sweat that he'd lose focus and would always be somewhat startled when he was called on for an opinion or information.

I suggested that Stuart attend his next meeting without trying to hold back the sweat. "Just let it go," I told him. Stuart was stunned that I hadn't given him some suggestions on how to control his excessive perspiration. He imagined that "letting it go" would translate into torrents of sweat. I explained that in trying so hard not to sweat he was actually using valuable energy that made him sweat even more.

At the next meeting, Stuart released himself from trying to prevent the sweat from coming. As a result, he was more relaxed and actually produced less sweat than he normally would have.

During a later session, we talked about why Stuart was so afraid of people seeing him sweat. He told me he believed that sweating was a sign of insecurity, vulnerability, and incompetence. I suggested alternative explanations for why people sweat—for one, because they are warm or hot. I also asked him if he'd ever seen a great performer—Elvis Presley, for example—sweat on stage. He said he had. When I pointed out that Elvis wasn't insecure, vulnerable, or incompetent when he performed, Stuart began to understand my point. Sweating didn't have to be associated with the negative traits he had assigned to it.

Just before Stuart began the series of interviews for the new position, he developed a routine. He planned to dress in the lightest clothes possible to prevent becoming overheated. He would also have a handkerchief handy to dab his forehead if necessary. He also practiced deep breathing and relaxation exercises daily, and planned to do them for five to ten minutes before his interviews. He also used imagery to practice "going with" his physical anxiety symptoms instead of fighting them. Every day, he imagined he was on an interview. When he would feel himself becoming anxious, he'd let his symptoms just happen. To his surprise, he discovered that they would diminish rapidly.

Stuart successfully interviewed for the position of project manager, and later, he held his weekly staff meetings with confidence.

The technique I had Stuart use is called "paradoxical intention"—a therapeutic technique in which the practitioner deliberately experiences or intensifies his or her symptoms to get them under control. In this case, you'd simply allow your anxiety symptoms to occur without trying to eliminate them. This will get you more used to them and how they make you feel. Surprise is a great thing for birthday parties, but you'll want to experience as little of it as possible during your interviews.

In Exercise 13.1, you will use the paradoxical intention technique to accustom yourself to your physical symptoms of anxiety. Rather than dreading them, you will actually try to accentuate them to help you get accustomed to them. Furthermore, you will see that by letting them occur, and even exaggerating them, it will actually lessen their effect on you.

EXERCISE 13.1. Using Paradoxical Intention

As you know from previous chapters, the way you manifest anxiety is unique to you, although there are many similarities among cases. In this exercise, modeled after the one suggested by Eloise Ristad in her book *A Soprano on Her Head*, you will be working with your particular case of interview-related anxiety. Begin by describing your symptoms of anxiety in the space provided below.

_____

_____

_____

When you practice your mock interviews, focus on your symptoms of anxiety. Look for them, and when you recognize them, try to intensify their effects. For example, if your hands shake slightly, will them to shake even more. If you begin to perspire, feel the sweat and imagine it pouring from you in streams. Whatever symptoms you experience, intensify them. Record the outcome in the space below.

_____

_____

_____

Feedback for Exercise 13.1

If your mock interviews are not causing you to feel the symptoms you think you'll experience on the actual interview, simulate the physical symptoms of anxiety by jogging in place. When the mock interview begins, you'll be flushed, out of breath, and weak in the knees. Practice interviewing under those conditions. When you go on the interview, your anxiety symptoms will feel like "old friends," and you'll know how to conduct yourself to counter their effects on you.

Even though you are relatively safe interviewing for a job, the situation is usually intimidating and nerve-wracking. If you practice interviewing while experiencing the symptoms of anxiety at their most severe, it will be easier for you to present yourself calmly and clearly during the actual interview.

Practice Your Relaxation Skills

When faced with an upcoming interview, put your deep-breathing and relaxation skills to good use. Practice the exercises described in Chapter 6 regularly. Then, a few days before the interview, visualize yourself in the reception area. Picture the setting—where and how you will sit, the receptionist, the lighting, the carpet, and so on. Visualize yourself calm and relaxed while you wait to be interviewed. When you arrive for the interview, visualize yourself relaxing at home. As you wait, release any tension in your muscles and take deep breaths to keep your mind alert.

You'll be surprised by how much pressure being able to relax in this setting takes off of you. If there's anything specific that helps you relax, do this activity the day before the interview. But be sure to avoid anything that may interfere with the interview even if you find it calming. For some examples, see "Beware of Comfort Foods and Habits" below.

RETHINKING YOUR INTERVIEW-RELATED FEAR-PROVOKING THOUGHTS

You've done a lot of work in this chapter to prepare for your upcoming interviews, and I'm certain you're feeling much better about the situation. You probably had a decent list of interview-related fear-provoking thoughts when you first turned to this chapter. In Exercise 13.2 on page 244, you'll have the opportunity to rethink those fear-provoking thoughts and come up with some positive predictions.

Beware of Comfort Foods and Habits

In an effort to calm yourself down before going on an interview, you may be tempted to turn to some deeply ingrained habits that bring you comfort—for example, eating certain foods, drinking alcohol, smoking, or chewing gum. Beware, however, that some of these habits can interfere with a successful interview.

For starters, eating sticky foods such as bananas or peanut butter just before an interview can interfere with smooth speech. It makes a lot more sense to eat something that lubricates your mouth, such as grapes. It's also a good idea to drink water, but watch out for bubbly water and other carbonated beverages. The carbonation can produce embarrassing gas—something you should definitely try to avoid during an interview.

Never smoke or chew gum during the interview, no matter how much these habits calm you. If you are a smoker, make sure you don't reek from smoke when you arrive for the interview. And, whatever you do, don't drink alcohol prior to the interview to alleviate your anxiety. Even having an alcoholic beverage the night before your interview can negatively influence your performance.

EXERCISE 13.2. Rethinking Your Interview-Related Fear-Provoking Thoughts

In this exercise, you'll be using the techniques you learned in Chapter 3 to identify counterevidence to refute any fear-provoking thoughts you have about interviewing for a job. Be sure to recall other job interviews in which you thought you did well to counter your negative predications. If interviewing for jobs is a new experience for you, you can use similar situations in which you feel you succeeded to dispute the validity of your fear-provoking thoughts.

1. Record your interview-related fear-provoking thoughts in the space below. Some examples might be "I won't be able to express myself clearly," or "My strengths won't be obvious enough," or "I don't know anything about the company."

   _____

   _____

   _____

   _____

2. For each fear-provoking thought, try to recall instances where that fear-provoking thought turned out to be a false alarm. For example, if you fear you will be unable to articulate your responses to the interviewer, record an occasion when you were able to respond to questions clearly and succinctly. If you feel you will be unprepared, be sure to record how much research and preparation you've done for the upcoming interview.

   _____

   _____

   _____

   _____

3. Challenge any all-or-nothing thoughts. If you're thinking that this will be your only opportunity to get a job like the one you're interviewing for, put things in perspective by identifying other companies that have similar job opportunities. Moreover, identify the many "one-in-a-million" opportunities you have experienced to date—there are probably very few. This should help you label this opportunity as "important" rather than as "crucial."

   _____

   _____

   _____

   _____

   _____

4. If you have experienced job-related disappointments or failures, try to identify the good things that came from it. For instance, if you had gotten that job working in the city, you may never have moved to the country where you are very happy. In other words, look for the silver lining.

_____

_____

_____

_____

_____

Feedback for Exercise 13.2

It's quite likely that several of your interview-related fear-provoking thoughts are the same or similar to the ones you identified in Chapter 2. As you prepare for each interview, keep a journal of your fear-provoking thoughts along with any information from your own history that reduces their validity.

Also, be sure not to overestimate the importance of any one interview. Push yourself to recall other instances in which you thought an opportunity would never come again and identify the accuracy of that assessment. Were you accurate? You may strongly believe that this particular interview is a once-in-a-lifetime shot, particularly if you got the interview through personal or family connections, or you happened to be at the right place at the right time. Put it in perspective. If it's meant to be and you prepare well, it should work out. If not, think about what you can learn from the experience and keep your eyes open for similar opportunities.

Although it isn't always pleasant to think back to failures and disappointments you have endured, try to identify something good that came out of them. Did you learn a valuable lesson? Did you come to any important realizations? There is a wonderful saying that covers this situation very nicely: "Experience is a lousy teacher . . . it gives the exams before the lessons."

THE WORST-CASE SCENARIO— IF ALL DOESN'T GO WELL

If you don't get the job, try not to personalize the results of the interview. There are many reasons why you may not get selected for a job, even if you interviewed well. For starters, the interview might have been conducted as a formality—the company could have had someone in mind to fill the position. In many cases, public companies and government offices must do a nationwide search due to contractual obligations, even though they intend to hire someone from the inside. In other cases, one of the candidates may have been more qualified than you. This doesn't mean you did anything wrong. It simply means that, on the surface, that person seemed better suited for the job.

The more insecure and vulnerable you are, the more you will want to self-blame and personalize the rejection. Try to overcome this. It is essential to judge your performance during the interview rather than the results of the interview. As you know, only your performance is directly under your control. If you don't get hired, ask for feedback and use it to improve your skills.

Self-reflection is also helpful and will make your next interview stronger. When you don't get a job, it can mean one of two things: 1) You were qualified, but someone was more qualified, or 2) You were deficient in some way. It is a good idea to take a careful look at the job requirements and determine the extent to which you fulfilled them. Next, play back the interview in your head and think about whether there was anything you might have done that kept you from succeeding. Self-reflection can sometimes be painful, but it often proves very helpful in your preparation for the next interview.

If you do very badly on an interview, it is extremely important to be forward-looking. You must think about how you will prepare differently for the next one. The best way to look for this information is by closely examining this interview. Try to list all of the "mistakes" you made so you can avoid repeating them. For example, if you determine that your research was inadequate, do more research the next time. If you felt unable to withstand the pressure, you may want to practice with more mock interviews and have the mock interviewer grill you even harder. You might also want to try going on interviews for jobs you don't necessarily want just for the practice. Good luck!

WHAT YOU HAVE LEARNED
AND WHERE YOU ARE GOING

Although you're not up on stage when you're being interviewed, it can certainly feel like it. Your audience of one can be just as terrifying as an audience of fifty. Compounding this fear is the fact that the stakes are generally higher because the consequences of your interview can affect your livelihood and future. The greater the risk, the more fear you will experience.

It should be clear that the key to overcoming interview-related anxiety is adequate preparation. And this is true for all forms of stage fright—even stage fright that occurs in social situations, better known as shyness. That's the subject of the next and last chapter.

14

The BIG Idea

By practicing basic social skills and preparing for social interactions, you can manage the effects of shyness and learn to "sound good" in social situations.

OVERCOMING SHYNESS

lthough most shy people have a fear of public speaking, not all people with a fear of public speaking are shy. Like stage fright, shyness is usually the result of fear-provoking thoughts, including the fear of being judged or evaluated in a negative way—in this case, in social situations. The stage fright that wells up in a person with a fear of public speaking when faced with speaking to a group in a formal setting is the same type of fear a shy person feels when he or she must speak to others, sometimes even just one person.

In *Self-Consciousness and Social Anxiety*, social psychologist Arnold H. Buss, Ph.D., points out that, in most cases, a shy person's fear-provoking, negative thoughts center on low self-esteem. Philip Zimbardo also acknowledges this relationship in his excellent book, *Shyness: What It Is, What to Do About It.* For a deeper look at shyness and low self-esteem, consider reading these two excellent books.

You may be surprised that shyness is actually a common trait. According to Zimbardo, 80 percent of people who took the Stanford Shyness Survey in the late 1970s reported being shy at some point in their lives. Forty percent reported being presently shy. That comes down to four out of ten people, or approximately 120 million people in the United States. Of this 40 percent, 25 percent reported being chronically shy. That's quite a large number of people who are afraid to share their feelings, thoughts, and observations with others.

Chances are if you're reading this chapter with great interest, you are one of those people—and this means that your fear of public speaking isn't limited to the podium; it occurs in many types of social situations. This chapter is designed to help you overcome this fear. You'll learn that

> "The way you overcome shyness is to become so wrapped up in something that you forget to be afraid."
>
> —*Claudia Lady Bird Johnson*

you can prepare for social interactions the same way you would if you were making a presentation to a group. When it comes to shyness and a fear of public speaking, the lines get blurred. If you are trying to get new clients by courting them with lunch dates, you are making a presentation. You are also making a presentation if you are asking your boss for a raise, asking someone out for a date, or just simply trying to make friends and acquaintances. Let's begin this chapter by taking a look at a classic case of shyness.

A CLASSIC CASE OF SHYNESS

Being shy can affect your life in many ways, even in ways that you aren't aware of. You are about to meet Stacey G. She was unaware of how her shyness was dictating who she would or would not let enter her life. This case shows how shyness can literally shape your life, even without your knowledge.

The Case of Stacey G.

Although Stacey G. initially came to me to regarding a fear of public speaking, it soon became clear that her problem was deeper than that. During one of our sessions, she blurted out an interesting lament: "How come the only men I ever attract are pushy, aggressive, and insensitive?" Very rarely were questions this easy to answer. In the two months since we'd been working together, we hadn't made eye contact more than five or six times—and the few times we did, it was fleeting. During our sessions, Stacey would practically curl up into a ball on the chair with her legs pulled up under her and her arms wrapped around her knees.

No matter where Stacey was, her outward behavior was the same. She would look down and avoid making eye contact with anyone in the room. If a nice young man wanted to meet her, he'd have to wait a long time for the opportunity to "catch her eye"—and, in most cases, that opportunity would never come. So what kind of men would be able to break through Stacey's carefully erected social wall? The type that doesn't need the reassurance of a friendly smile or prolonged eye contact. The only men brave enough to approach an unapproachable woman were pushy, aggressive, and insensitive. This answered Stacey's question. By becoming aware of this, Stacey became motivated to make herself more socially available so it would be more likely that the types of people she wanted in her life would approach her. We worked on simple behaviors like making eye contact and smiling. She soon discovered that this approachable behavior paid off handsomely. She extended some of these principles to her fear of public speaking, and we had killed two birds with one stone.

SHYNESS VERSUS A FEAR OF PUBLIC SPEAKING

Although stage fright is more common than shyness, the two are closely related. In fact, both are often classified under the general heading of "social anxiety" or "social phobia." Shyness generally comes into play in social situations that require a mutual give and take or any type of interaction with people. Stage fright, on the other hand, usually involves a single performer and an audience, with limited interaction. Still, when given a choice, most people would rather interact with a stranger than speak in public. But this isn't necessarily true for someone who is shy. Although they share the fear of negative evaluation, the roots of shyness are deeper than the fear of public speaking. And while avoidance of stage fright by not speaking in public can have negative consequences on certain areas of one's life, avoiding common social interactions due to shyness can affect nearly every aspect of one's life and seriously threaten the quality of that life. Clearly, shyness can have more serious and frequent negative consequences than a fear of public speaking. If you are shy and want to overcome or manage it, you'll need to understand what shyness is all about. Let's take a look.

> "My first language was shy. It's only by having been thrust into the limelight that I have learned to cope with my shyness."
> —Al Pacino

WHAT SHYNESS IS ALL ABOUT

According to studies performed by Arnold Buss and colleagues at the University of Texas, shyness is not due to a desire to avoid people, as you probably know. On the contrary, shy people want to be with other people; they are just afraid to interact with them. Shyness is a feeling of varying degrees of discomfort in social situations, particularly with unfamiliar people. It can be expressed three ways: by emotional reactions, by fear-provoking thoughts, and by a failure to interact.

Shy people usually experience two types of emotional reactions—fear and self-consciousness. If fear is the predominant trait of shyness, the sympathetic nervous system reacts with quickened heartbeat, elevated blood pressure, and sweating. It is a mini fight-or-flight response. On the other hand, self-consciousness as the predominant trait of shyness doesn't get the body into high gear for a fight-or-flight reaction. It has an opposite effect: it freezes you in your tracks like a deer in headlights.

When a shy person finds him- or herself in an anxiety-provoking social situation, thoughts ranging from panic to fear are not uncommon. That person may also worry about upcoming social situations. Self-consciousness can cause one to feel exposed and vulnerable in the presence of others. Worrying about being inept and doing something wrong or embarrassing may take over. When a person is this self-conscious, it's likely that these worries are being exaggerated.

In groups, people who are shy usually stay on the fringe and respond to others in the most minimal ways. When someone asks them a question, they speak softly, may even mumble, and often give one-word answers to questions.

Novelty is the leading cause of shyness. New people and new situations will heighten the novelty of any situation. Even if you don't consider yourself a shy person, you've probably experienced it yourself—for example, if you've ever moved to a new neighborhood or started a new job where you met many new people, you probably found yourself being shy or reserved. The more you assume new social roles, the more the novelty (and shyness) increases.

There are four major factors that seem to be involved in shyness— 1) a fear of people, 2) a fear of a negative evaluation in certain situations, 3) having low self-esteem and feelings of unworthiness, and 4) a perceived lack of social skills. Let's take a look at them.

A Fear of People

Shyness is basically a fear of people, or specifically strangers. This is illustrated by the results of Phillip Zimbardo's survey of hundreds of college students: 70 percent reported feeling shy around strangers, and 68 percent reported feeling shy around members of the opposite sex. When it came to authority figures, 55 percent of the students reported feeling shy around them by virtue of their knowledge. As you know, the fear of negative evaluation plays a strong role in shyness and in stage fright in general. Because authority figures are good at identifying an inadequate performance, it's no surprise they elicit shyness so frequently.

How many times have you avoided doing or saying something because you would be observed by complete strangers? How many times have you found yourself clamming up in the presence of an authority figure? If this a frequent occurrence in your life, you're probably relieved to know that you're not alone. More than half of the students surveyed—as well as countless other people—know how you feel.

A Fear of Negative Evaluation in Certain Situations

As a general rule, as the formality of a situation increases, shyness increases with it. Formal situations in which shyness is greatly intensified may include graduations, funerals, weddings, and public events. When there are many rules of etiquette and instances in which they must be followed, there is a greater fear, and likelihood, of saying or doing the "wrong" thing. These situations can lead to feelings of exposure and humiliation. For instance, fumbling with your words around a grieving widow, especially if other people are present, can be very embarrassing, and thoughts of that "ridiculous" thing you said in front of "all those people" can be persistent.

It's likely that the more public an event is, the more exposed and vulnerable you will feel. This is because there are more people around to judge how you behaved or what you said or didn't say. Also, gatherings in which there is a lot of social attention or none at all can also intensify shyness. Being overlooked at a party can be just as difficult and embarrassing as being in the spotlight.

It should also go without saying that a breach of privacy can invoke shyness—in anyone. If you are doing something you would normally do in private, and suddenly the public/private barrier is somehow lowered, you would surely suffer a great deal of embarrassment.

Low Self-Esteem and Feelings of Unworthiness

People who have a low self-esteem and/or feelings of unworthiness tend to be less willing to interact with others. If you have such feelings, your predictions concerning the outcome of your social interactions tend to be negative. If your head becomes full of fear-provoking thoughts—*I'm not as sophisticated as that group of people* or *I'm not as smart as that person* or *I'm just not as pretty as those women*—you'll scare yourself so much that you won't even give yourself a chance to socialize. For example, if you think you are particularly unattractive, you might be afraid to ask someone you think is attractive out on a date. If you've convinced yourself that you're boring and have nothing important to share, you'll avoid intimate dinner parties. In fact, low self-esteem and feelings of unworthiness will have you avoiding countless social situations. Again, if you recognize yourself here, you may want to look through the two books mentioned earlier.

A Perceived Lack of Social Skills

In our society, social skills are very important. Being able to interact with people is a virtual necessity of life. Shy people often believe that they lack social skills, which causes them to feel inadequate or deficient. In many cases, they simply do not have enough experience socializing to have the proper skills. Fortunately, social skills can be learned. The Case of Steve N. is a classic example of someone who lacked experience with social encounters and, as a result, lacked the necessary skills to feel comfortable in social situations.

You Can Do It . . .
With Some Practice
Shy people often believe they lack social skills, which causes them to feel inadequate or deficient. Fortunately, social skills can be learned and practiced.

The Case of Steve N.

Steve N. was brought up in a family where a lack of intimacy and communication was the norm. As a youngster, he preferred the company of machines to other kids. As an adult, he chose the solitary profession of an accountant, where most of his interactions would be with computers and numbers. Although he eventually married and had three children, he was an outsider in his family unit. His wife and children complained of his lack of emotion toward them. When things got emotionally tough, they said, he'd go work on his computer. What made matters worse in the eyes of his family was that Steve had no problem being extremely affectionate with the family dog.

During our first session, Steve clearly stated that he felt very awkward in social situations, so it was much easier to deal with the consequences of walking away than looking awkward and being embarrassed. He avoided interacting with people because he believed he'd lose more by communicating badly than by not communicating at all. This major skill deficit needed to be resolved for Steve to have a fulfilling family life.

Steve's upbringing by parents who lacked intimacy and communication skills is consistent with research showing that parents with shy children tend to be shy themselves, while parents of uninhibited children do not tend to be shy. In *Frames of Mind*, psychologist Howard Gardner discusses a specific form of social IQ referred to as "interpersonal intelligence," which seems to have some genetic basis. Through information like this, Steve came to understand that his shyness was probably due to how he was raised combined with his genetic structure. He believed that this was something he could learn to overcome.

With a little help, Steve started talking to his family members one at a time to make a connection. He stayed away from emotionally charged topics at first. Then, he began taking some small risks and saw that nothing bad happened to him as a result. Eventually, Steve graduated to participating in "family talks" about difficult issues.

As it was in Steve's case, shy people often exaggerate how others will perceive their efforts at social interaction and, therefore, fail to take even the slightest risks. But to overcome shyness you need to take risks, and you can do this in small steps by setting achievable goals. There will be more on goal setting later in the chapter. For now, I want you to consider the consequences of shyness so you can set your mind to avoiding them.

HOW SHYNESS CAN AFFECT ONE'S LIFE

If shyness is permitted to go unchecked, and becomes more ingrained and chronic, it can eventually lead to loneliness and depression. People who are shy generally hold back in their relationships and, as a result, tend to have fewer friends and romantic partners. They usually keep their feelings, wants, and even their complaints to themselves, and prefer the security of not asking or telling over the risk of getting hurt. They often choose protective isolation because they feel their reactions in social situations are inappropriate. As you can well guess, being shy can also lead to boredom. Because social interactions are often avoided, a shy person can wind up having a very repetitive lifestyle, based more on safety needs than on pleasure seeking. New events, activities, and social circles are often avoided out of fear.

People who are shy also have a tendency to be self-preoccupied, which takes attention away from the task at hand, in much the same way self-monitoring distracts a speaker from his or her speech. When a person is preoccupied with him- or herself, it can interfere with job performance and relationships. Interestingly, the majority of people who report being shy admit that they are excessively preoccupied with themselves. Although self-examination and self-analysis are generally healthy signs of psychological functioning, these tendencies tend to be dysfunctionally obsessive in very shy people.

If you are shy, you are probably familiar with some of the above. Keep in mind, however, that the consequences you suffer as a result of your particular case of shyness may not be a severe as a life of lonely solitude. Whatever the case and whatever the degree of shyness you think you have, you can overcome shyness with a little effort and some practice, the same way you can overcome your fear of public speaking. Moreover, you can learn to put your fear-provoking thoughts about social interactions into the proper perspective.

> "Scientists have found the gene for shyness. They would have found it years ago, but it was hiding behind a couple of other genes."
>
> —Jonathan Katz

WHAT TYPE OF FEAR-PROVOKING THOUGHTS CAUSE YOUR CASE OF SHYNESS?

The first step to overcoming shyness is learning to identify the fear-provoking thoughts that make you want to avoid socializing. When you are faced with a social situation, what thoughts are running through your head? If you haven't been paying attention to them, now's the time to put words to them. Exercise 14.1 on page 254 can help you out here, but you'll need to do the real work.

MANAGING YOUR SHYNESS

It's time for you to develop a plan for managing and overcoming your shyness. One of the best ways to do this is to focus on removing obstacles in your life and receiving the rewards that come from removing those obstacles. In Exercise 14.2 on page 255, you will identify what you would do if your shyness had no hold over you, and you'll make these actions possible by setting smaller goals leading up to them. Remember, this process will require you to take some risks.

EXERCISE 14.1. Identifying Your Shyness-Related Fear-Provoking Thoughts

Listed below are some common fear-provoking thoughts shared by people who are shy. Place an "X" next to any that sound familiar to you. Add any of your own specific fear-provoking thoughts in the space provided.

____ I'm not good at anything.

____ People just don't seem to like me.

____ I'll make a bad impression on those people.

____ I'm not stylish or contemporary and won't blend in.

____ I'm boring and having nothing interesting to say.

____ I'm unattractive.

____ I always come across as negative and pessimistic and bring people down.

____ I don't have good social skills.

____ I can't be intimate with people.

____ I hate being the center of attention.

____ I can't stand being compared to others.

____ People will judge what I say and do.

____ I'm hopeless when it comes to the opposite sex.

____ I don't know how to strike up a conversation.

____ I'm too skinny/fat/tall/short and stick out like a sore thumb.

____ I always look awkward when I try to do what others are doing.

____ I'm too plain.

_____   _____

_____   _____

_____   _____

_____   _____

_____   _____

_____   _____

Feedback for Exercise 14.1

If you checked more than one-third of these items and had some of your own to add, you are probably more than moderately shy. To understand yourself better, review the checked items to see if there's any pattern—for example, did you check mostly items that are related to your appearance or to how you think others perceive you? Now, identify the fear-provoking thoughts you find most upsetting. Start by attacking those by looking for solid evidence to support them. Chances are you will have very little solid evidence and will be able to diminish their power over you. Turn back to Chapter 3 for some helpful advice on evaluating and disproving your fear-provoking thoughts, and get to it!

EXERCISE 14.2. Goal Setting to Overcome Shyness

In this exercise, you'll list five things you would like to accomplish if your shyness did not keep you from achieving it. Express your goals in terms of actions you can take that are under your direct control—for example, "Take a course in something that interests me at my local college," or "Invite Jack and Diane over for dinner," or "Go to that office party next week."

1. _____

_____

_____

2. _____

_____

_____

3. _____

_____

_____

4. _____

_____

_____

5. _____

_____

_____

6. _____

_____

_____

Feedback for Exercise 14.2

Arrange the items from easiest to hardest in terms of what it would take to accomplish them. Then, review Chapter 5, which discussed goal setting, and create smaller goals that will lead to your ultimate goal. For example, "Call my local college and request a catalog" would be one of the subgoals of eventually taking a college course and "Having coffee with Jack or Diane" would be a subgoal of inviting the couple over for dinner. Make sure all of your goals and subgoals are under your control. Be sure to indicate how you can tell if your goals have been met.

LEARNING AND PRACTICING NEW SOCIAL SKILLS

Most of the techniques described in the earlier chapters can also be applied to shyness. This section, however, provides another approach specifically for overcoming shyness: learning and practicing social skills. Doing both can go a long way in helping you to control your social anxiety. Chances are, you already have the skills; you just don't use them often. If this is the case, practicing will help you overcome your fear. If you feel that you are lacking some skills—such as conversational skills—you'll find the sections to follow very helpful.

Conversational Skills

Of all the social skills that are useful in overcoming shyness, conversational skills are close to the top. Shy people often think they have nothing to say. Even though they may be intelligent, the pressure of a conversation can reduce them to monosyllables. I remember a cartoon from the *New Yorker* that showed a circle of people having a discussion. An outsider who was about to enter the conversation was told, "If you don't have a Ph.D., scram!" Many people find it difficult to enter into a conversation. Ron M. experienced this fear regularly.

The Case of Ron M.

One of the most socially awkward situations for Ron M., he said, was joining a group of people who were engaged in a conversation in which he'd like to participate. In the past, when he made attempts to do this, he felt like he drew too much attention to himself and made everyone in the group uncomfortable. Most of the time he felt like he didn't know the right thing to say—and even if he did know what to say, he wouldn't know the right time to say it. Ron learned many of the skills discussed below. They gave him the confidence to enter into conversations. He increased his sensitivity to group interactions and developed a great sense of timing for entering into a conversation.

Like Ron, many people feel awkward joining a conversation in progress. In fact, I've met plenty of people who dread going to parties or other functions for this very reason. *What to say? How to say it? When to say it?* There's actually a process involved, which you can easily learn. As your skills improve through learning and practice, you'll see your social behavior changing at work, parties, and maybe even while waiting on the supermarket checkout line.

How to Enter Into a Conversation

In learning this skill, there are three things to think about: where to stand, what to say, and when to say it.

• **Where to stand.** When you first approach a group, stand one small step outside the circle of people. Here, you are in a position to listen to the conversation, but you're not conspicuously trying to become part of the group. When you are ready to make your entering statement (discussed below), you'll only need to take a small step to take your position within the group.

• **What to say.** Before you attempt to join the conversation, listen to what the group is saying, both in terms of content and tone. For example, if the conversation is light hearted, you wouldn't want to enter it with a statement of doom and gloom. If the matter is a serious one, you wouldn't want to make a joke. After you've listened to the conversation for a little while, think of and rehearse an appropriately interesting comment or question for your opening statement. For example, I was at a party where there were many psychologists, but I only knew the host. I walked over to a small group of people who were discussing the relative merits of natural supplements for relaxation such as valerian root versus pharmaceutical drugs such as Xanax. I listened for a few minutes to formulate my opening statement. I decided to ask a question rather than state my personal opinion on the subject. Since I wasn't taking sides, I had a better chance of being accepted by the entire group. "Do you think there will ever be as much research on herbal remedies in the U.S. as there is in Europe?" I asked. A few of the members addressed my question, and I was *in*.

• **When to say it.** When your statement is timely and relevant . . . make your move. Step forward and make your statement. As you work on this skill, you will become more sensitive to when there is a natural pause in a discussion. This will make it much easier to enter into the conversation.

Be sure to practice these three steps as often as possible. When you are around people you feel very comfortable with and would normally think nothing of barging into the conversation, use that as an opportunity to practice entering into a conversation with people you don't know so well. As explained above, listen for a while, find the right opening, and then enter. Watch and listen for feedback from the group. As you improve, you'll see that people may agree more often with what you say, or they may compliment you on your insightfulness, or they may be interested in further discussion.

Preparing a Dialogue in Advance

Quite often the stress of being in a new social situation can feel overwhelming. It will be much easier to cope with if you have some dialogue prepared in advance. You can do this by paying attention to current events, learning a few funny jokes, or preparing a little lecture on the more interesting aspects of your work or hobby.

Also, prepare a list of conversation-starting remarks. There are a number of sources for these. Try to think of your own (this is a lot easier when you are not under stress), ask friends for the remarks they use, see what others use on you, or watch television and see what your favorite characters use.

How to Ask Open-Ended Questions

Some people are easy to talk to and keep the conversation going, while other people make it very difficult to converse at all. Likewise, some people have absolutely no trouble talking to anyone who comes their way, while others just can't find the right words. Take the case of Jerry C., for example. He just couldn't get the conversation he was trying to have with Alice, a woman he'd just met, off the ground:

Jerry C.: Are you having a nice time at the party?

Alice: Yes.

Jerry C.: Do you know many people here?

Alice: Yes.

Jerry C.: Did you come here straight from work?

Alice: No.

Jerry C.: Do you work close by here?

Alice: Yes.

While it seems as if Alice was responsible for the dull exchange, it was the way Jerry C. phrased the questions that was the real culprit. Jerry had not mastered the skill of asking open-ended questions—questions that cannot be answered with a single word. His questions where phrased in such a way that each answer could potentially terminate the discussion. Meanwhile, the pressure remained on him to come up with more questions if he wanted to keep the conversation going. What's worse, he learned very little about Alice from each of her answers.

Instead of asking Alice if she knew anyone at the party, Jerry could have asked who she knew. Alice would have responded by telling him the names of the people she knew. Then, he could have taken that further and asked how she knew them. Also, rather than asking if she worked close by, he could have asked her what type of work she does. Open-ended questions like these might have helped Alice open up enough to allow Jerry to get to know her. You can practice coming up with some open-ended questions of your own in Exercise 14.3.

When asking open-ended questions, the answers people give you may contain "free information"—in other words, the response you receive will include details that weren't requested but are helpful in getting to know the person better and keeping the conversation going. You can use the free information to formulate your next question.

When you ask open-ended questions and receive this free information, you'll come to appreciate the offering. Return the favor and give others free information when they ask you questions. In fact, even if their question could be answered with a simple yes or no, offer some free information to make it easier for the person to ask his or her next question. Also, by offering free information, you can steer the conversation to topics that interest you or that you'd like to discuss.

EXERCISE 14.3. Asking Open-Ended Questions

As you now know, open-ended questions are questions that can't be answered with a simple yes or no, or single-word, answer. Being able to ask these types of questions is an important conversational skill.

Imagine that you're at a business lunch or a social gathering, and think of at least five open-ended questions you can ask people to get the conversation flowing. Record them in the space provided.

1. _____ ?

2. _____ ?

3. _____ ?

4. _____ ?

5. _____ ?

Feedback for Exercise 14.3

Ask yourself each of the five questions you recorded above and note your responses. Can you answer any of them with a simple yes or no or with some other one-word answer? If you can, you'll need to revise them. Keep revising them until the questions get you to reveal something interesting about yourself.

Once you know that your questions work, practicing asking them whenever you get the chance. Be sure to listen for free information to use for further questions.

Giving and Receiving Compliments

"I can live for two months
on a good compliment."

—Mark Twain

Compliments are great conversation starters, whether you are on the giving or receiving end. Although you might think that giving and receiving compliments are easy enough tasks, this isn't always the case. To master the art of giving and receiving compliments, consider the following factors:

• **Carefully select the compliment through observation.** Before you give a person a compliment, carefully identify something that seems to matter to that person or take note of what he or she has just done. For example, when preparing to give a compliment to a stranger, first observe that person to determine what type of compliment you think he or she would appreciate. For example, if a person is very well dressed or is wearing a lot of jewelry, appearance is probably important to him or her. In this case, that person's appearance would make good compliment material. Or, if you wish to compliment a speaker whose presentation you enjoyed, and that speaker used a very broad, expansive vocabulary, he or she is probably proud of her use of the language. Compliment it.

In the beginning, giving compliments to strangers is good way to practice the skill of compliment giving. Since you will most likely not be seeing that person again, there's little risk involved. (See Exercise 14.4 on page 262.)

• **Make your compliments specific.** An important key to successfully giving a compliment is to make it as specific as possible. When your compliments are specific, it's clear that you are not simply trying to flatter the receiver. A specific compliment shows that you really paid attention. Look at the following three examples and note how much more specific the second and third are than the first.

That was a great talk you gave this afternoon.

The examples you used in your talk made everything so clear. I especially liked the one about—

That was a great opening. You grabbed the audience's attention right away.

• **Carefully choose words that are clear, unambiguous, and complimentary.** Once you know what you'd like to compliment about a person, choose your words carefully. Compliments are meant to make the receiver feel good, so make sure that's what your compliment will do. You might think giving a compliment is simple—for example, how hard is it to say something like "I really enjoyed your talk!" You'll be surprised, however, to discover how easy it is to botch compliment giving. Consider these examples:

Kevin: I'm terrible at giving speeches, but you did a great job.

Janet: I'm sure you're a good speaker!

While attempting to compliment Janet on her great speech, Kevin tore himself down. Before Janet could enjoy Kevin's compliment (if she ever would), she first had to build Kevin back up.

Brian: That was *some* speech.

Steve: Uh, thanks, I guess.

Brian's compliment was ambiguous. Steve had no idea what he was trying to say. If Brian's tone was sarcastic, his statement was not a compliment; it was an insult.

Darlene: A lot of people seemed bored by your talk, but I can't understand why. I thought you did a great job.

Nick: You think a lot of people were bored by my talk?

Darlene's compliment to Nick came in the form of a mixed message. It very possibly had hostile undertones. Always be sure your compliment is complimentary!

• **Receive compliments graciously.** When a person pays you a compliment, graciously accept it and thank the person. Many people think that if they accept a compliment, they will seem arrogant or conceited. They've been taught to show modesty and protest a little. However, by belittling someone's compliment, you are discounting their opinion. Consider these examples:

Joe: You gave a really great talk yesterday.

Mary: It was no big deal. It was rather ordinary, really.

Instead of graciously receiving the compliment, Mary denied the accuracy of the compliment, thereby discounting Joe's opinion.

Susan: Hey, that's a great looking suit!

Beth: Oh, so's yours.

In this case, Beth is diverting the attention away from the compliment and gives Beth an obligatory compliment in return. The return compliment seems stiff and formal, and could make Susan uncomfortable for having made the original compliment.

So, avoid making the person who compliments you feel foolish for giving you a compliment and accept the comment. I'm certainly not saying you should go with the other extreme: "Yes I did give a great speech! Didn't I?—I always do!" There is a middle ground that permits you to say, "Thank you, that's great to hear. I've been preparing that talk for the past three weeks."

Now that you have some idea how to give and receive compliments, you'll want to practice this skill—especially when it comes to compliment giving. In Exercise 14.4, you'll be selecting strangers at random and complimenting them on things you think might matter to them. When it comes to receiving compliments, simply practice saying, "Thank you," and leave it at that until you feel comfortable saying more.

EXERCISE 14.4. Giving Compliments

In this exercise, you will be giving out four compliments to people you don't know in the next few days. Jot down the compliment and take note of their replies and reactions. For example, did they smile? Were they embarrassed? Were they gracious about receiving the compliment?

Compliment: _____

Response: _____

Compliment: _____

Response: _____

Compliment: _____

Response: _____

Compliment: _____

Response: _____

Feedback for Exercise 14.4

Did you observe some aspect of the person you could compliment? How comfortable were you when giving the compliment? Did your comfort level change after you did it a few times? Once you have done this exercise with strangers, try it on people you know. Remember that the key to being successful is to select areas that the person cares about and will enjoy that he or she is being noticed in that area.

Assert Yourself!

When you're trying to overcome shyness, being able to assert yourself is an important social skill to have. Many people think it's better to do something they don't want to do than risk being disliked for not doing it. For them, saying no isn't worth the guilt and alienation they think it will cause.

Since a full discussion on this topic could fill a whole book (or volumes) of its own, I'll make this quick and simple. If you're interested in investigating assertion training, I recommend that you read Manual J. Smith's wonderful book *When I Say No, I Feel Guilty.*

PRACTICING YOUR SOCIAL SKILLS

There are many times when you may have the necessary skills to do something, but you don't use them. This usually occurs because you haven't practiced a skill enough to feel confident of the outcome. Most skills must be practiced if they are to remain effective. At first, they should be practiced in an environment that is as nonthreatening as possible. If your ultimate wish is to meet new people and begin dating, do not begin practicing conversational skills on potential dating partners. Begin with people you consider "safer." As your skill level increases, move on to the type of people you want to date.

Take every opportunity to practice your skills. For example, it can be on line at the supermarket or at the bank. Lines are a great place to start conversations because nobody enjoys standing and waiting, and you can always easily begin by getting others to join you in complaining about the situation. You can put your goal setting to work here, too: for example, tell yourself you'll try to strike up a conversation with two strangers today. Tomorrow, you can make it three. Just keep practicing.

WHAT YOU HAVE LEARNED
AND WHERE YOU ARE GOING

In this chapter, you learned that you don't have to give in to your shyness. You can overcome this trait by practicing specific social skills and by taking a few minor risks. If you do this, you can expect big payoffs! You'll feel less awkward and perhaps less lonely as you willingly invite new people and situations into your life. This type of stage fright doesn't have to hold you back—go out and get what you want from life!

CONCLUSION

You began this book by assessing your AQ. Now that you've reached the end, I want you to retake the quiz so you can see how far you've come. When you see how much progress you've made, you'll want to uncork that bottle of Champaign that's been waiting for you in the fridge! Take the quiz right now, and then turn back to this conclusion because I'm going to let you in on a little secret. Don't read on until you've taken the quiz.

Here's the secret: The statements in the test fall into six separate categories. When you total the scores for the individual groups, you can pinpoint what aspect of public speaking is still causing you the most anxiety. This information is presented here at the back of the book rather than in the beginning because I wanted you to read the *whole* book, not just the chapters you thought were relevant to your case of stage fright. All of the chapters hold essential information that I want you to be familiar with—so don't take any shortcuts!

Total your scores for statements 1, 20, and 29. These statements center on *fears related to avoidance and adequate preparation.* If your score is 4 or greater, reexamine this area carefully. It seems you are still trying to get out of making presentations or speeches whenever you can. Go back and reread Chapter 7.

Total your scores for statements 2, 5, 8, 14, 17, 23, and 26. These statements center on *fears related to your competence.* If your score is 10 or greater, reexamine this area carefully. It means you still have doubts and fears about your ability to make a good presentation. Go back and reread Chapters 1, 2, 3, 4, 5, 6, 8, 9, and 10.

Total your scores for statements 3, 6, 9, 12, 15, 18, 21, and 24. These statements center on *fears related to being accepted by your audience.* If your score is 12 or greater, reexamine this area carefully. It means you still have fears about whether the audience will like you and what you say and do. Go back and reread Chapters 1, 2, 3, 4, 6, 11, and 14.

Total your scores for statements 4, 7, 19, and 22. These statements center on *fears related to physical symptoms.* If your score is 6 or greater, reexamine this area carefully. It means you are still focusing on the physical symptoms of your stage fright. Go back and reread Chapter 6.

Total your points for statements 10, 13, and 30. These statements center on *fears related to specific situations and audience characteristics.* If your score is 4 or greater, reexamine this area carefully. It means you are still worrying about the audience and the environment in which you will be presenting. Go back and reread Chapters 10, 11, and 13.

Total your points for statements 11, 16, 25, 27, and 28. These statements center on *fears related to self-monitoring.* If your score is 7 or greater, reexamine this area carefully. It means that you are still distracting yourself by examining how you are doing and what physical state your anxiety level is at. Go back and reread Chapters 1, 4, 6, 9, and 11.

The goal of this book is not just to get you comfortable with public speaking, but also to help you eventually look forward to it. Trust me: as you become more comfortable, you will begin to enjoy it more. But remember, you have finished the book not the training. You must continue to hone the skills you have learned here. Continue to do your relaxation techniques on a daily basis—not just when you are faced with public speaking. Practice your presentation skills every day, whether you are speaking one on one or to a group.

If there are times when you still feel anxious before speaking, recognize your fear for what it really is: excitement. Without it, there would be little pleasure for a job well done.

Appendix A

A CRASH COURSE IN PUBLIC SPEAKING

Chances are, if you've skipped ahead to this section, you are going to be giving a speech very soon, maybe even tomorrow. You probably avoided preparing for it, and now the day of reckoning is here, and you can no longer put it off. Good news! This crash course is designed to get you through the experience intact. It's sort of like going straight to the emergency room—it will save you and get you through the experience. Later, however, you really should see your doctor—or read the rest of the book!

You must begin by preparing your presentation or speech. Without that, you obviously cannot make your presentation. You will then practice a failsafe technique for giving your presentation so that no matter what happens, you can get through it. That, in itself, will be very calming. Then you will learn about how fear gets in your way and some quick strategies to minimize its effects. You will also learn how to relax your body and make presenting easier.

DESIGN THE PRESENTATION OR SPEECH

The first thing you must do is make sure you know what you are going to say. After you have completed this first section, you will be able to survive your presentation, even if you go no farther. If you have already designed your speech or presentation, outlined it, or sketched out a few ideas for it, good for you. If not, take the steps below:

1. Define Your Overall Intention

You have a specific reason for giving your speech or presentation. What is it? If you don't know, try to figure it out. Identify the desired outcome of a successful talk. Also, identify specific events or benchmarks to indicate what the outcome(s) would be. For example, would you get hired for a consulting job, be asked to speak again, receive luncheon invitations, and so on? This will help you evaluate your talk, but more important, it will give you a target for which to aim while developing your speech. *Everything* you say in your speech should be related to your purpose.

2. Creating Your Outline

With your purpose in mind, create an outline. Make a complete list of *all* the possible topics you would like to cover. Prioritize the items by ranking them from most important to least important. Eliminate any item that is not *essential* to achieving your purpose. The less content you have to present, the better you will be able to present it. Focusing on a few important things will give you the opportunity to include examples, stories, and/or anecdotes to get your point across. Arrange the items in the order you would like to present them.

3. Collect the Information for Your Talk

Write out all the basic information for each point you wish to cover. If you need to research any of the topics further, do so, and enter the results of that research. You can quickly search the Internet for relevant information. For each point, identify one or two good examples/stories/anecdotes that will increase the audience's interest in that point. If you are going to use media such as a PowerPoint presentation, gather all of your media files including graphics, photos, video, and audio files. If you're preparing a presentation at the last minute, make it as simple as possible.

4. Write Out the Complete Text of Your Speech

Write or type the entire speech as if you were going to read it. Make sure it is written in a conversational manner. Insert your outline in the left-hand margin of the printout. Place each point you want to cover next to the complete text that corresponds to that point. Make the text large enough so that a quick glance is all you need to be able to read it easily.

Once you've taken the four steps above, you must practice your speech. Put this book down and go get your presentation ready. Don't rush through it! Then come back to the book.

PRACTICING YOUR SPEECH

Read your speech a few times *out loud*. Then, look only at the items outlined in the left-hand column. Try to improvise your speech by looking only at the outline. If you are very familiar with the material, this may be all you need. You will just need your outline to remind you of what comes next. Go back and forth between reading the entire speech and improvising with your outline. Once you've read the speech aloud at least five times, you should be getting pretty comfortable with the content. Phrases become familiar and certain sections will almost jump off the page.

Once you feel very comfortable reading the presentation, try it again in your own words with just the outline to guide you. This time, stop in the middle of your speech, look away, and then try to determine where you left off. Practice "losing" your place and then finding it until you feel that you can rely on your outline to be your "safety net" during the actual speech. If at any time during the presentation you become very distracted and really do "freeze up," you can always refer to your outline and begin reading the complete text. To get away with this, create a few transition lines to explain to your audience why you're reading. For example you might say, "The information I am now going to present is so important that I want to make sure I give it to you exactly as I prepared it." This puts the emphasis back on the information, not on your temporary lack of focus. With luck, you won't have to read your speech, but it's good to know it will be available if necessary.

There are a few basic rules to follow when you are practicing. The most important one is to practice as much as you can. The more times you go through your presentation, the better you will know it and the less likely you will be distracted and forget important information. When you practice, try to match the conditions under which you will be presenting—in other words, practice as you will perform.

Try to simulate the conditions you will be speaking in as closely as possible. If you will be using a microphone, practice using a microphone if you have one available on such short notice. Practice while you are wearing the clothes you will be presenting in. You may practice in comfortable clothes and then find that a shirt and tie or uncomfortable heels distract you. Get used to the way the clothing you wear will feel.

Practice incidentals. Practice walking up to the podium and looking at the audience before you begin. If you will have a spotlight, practice with a light shining in your face. If you will receive an introduction, practice thanking the person who introduced you. If you have to get the audience to stop talking and listen to your talk, practice that. The idea is to reduce the number of surprises as much as possible.

Practicing With Distractions

There are two kinds of distractions you will have to face—internal and external. The internal distractions come from self-monitoring—in other words, from assessing how you are doing and feeling. This is one of the biggest causes of stage fright. Once you begin to get anxious, you will surely notice your physical symptoms of anxiety. Focusing on them will distract you from your speech. Also, evaluating how you are doing by paying close attention to the audience's reaction to what you are saying and doing can also take much-needed attention away from your speech. In other words, if you start focusing on anything but what you are saying and doing, your speech will be difficult to get through. It will be easy to lose your place, make mistakes, and forget what you are going to say.

The two keys for handling this situation are 1) learning to use your outline so you always know where you are, and 2) practicing how to refocus on your speech if your mind starts wandering. While you are practicing your speech, intentionally focus on something else so you can practice getting back on track. Do this until you can quickly find your place and resume your speech.

Shout It Out!

You must practice your speech out loud. Reading it silently to yourself will *not* help. Also, if you will be speaking to a small or medium-sized group without a microphone, practice reading it with the same loud voice you will be using when you actually give it. Get used to hearing how your voice sounds when you project it.

External distractions come from outside of you. You can pretty much guarantee that there will be external distractions during your speech. Waiters drop dishes, people sneeze way too loud, babies cry, equipment fails, air conditioning stops working, and a few thousand other things can happen. To help with these types of distractions, schedule some actual distractions while you are practicing your speech. You can ask friends or family to walk in or call while you are practicing. You can set your alarm clock to go off during your practicing. Use these opportunities to practice refocusing on your talk.

Practice With a "Real" Audience

If time permits, ask a few friends, family members, or colleagues to listen to your speech. This will get you used to presenting in front of people. If you make a mistake, do not start over, just keep going as if this were your real audience.

If you have time, videotape your speech and review it. The recording can provide you with some good feedback. Try to determine if there are any slow spots, difficult areas where you need more work, or any other possibilities for improvements. Another good idea is to make an audio recording of your speech. You can play this in your car, during your bath, or while you are preparing dinner. This will help reinforce the material you'll be presenting.

WHAT'S FEAR GOOD FOR?

If you've done what I've suggested so far in this crash course, you'll get through your presentation no matter how nervous you are. So, let's turn our attention for a moment to the fear and anxiety you're feeling. The fear and anxiety we feel in dangerous situations is often referred to as the fight-or-flight response. This is how we respond

to danger; we either run away or stay and fight. As soon as your brain perceives danger—*even if it's false danger*—it gets your body ready for action. It gets your heart pumping more quickly, it increases your breathing rate, it puts your sweat glands into overdrive, and so on. This is great if you are facing a mugger or a dangerous beast, but it is actually quite uncomfortable if you are presenting yourself to an audience. Be aware that you will most likely experience the symptoms of anxiety so they don't come as a shock to you. These symptoms do not have to interfere with your presentation if you can learn to expect them and manage them.

THINKING YOUR WAY THROUGH ANXIETY

Put your anxiety-producing thoughts into perspective by examining their accuracy. What do you fear most about being up in front of an audience? Put words to the fear. You may worry that you will forget everything you are going to say. Examine your history. Have you ever forgotten everything you had planned to say? Chances are it hasn't happened. If it has, remember that you have the entire text of your talk available to you in this particular situation. There's no chance you'll fall completely silent.

Do this for each of your fears until you can either disprove them or reduce their severity. Keep in mind that some of your anxiety-producing thoughts are probably exaggerations of what's likely to happen. Try to identify all-or-nothing thoughts, and remind yourself that not everything in life is black or white. For example, if you're thinking that if your talk is not great it will be a disaster, remind yourself that there is a middle road: your talk can end up being somewhere in the middle, which isn't so bad. Likewise, are you thinking in extremes? Watch for statements

Simulating the Physical Symptoms of Anxiety

A great technique for learning to deal with distractions caused by your physical symptoms is to simulate them through exercise. Before your practice sessions, jog in place long enough to get your heart rate up. Your breathing should be somewhat labored, your skin should be flushed and warm, and your hands should be shaking just a bit. These are very similar to the physical symptoms of anxiety you may feel right before you begin talking and during the first few minutes of your speech—the two most frightening times for most public speakers. If you can train yourself to speak clearly under these conditions, you'll find it easier to perform while experiencing them in the actual situation.

such as, "I'm going to forget everything" or "Everyone will be bored by my talk." You might forget a few things, but if you've practiced your speech and have your outline handy, you won't forget *everything*, maybe just a couple of things. And yes, chances are you'll bore someone out there in the audience but not *everyone*. Again, look for the shades of gray. Also, watch out for words like "always" and "never." For example, "I always screw up," or "I never get my points across." Don't overgeneralize. Identify times when you did, in fact, get your points across and all the times you didn't screw up.

Rate your fears on a scale of 1 to 100 with 1 representing total calm and 100 representing total panic. This will help you get away from that all-or-nothing and extreme thinking. It also gets you to look within and examine how anxious you actually are. When you've done this, you'll likely realize that it's really not as bad as you thought. Then, once you have gotten a handle on your anxiety-producing thoughts, learn to relax.

LEARNING TO RELAX

The physical symptoms of anxiety tend to make us even more anxious. Learning how to control these symptoms can reduce your fear and help your concentration. Like any physical skill, it improves with practice, but since you have limited time, make the most out of the following exercise:

Find a comfortable place to sit or lie down. Take a few seconds to adjust your position until you feel that your body is totally supported. Inhale and exhale through your nose. Say the number ten to yourself and take a slow, deep breath. Exhale slowly and completely, consciously letting go of any tension you feel. Now, say the number nine to yourself and take a slow, deep breath. Exhale slowly and completely, letting go of any tension you feel. As you exhale, say the following: "I am more relaxed now than I was at number ten." Say the number eight to yourself and take a slow, deep breath. Exhale slowly and completely, letting go of any tension you feel. As you exhale, say the following: "I am more relaxed now than I was at number nine." Repeat this exercise until you count down to the number one.

Since you have such a short time, practice this exercise as many times as you can. Once you've done it a few times, do the exercise while sitting in a straight-back chair. This will get you ready to do the exercise while you're waiting to speak or make your presentation. Since the few minutes before you are to make your speech often cause the most anxiety, this exercise will help you restore calm and focus.

If you follow the suggestions in this crash course, you should be able to get through your presentation with a minimum amount of discomfort. Even if you have to give it tomorrow, you have enough time to try out each technique described here. Hopefully, the discomfort you have gone through by avoiding the task until now will give you the incentive not to wait until the last minute again. When you have a chance, read the entire book so that you can reap the benefits of being able to make presentations comfortably and competently . . . and most of all, enjoyably.

Appendix B
RELAXATION
TRANSCRIPT

Record the transcript in this appendix in a quiet setting. Before you begin to record the material, practice your relaxation exercises so that your voice will be soothing and calming to the "you" who will be listening to the recording later. Don't rush through it. As you record each instruction, give your future self some time to actually carry it out. Keep your voice soft, low, and breathy. You'll thank yourself later.

Let's relax. (pause)

Find a place where you're going to be really comfortable . . . a recliner, a bed, a couch. (pause)

Lie down and get comfortable . . . make sure your legs are well supported. (pause)

Lean your head back . . . feel that it is supported . . . feel that your shoulders are supported. (pause)

Notice now that you can let any tension in your neck melt away. (pause)

Just let your body sink in. (pause)

Now, wherever your eyes happen to fall . . . select one spot. (pause)

And from now on, just gaze only at that spot. (pause)

If at any time your eye muscles get tired . . . slowly close them (pause) but as long as they're open . . . keep gazing at that one spot. (pause)

All the time you're breathing, you're going to be breathing in and out slowly through your nose. (pause)

So, begin now by exhaling, sucking your stomach in like a pump to push out the air. (pause)

And then slowly inhale, first into your stomach, and then all the way up your chest. (pause)

And then slowly exhale. (pause)

This is the way you're going to be breathing the whole time. (pause)

Place all of your attention on your breathing. (pause)

Feel the air coming slowly into your stomach. (pause)

When it's comfortably full, take it all the way up your chest . . . and then slowly exhale. (pause)

Notice that as you keep softening your muscles,

273

and that every time you take an inhale, there's just a little bit of tension on the inhale because your muscles are contracting. (pause)

It's when you exhale that you let everything go. (pause)

Try to make your exhales longer and slower than your inhales. (pause)

That's how you really get comfortable and feel good while you're relaxing. (pause)

Keep focusing your attention on your breathing. (pause)

Always know where the breath is as it's rising, coming in. (pause)

And slowly, on how you exhale. (pause)

And every time you exhale . . . sink back even more. (pause)

Think back to when you were a young child, and somebody wanted to pick you up. You didn't want to be picked up . . . so you just let your body go limp . . . sort of a "sack of potatoes" feeling . . . and just let everything go. (pause)

Just be floating . . . no tension in your body. (pause)

You're still focusing on the breath coming in slowly, using the muscles that you're using to breathe with, getting them to relax and soften. (pause)

And then a slow, slow exhale, and you really let go. (pause)

You really let your body go limp. (pause)

Now what I want you to do is, the next time you begin an inhale . . . start a slow, rhythmic count . . . just to see what number you get up to; there's no right or wrong here. (pause)

And then, as you start your exhale, use the same rhythmic count to keep track of your exhale. (pause)

Try to make your exhale one-and-a-half times as long as your inhale. (pause)

If you count six on your inhale, on the way up, count nine on your exhale, on the way down. (pause)

We want to spend as much time relaxing as possible. (pause)

Start counting. (pause)

Remember that your attention is always on the breath. (pause)

And where it is in your stomach and chest. (pause)

And you're constantly softening your muscles. (pause)

Now, with each inhale and exhale, keep counting. (pause)

Now, when I tell you, I want you to begin the same slow, rhythmic count. (pause)

But this time when you finish your inhale, stop for one beat, then start your exhale . . . when you finish your exhale . . . pause for one beat. (pause)

So there will always be one beat at the end of the inhale and at the end of the exhale when you're totally still. (pause)

Notice what effect this has on your breathing. (pause)

Once you finish exhaling with your count, you can stop counting. (pause)

And just keep breathing. (pause)

Continue to let go as you breathe. (pause)

Feel your body totally supported. (pause)

Keep leaning back. (pause)

Let yourself go. (pause)

Notice the temperature of your hands. (pause)

You're still following the airstream. (pause)

All your attention is on your breath. (pause)

Now feel the weight of your body. (pause)

Take three more slow, deep breaths. (pause)

Open your eyes. (pause)

Sit up slowly. (pause)

How do you feel now?

How alert do you feel?

RECOMMENDED READING

Beyond Bullet Points: Using Microsoft PowerPoint to Create Presentations That Inform, Motivate, and Inspire by Cliff Atkinson (Redmond: Microsoft Press, 2005).

Blink: The Power of Thinking Without Thinking by M. Gladwell (New York: Little Brown and Company, 2005).

Changing Minds: The Art and Science of Changing Our Own and Other People's Minds by Howard Gardner (Boston, MA: Harvard Business School Press, 2006).

Feeling Good: The New Mood Therapy, Revised and Updated, by David D. Burns (New York: Avon, 1999).

Influence: Science and Practice, Fourth Edition, by Robert B. Cialdini (Needham Heights, MA: Allyn and Bacon, 2000).

Podium Humor, Reissue Edition, by James C. Humes (New York: Collins, 1993).

Presentations That Change Minds: Strategies to Persuade, Convince and Get Results by Josh Gordon (New York: McGraw-Hill, 2006).

The Relaxation Response, Expanded and Updated Edition, by Herbert Benson, MD, with Miriam Z. Klipper (New York: Harper Paperbacks, 2000).

Self-Consciousness and Social Anxiety by Arnold H. Buss, PhD. (New York: W.H. Freeman and Company, 1980).

Self-Presentation: Impression Management and Interpersonal Behavior, Reprint Edition, by Mark M. Leary (Boulder: Westview Press, 1996).

Shyness: What It Is and What to Do About It, Reissue Edition, by Philip G. Zimbardo (Boston, MA: Addison-Wesley Publishing, 1990).

The Speaker Survival Guide: 101 Eloqui Tips for Successful Public Speaking by D. Booth and D. Shames (Calabassas, CA: Eloqui, 2007).

The Story Factor: Inspiration, Influence, and Persuasion Through the Art of Storytelling by Annette Simmons (New York: Basic Books, 2006).

SELECTED REFERENCES

Aaron, S. *Stage Fright: Its Role in Acting.* Chicago: Chicago University Press, 1986.

Altmaier, E., Leary, M., Halpern, S. and Sellers, J. "Effects of stress inoculation and participant modeling on confidence and anxiety," *Journal of Social and Clinical Psychology* 1985; 3(4): 500–505.

Atkinson, C. *Beyond Bullet Points: Using Microsoft PowerPoint to Create Presentations that Inform, Motivate and Inspire,* Redmond: Microsoft Press, 2005.

Beatty, M., and Payne, S. "Speech anxiety as a multiplicative function of size of audience and social desirability," *Perceptual and Motor Skills* 1983; 56(2): 792–794.

Beck, A., and Emory, G. *Anxiety Disorders and Phobias: A Cognitive Perspective,* New York: Basic Books, 1985.

Benson, H. *The Relaxation Response,* New York: Morrow Books, 1975.

Booth, R, Bartlett, D., and Bohnsack, J. "An examination of the relationship between happiness, loneliness, and shyness in college students," *Journal of College Student Development* 1992; 33(2): 157–162.

Burns, D. *Feeling Good: The New Mood Therapy,* New York: New American Library, 1980.

Buss, A. *Self-Consciousness and Social Anxiety,* San Francisco: W.H. Freeman and Company, 1980.

Caldwell, R. *The Performer Prepares,* Dallas: PST Inc., 1990.

Caspi, A., Elder, G.H., and Bem, D.J. "Moving away from the world: Life-course patterns of shy children," *Annual Progress in Child Psychiatry and Child Development* 1989; 275–293.

Cialdini, R.B. *Influence: Science and Practice,* Needham Heights, MA: Allyn and Bacon, 2001.

Dawson, R. "Comparing contributions of cognitive behavior therapy strategies in the treatment of speech anxiety," *Australian Journal of Psychology* 1982; 34(3): 277–308.

Desberg, P., Marsh, G., and Crandell, C. "Dispositional correlates of audience anxiety," Paper presented at the Western Psychological Association Meetings, Los Angeles, 1984.

Ellis, A. *Reason and Emotion in Psychotherapy,* New York: Lyle Stuart Press, 1962.

Fredrick, G., and Goss, B. "Systematic desensitization in avoiding communication," in *Avoiding Communication: Shyness, Reticence, and Communication Apprehension.* Daly, J. and McCroskey, J. (Eds.) Beverly Hills: Sage Publications, 1984.

Fremouw, W. "Cognitive-behavioral therapies for modification of communication apprehension," in *Avoiding Communication, Shyness, Reticence, and Com-*

munication Apprehension, Daly, J. and McCroskey, J. (Eds.), Beverly Hills: Sage Publications, 1984.

Freud, S. *Jokes and Their Relation to the Unconscious.* New York: Norton Books, 1905.

Gardner, H. *Changing Minds,* New York: Oxford University Press, 2004.

Gross, R., and Fremouw, W. "Cognitive restructuring and progressive relaxation for treatment of empirical subtypes of speech anxious subjects," *Cognitive Therapy and Research* 1982; 6(4): 429–436.

Hayes, B., and Marshall, W. "Generalization of treatment effects in training public speakers," *Behavior Research and Therapy* 1984; 22(5): 519–533.

Hekmat, H., Lubitz, R., and Deal, R. "Semantic desensitization: A paradigmatic intervention approach to anxiety disorders," *Journal of Clinical Psychology* 1984; 40(2): 463–466.

Humes, J.C. *Podium Humor,* New York: Harper and Row, 1975.

Jackson, J., and Latane, B. "All alone in front of all those people: Stage fright as a function of number and type of co-performers and audience," *Journal of Personality and Social Psychology* 1981; 40(1): 73–85.

Jaremko, M., Hadfield, R., and Walker, W. "Contribution of an educational phase to stress inoculation of speech anxiety," *Perceptual Motor Skills* 1980; 50(2): 495–501.

Johnson, R.L., and Glass, C.R. "Heterosocial anxiety and direction of attention in high school boys," *Cognitive Therapy and Research* 1989; 13(5): 509–526.

Kelly, L. "Social skills training as a mode of treatment for social communications problems," in *Avoiding Communication, Shyness, Reticence, and Communication Apprehension.* Daly, J. and McCroskey, J. (Eds.), Beverly Hills: Sage Publications, 1984.

Kirsch, I., Wolpin, M., and Knutson, J. "A comparison of in-vivo methods for rapid reduction of "stage fright" in the college classroom: A field experiment," *Behavior Therapy* 1975; 6: 165–171.

Klatzky, R. *Human Memory: Structures and Processes,* San Francisco: W.H. Freeman, 1980.

Koudas, O. "Reduction of examination anxiety and stage-fright by group desensitization and relaxation," *Behavioral Research and Therapy* 1967; 5: 275–281.

Leary, M. *Interpersonal Rejection,* New York: Oxford University Press, 2001.

Leary, M. *Self-Presentation: Impression Management and Interpersonal Behavior,* Boulder: Westview Press, 1996.

Leary, M. *Understanding Social Anxiety: Social, Personality and Clinical Perspectives,* Beverly Hills: Sage Publications, 1983.

Lent, R., Russell, R., and Zamostny, K. "Comparison of cue controlled desensitization, rational restructuring and a credible placebo in the treatment of speech anxiety," *Journal of Consulting and Clinical Psychology* 1981; 49(4): 608–610.

Lucas, J., and Lorayne, H. *The Memory Book,* New York: Ballantine Books, 1985.

Markway, B.G., Carmin, C.N., Pollard, C.A., and Flynn, T. *Dying of Embarrassment: Help for Social Anxiety & Phobia,* Oakland: New Harbinger Publications, Inc., 1992.

Marsh, G., Desberg, P., and Crandall, C. "Effects of social anxiety on memory for names," Paper presented at the Western Psychological Association meeting, San Francisco, 1983.

Marshall, J.R. *Social Phobia: From Shyness to Stage Fright,* New York: Basic Books, 1994.

Marshall, L., Parker, L., and Hayes, B. "Treating public speakers problems: A study using flooding and elements of skills training," *Behavior Modification* 1982; 6(2): 147–170.

McCrosky, J. "Oral communication apprehension: A summary of recent theory and research," *Human Communication Research* 1977; 4: 78–96.

McKinney, M., and Gatchel, R. "Comparative effectiveness of heart rate, biofeedback, speech skills training and a combination of both in treating public speaking anxiety," *Biofeedback and Self-Regulation* 1982; 7(1): 71–87.

McKinney, M., Gatchel, R., and Paulus, P. "The effects of audience size on high and low speech anxious subjects during an actual speaking task," *Basic and Applied Social Psychology* 1983; 4(1): 7H7.

Medley, H.A. *Sweaty Palms: The Neglected Art of Being Interviewed*, Berkeley, California: Ten Speed Press, 1984.

Melchior, L.A., and Cheek, J.M. "Shyness and anxious self-preoccupation during a social interaction," *Journal of Social Behavior and Personality* 1990; 5(2): 117–130.

Montgomery, R.L., Haemmerlie, F., and Edwards, M. "Social, personal, and interpersonal deficits in socially anxious people," *Journal of Social Behavior and Personality* 1991; 6(4): 859–872.

Norton, G., MacLean, L., and Wachna, E. "The use of cognitive desensitization and self directed mastery training for treating stage fright," *Cognitive Therapy and Research* 1978; 2(1): 61–64.

Olivier, L. *Confessions of an Actor: An Autobiography*, New York: Simon and Schuster, 1982.

Osberg, J. "The effectiveness of applied relaxation in the treatment of speech anxiety," *Behavior Therapy* 1981; 12(5): 723–729.

Rickman, M.D., and Davidson, R.J. "Personality and behavior in parents of temperamentally inhibited and uninhibited children," *Developmental Psychology* 1994; 30, N3: 346–354.

Ristad, E. *A Soprano on Her Head*, Moab, Utah: Real People Press, 1982.

Ross, J. *Triumph Over Fear*, New York: Bantam Books, 1994.

Smith, J. *Relaxation Dynamics: Nine World Approaches to Self-Relaxation*, Champaign, Illinois: Research Press, 1975.

Smith, M. *When I Say No, I Feel Guilty*, New York: Dial Press, 1975.

Snyder, M. *Public Appearances/Private Realities: The Psychology of Self-Monitoring*, New York: W.H. Freeman and Company, 1987.

Wallace, A., Wallechinsky, D., and Wallace, I. *The Book of Lists*, New York: Morrow Books, 1983.

Watson, D., and Tharp, R. *Self-Directed Behavior: Self-Modification for Personal Adjustment*, Monterey, California: Brooks-Cole, 1977.

Weissberg, M. "A comparison of direct and vicarious treatments of speech anxiety: Desensitization, desensitization with coping imagery and cognitive modification," *Behavior Therapy* 1977; 8: 606–620.

Worthington, E.C. "Speech and coping skills training and paradox as treatment for college students anxious about public speaking," *Perceptual Motor Skills* 1984; 59(2): 3394.

Woy, J., and Efran, J. "Systematic desensitization and expectancy in the treatment of speaking anxiety," *Behavioral Research and Therapy* 1972; 10: 43–49.

Yate, M.J. *Knock 'em Dead: With Great Answers to Tough Interview Questions*, Boston: Bob Adams, Inc., 1995.

Zettle, R.D., and Hayes, S. "The effects of social context on the impact of coping self-statements," *Psychological Reports* 1983; 52(2): 191401.

Zimbardo, P. *Shyness: What It Is, What to Do About It*, Reading: Addison-Wesley Publishing Company, 1977.

ABOUT THE AUTHOR

Peter Desberg, PhD, received his doctorate from the University of Southern California. He is a professor of psychology at California State University, Dominguez Hills, as well as a licensed clinical psychologist. For over twenty-five years, he has carried out research in the area of performance anxiety and stage fright. He is an active consultant and has conducted seminars and workshops on controlling stage fright for corporations, actors, musicians, athletes, job applicants, and public speakers. Dr. Desberg is the author of sixteen books and numerous articles. He is a sought-after speaker and has appeared on numerous television and radio programs. He and his family currently reside in the Los Angeles area.

INDEX